A Sunrise Book

E. P. DUTTON | NEW YORK

THE
BOOK
OF
ROUNDS

Mary Catherine Taylor

and

Carol Dyk

Setting of music and lyrics by Nicholas Skedgell

Library of Congress Cataloging in Publication Data
Main entry under title:

The Book of rounds.
"A Sunrise book."
Includes index.
1. Glees, catches, rounds, etc.   I. Taylor,
Mary Catherine, 1903-   II. Dyk, Carol.
M1578.B725   784'.1   75-11765

ISBN: 0-87690-182-8

Published simultaneously in Canada by Clarke, Irwin & Company Limited,
Toronto and Vancouver

10   9   8   7   6   5   4   3   2   1
First Edition

Designed by The Etheredges

CONTENTS

INTRODUCTION

Round, catch, canon, fuga, rota, *caccia* (Ital.), *chace* (Fr.), roundel and roundelay are various names that have been given at various times over the past few hundred years to essentially the same form of music. And what exactly is this particular form of music?

Edward F. Rimbault, in his collection, *The Rounds, Catches and Canons of England of the 16th, 17th and 18th Centuries*, published in 1863, gave this definition: "A round is a species of canon in the unison, so called because the performers begin the melody at regular, rhythmical periods, and return from its conclusion to its beginning, so that it continually passes round and round from one to another of them." You can see that trying to define a round is rather like trying to describe a circle without using your hands.

Basically a round is a simple fugue, as "canon in the unison" indicates. Canons *not* in the unison are more complicated and are represented here by only one example, "Hey, Down a Down, Behold and See" (p. 127-128) which "is in three voices, at the 5th and 9th" and explains itself when looked at. Therefore, we can say all rounds are a form of canon but not all canons are rounds. A further distinction between them is that in a canon the voices can follow one another as closely as one measure apart, or even just two or three notes, whereas in a round the first voice completes a statement before the next voice enters.

What then is a catch? It is a round more concerned with the words than the music, with the "narrative" interrupted by rests inserted in such a way that, as the voices weave in and out, the original meaning of the words becomes entirely altered. A perfectly straightforward, "innocent" verse such as "Have You Sir John Hawkins' History?" (p. 111) refers to the publication, in 1776, of two massive histories of music, one by Sir John Hawkins, the other by Dr. Charles Burney, both men eminent in music circles. In this catch you will see how "Burney's History" becomes "Burn His History," referring to the Hawkins opus.

Many catches were far from innocent, however. In the majority of those using the interwoven words, the hidden and secondary meanings are often quite salacious. In "Twixt Dick and Tom" (p. 217) the double meaning is very apparent. Eventually, though, as collections of rounds proliferated (and that they certainly did), the words "round" and "catch" became virtually synonymous.

The very earliest meaning of the word catch had nothing to do with double meanings or jumbled words. It indicated that the singers were instructed to "catch" their parts by listening carefully, to make sure they joined in at the right place. Rounds originally were learned only by ear, in true folk tradition, and for over 200 years no one bothered to write them down. Many references are made to them in the literature of the period, during which many other kinds of music were recorded. But not rounds.

To trace the history and development of rounds is not easy. Perhaps someday someone will find an old manuscript that will fill in some of the gaps. The first round on record goes back to the 13th or 14th century. Not until the middle of the 19th century was a date assigned to this especially beautiful composition, "Sumer Is Icumen In" (p. 171), which had reposed undiscovered in one of the Harleian manuscripts in the British Museum. In the 1850's there was a tremendous surge of interest in medieval music and many scholars worked enthusiatically on deciphering and transcribing the masses of manuscripts that had lain ignored in various libraries for several centuries.

The then Keeper of Manuscripts in the British Museum, Sir Francis Madden, decided by a series of deductions and extrapolations that "Sumer" had probably been written between 1227 and 1240. His assumption was widely accepted by many music savants. But in 1944 this was challenged by Manfred Bukofzer in a scholarly treatise, "*Sumer Is Icumen In*, A Revision" (Univ. of Calif. Publications in Music, Vol. 2 No. 2). He explained why it could not have been written before the early 1300's, which in no way detracts from its remarkable intrinsic beauty and value; but it does narrow the gap between its appearance and the next example of this form, so that it is not quite so inexplicably isolated as at first believed. "Sumer" still remains a "first" in several categories. It is the first specimen of a canon and the first canon to have had secular words. It became so popular that sacred words, "Perspice Christicola," were added later. They were no match for the joyous original ones but were probably demanded by some sternly inflexible ecclesiastic, to make the song acceptable in church. It is also the first known composition for six voices. Lastly, and perhaps most importantly to us, it is the earliest known harmonized music that is still widely enjoyed today.

Following "Sumer Is Icumen In," we look in vain for specimens of rounds *musically notated* and not just referred to in other books. Dr. Rimbault, in his book, casually mentions that he "fortunately discovered a very interesting roundel of the 14th century, of which the following is the history: 'In 1453, Sir John Norman, being the first Lord Mayor of London who brake that anncient and old continued custome of riding with great pomp into Westminister. . . choosing rather to be rowed there by water, the watermen made to him a roundel or song to his great praise.' " The round is "Row the Boat, Norman, Row," listed herein as "Heave Ho and Rumbelow" (p. 6), with a second set of words, "Turn Again Whittington." As I have written elsewhere:* "Dick Whittington who was 'thrice Lord Mayor of London' was first elected to that office in 1397, fifty-six years before Norman's term. This adds one more mystery to the history of rounds. If, as seems probable, rounds were popularly sung and handed down by ear from generation to generation long before anyone wrote them down, it is quite possible that the tune may have been composed for Whittington and passed on as 'The Lord Mayor's Roundell,' with new words put to it as occasion demanded. On the other hand, perhaps the Whittington words were not set to the tune until Elizabethan times—more than 150 years after his death— when his story caught the popular fancy and acquired many legendary variations that had no foundation in fact." So the date of that round remains uncertain, but it is the only one for which the music is known to have been written down between "Sumer" and the first collections of rounds that appeared in the early 17th century.

England was a nation spilling over with brilliant music throughout the 15th and 16th centuries. Three of the Henry's were musicians: Henry V (reigned 1413–1422) maintained a very large musical establishment as part of his Chapel Royal; Henry VI (reigned 1422–1453) was a composer of considerable

---

Rounds and Rounds (published in 1946 by William Sloane Associates and reissued in paperback by Hargail Press).

merit; and Henry VIII (b. 1491– d. 1547) was instructed in music as an essential part of his education to become the ecclesiastic he was destined to be. When his elder brother died he ascended to the throne and remained an ardent lover of music and a skillful composer and performer. Elizabeth, too, loved and encouraged music throughout her long reign and undoubtedly knew many rounds if we are to judge by the recurring references to them in books and plays of the time:

In Beaumont and Fletcher's "Coxcomb" (1610) we find: "They were like careful members of the city/Drawing in diligent ale and singing catches"; Shakespeare's "Twelfth Night" has three references to catches as do many of his other plays. In Ben Jonson's "New Inn" (1626) there is the following:

BARNABY.—*How does old Staggers the smith and Tree the sadler? Keep they their penny club still?*
JORDAN.—*And the old catch, too, of "Whoop Barnaby"!*
BARNABY.—*Do they sing at me?*
JORDAN.—*They are reeling at it in the parlor now.*

Reference to "Whoop Barnaby" is made in a number of places, by different authors, but no trace of the round itself has been found, which is too bad because it must have been amusing to have been so popular.

In William Chappell's book, *Popular Music of Olden Times* (2 vols., 1855–1859) he wrote, "Tinkers, tailors, blacksmiths, servants, clowns and others are so constantly mentioned as singing music in parts, and by so many writers, as to leave no doubt as to the ability of at least many among them to have done so. . . . Perhaps the form of round or catch was more generally in favor, because, as each would sing the same notes, there would be but one part to remember, and the tune would guide those who learnt by ear."

Some people, obviously, discovered how to construct simple melodies that produced felicitous harmonies when put together in a certain way. These intuitively musical people, possibly illiterate otherwise, would teach the melodies to companions who would in turn, teach them to others. Thus rounds spread. This is speculation, of course, but it seems a logical assumption. Yet isn't it strange that it was not until five years after Elizabeth's death that the first *musically printed* rounds reached the light of day?

Two musicians of that period, David Melvill in Scotland and Thomas Ravenscroft in England brought out, almost simultaneously, huge collections of this delightful form of music. There is no indication that they knew or had even heard of each other, but Ravenscroft's three collections (*Pammelia* 1609, *Deuteromelia* 1609, and *Melismata* 1611) and Melvill's *Buik of Roundels* 1612 contain so much of the same material it is an inescapable conclusion that rounds had been around for a long time, handed down only aurally and perhaps not taken seriously enough to be "preserved" in print. These rounds paint a picture of a rough, jolly, virile time, reflecting the emotions and native wisdom of people whose naturalistic values saw nothing incongruous in having deeply felt religious songs alongside audaciously wanton ones.

Quite a lot is known about Thomas Ravenscroft, (c.1590–c.1633). He appears to have been something of a child prodigy. Records show that he took a degree in music at Cambridge in 1605, making him around 15. He became a chorister at St. Paul's and later, musicmaster at Christ's Hospital. During this time he was doing a lot of composing and was demonstrably capable of writing the kind of madrigals, ayres, canzonets, anthems, etc. that were being published by his more conventional contemporaries (Cavendish, Cranford, Dowland, Farnaby and Morley, to name a few). But he seems to have fallen in love with rounds. His collection *Melismata* is subtitled *Musical Fantasies, Fitting the Court, Citie and Country Humours*, which reveals his broad sympathies with all kinds of people.

About David Melvill very little is known beyond the fact that he was the elder brother of James Melvill, 1556–1614 (a well-known Scottish divine and writer), and inherited the family estate where he lived a quiet life, occupying himself with agriculture and the pursuit of music, including the collecting of rounds. He noted that it took him twelve years to assemble his collection.

Brother James, meanwhile, got into the act by writing a round entitled "As I Me Walked on a May Morning" (p. 157) which is a fragment of a poem that appeared in his book, *The Spiritual Propine Of A Pastour To His People* 1598 (the literal meaning of propine is "a gift of money, esp. drink money"). David's book contained a notation at the end of the brief round, "Finis quoth M. James Melvill." The extraordinary thing about this is that "As I Me Walked" appeared first in *Pammelia* in 1609 (without the "finis" notation) three years before David's book came out. Evidently word of mouth speeds the broadcast of a popular song just as well as radio, and Ravenscroft must have picked up the tune and included it in his first collection before David got his all put together.

Church bells played an important part in people's lives, as shown by the number of rounds written about them. Apart from the "Ding-Dongs," "Bim Boms," "Tingle Tingle Tings" and so on, there are the "Peals." I used to think that "pealing bells" was just another way of saying "ringing bells" but that is not the case. First of all, a "peal of bells" is a set of bells tuned to the notes of the major scale, whereas "peals" are successive changes rung on such sets. "Ringing the changes" or "change-ringing" was practiced only in England and is not to be confused with the carillon music so popular in Europe. Carillon music employs many more bells and is played on a console arranged like the manuals and pedals of an organ, with the ropes attached to the bells' clappers, while the bells themselves are rigidly fixed in place. Change-ringing, on the other hand, is achieved by pulling on ropes attached to the tops of free-swinging bells which revolve in a sort of ball-bearing arrangement called a gudgeon.

There were individual and well-established peal patterns for births, deaths, marriages, victories, church holidays or anything else that needed celebrating. On births different peals were rung for boys and girls; likewise on deaths one set signified a man, another a woman, with the age of the deceased tolled out as well.

In the chapter headed "Bells" you will find all sorts of references to pealing. "All in to Service" I and II (pp. 18 and 19) refer not to a church service, as I once thought, but to a special peal pattern played between switching over from one peal to another. "Tenor" in "The Great Bells of Oseney" (p. 18) and "Tom" in

"Great Tom Is Cast" (p. 19) refer to different sized bells in the sets. Incidentally, "Great Tom Is Cast" was written by Dr. Henry Aldrich, dean of Christchurch at Oxford. You will find other compositions of his scattered throughout the book, some rather surprisingly ribald for a clerk.

The short and long versions of "Let's Have a Peal for John Cooke's Soul" (pp. 69 and 23) give an indication of how the ringers refreshed themselves during the hours of a long peal. Plenty of drink was provided, and there was always a spare man to climb down from the bell-tower to go for ale to refill the bowls, tankards and cans, or to spell anyone who collapsed.

John Cooke must have been a well-loved character to have had two peals dedicated to him at his death and still another directed at him while alive. The rather strangely titled "I.C.U.B.A.K." (p. 272) has been interpreted by some to mean "I See You Be A Knave." But in those days the letters I and J were used interchangeably so it could also stand for "John Cooke You Be A Knave," since he is named in the round. The term knave was used affectionately, much as we use the word rascal today.

While assembling this collection it was hard to limit the selections from Ravenscroft and Melvill, but their books were only the beginning of a wave of collections of rounds. From about 1648 to the early 1700's the name of Playford was a familiar one to music lovers. John Playford founded the music publishing company that bore his name and he handed it on to his son Henry, who retired from music publishing around 1707 and sold his stock to a John Cullen. Pepys was a good friend of John Playford, who often gave him complimentary copies of his publication in order to get Pepys's respected opinion.

The list of Playford's rounds, catches and canons publications begins in 1651 when he brought out his *Musical Banquet*, and the next year published John Hilton's *Catch That Catch Can*, subtitled *A Choice Collection of Catches, Rounds and Canons for 3 and 4 Voices*. The latter contained much of Ravenscroft's material as did succeeding editions, year after year, but without giving Ravenscroft any credit. In 1672, 1673, 1685, 1686 and 1687 more collections were introduced, all bearing the titles *Catch That Catch Can, The Musical Companion* or *Pleasant Musical Com-*

panion. Long after the death of both Playfords, up until 1740, more editions and reprints under the name Playford were welcomed by what seems to have been an insatiable public.

Perhaps the prohibition of church and theatre music during Cromwell's time caused the sharp rise in "secular" and "domestic" music. Antonia Fraser, in her biography of Cromwell, advances such a theory and the staggering amount of music publication would seem to prove it. Just the continuing flow of rounds, catches and canons, which was the merest fraction of the totality of music published, showed a "strong inclination of the citizens to follow Musick," as Roger North observed in his *Memoires of Musick* (written in 1782 but not published until 1842), adding that "in a lane behind St. Paul's . . . some shopkeepers and foremen came weekly to sing . . . and enjoy ale and tobacco."

In 1672 Edward Ravenscroft, possibly a descendant of Thomas because it was not a common name, wrote a comedy called "The Citizen Turned Gentleman," in which the citizen is advised that in order to appear a man of consequence he "must have a music club once a week at his house." Thus, singing had indeed become "so goode a thing," as William Byrd had written long ago in 1588 when he wished "all men would learn to sing," that most of them, of all classes, did, and competently too, judging from accounts of the time.

During this period "Catch Clubs" began springing up all over the country. In the fourth edition, "corrected and much enlarged," of Playford's *Musical Companion*, there was this new and interesting title page: ". . . being a Choice Collection of Catches for 3 and 4 Voices. *Published chiefly for the Encouragement of the Musicall Societies which will be speedily set up in all the Chief Cities and Towns in England.*"

All activities of life were celebrated in rounds, or catches, as they were now generally called. Many of the composers paid homage to the jovial god, Bacchus, which is reflected in the profusion of drinking songs. Thomas Brewer, author of "Blest, Blest Is He" (p. 97), had, according to John Jenkins, "through his proneness to good felloweship attained to a rubicund nose." So much so, that Dr. Aldrich (mentioned above) was inspired to write "Tom's Jolly Nose" (p. 257), whereupon Jenkins replied with "An Answer to Tom's Jolly Nose" (p. 258).

This same Jenkins, from 1660 to 1666, was music teacher in residence at the home of Lord North, whose second son, the Hon. Roger *(Memoires of Musick)* wrote affectionately of him in his *Autobiography*: "He was a man of much easier temper than any of his faculty, being neither conceited nor morose, but much a gentleman . . . and superinduced an airy sort of composition, wherein he had a fluent and happy fancy." Two of Jenkins's catches included here are "A Boat, A Boat" (p. 241) and "Come Pretty Maidens" (p. 32).

The 17th century might well be called "The golden age of rounds." Beginning with William Byrd (1545–1623) and his canon "Hey Ho ! To the Greenwood" (p. 165) and Jenkins (1592–1678) we go to John Hilton (1599–1656), the Lawes brothers, William (1598–1645) and Henry (1596–1656), Simon Ives (1600–1666), Thomas Brewer (1611– ?), Mathew Locke (1630– ?), John Blow (1648–1708), Michael Wise (1648–1687), William Turner (1651–1739), John Lenton (1656– ?), Henry Purcell (1658–1695), Richard Browne (? –1664), John Jackson (? –1688), John Reading (? –1692) and Henry Aldrich (1647–1710). Examples from all of them can be found throughout the book.

Lamentably, the majority of the rounds do not name a composer, and I have made no attempt to list a source (other than Melvill's and Ravenscroft's) because so many of them appear over and over again in collection after collection. I have noted the composer wherever possible.

The foundation of "The Noblemen and Gentlemen's Catch Club" in 1761 gave a new impetus to catch-composing so that fresh material began to be printed, taking the place of the oft-repeated older collections. This particular Catch Club was formed with the announced intention of "encouraging the composition and performance of catches, cannons and glees." (Why "glees" were included in a Catch Club repertoire is somewhat inexplicable because they are just part-songs put together with massive blocks of harmony. Many of them are very pretty but they are *not* catches or canons. The word "glee" itself does not necessarily characterize a song of cheerful nature. It comes from the Anglo-Saxon "gligge" meaning, simply, music.)

The Club became very fashionable, with most of the noble music amateurs of the day being active members, as well as various royalty. The Prince of Wales, later George IV, and the Duke of Clarence, later William IV, entered enthusiastically into the singing and drinking but not the composing. One nobleman, whose work is included in this book, is the Earl of Mornington (1735–1781), who also founded the Academy of Music, another amateur Society in which, for the first time, ladies were allowed to sing.

Some of the well-known professional members of the club whose works are represented are Sir John Hawkins, of the famous *History* (1719–1789), William Hayes (1707–1777), William Boyce (1710–1779), John Callcott (1766–1821), Thomas Arne (1710–1778), Samuel Arnold (1740–1802), John Alcock (1715–1806), Luffman Atterbury (? –1849), Jonathan Battishill (1739–1801), Joseph Baildon (c.1727–1774) and John Danby (1757–1798).

In 1763 the Club introduced the custom of offering prizes for the best catch, canon and glee. In 1787, as a consequence of Dr. Callcott entering nearly 100 compositions in the contest, the judging committee decided that a line had to be drawn somewhere, so a limit of four in each category was set. The next year Dr. Callcott submitted twelve compositions and took all the prizes.

There were a number of other rules instituted by the Club. The president selected who should sing. If, for any reason, the member failed to perform his part to the satisfaction of the president, he was "fined" by having to toss off a half-pint bumper of wine. Since the judgment of "failure," whether a false note, a missed beat, a faulty pronunciation or anything else, was purely at the discretion of the president, he could, if he were one of the more convivial members, find plenty of reasons to impose the fine. As most of them *were* convivial they rarely ended an evening sober.

Thomas Warren, as the first secretary of the Club, has left a priceless body of work as a testament to the quality of music that membership in the Club engendered. From 1763 to 1794 (probably the year of his death) he published a yearly collection, a total of thirty-two volumes, of the catches, canons and glees that took the prizes in those years. Thomas Greatorex (1758–1831), organist, composer, conductor and writer, compiled an index to the whole lot.

Meanwhile, as various Italian, German and American musicians visited or settled in England, the popularity of rounds was not lost on them. Haydn, Mozart, Beethoven, Mendelssohn, Cherubini and others were all intrigued enough to try their hands at this form with beautiful results. You will find quite a few of their rounds in the chapter entitled "Great Masters, so-called."

As time moved on, public taste drew from the rude toward the decorous, and eventually to the depressingly prudish. William IV, who had been a somewhat reluctant king but a lusty rounds singer in the Catch Club, was succeeded in 1837 by his young niece, Victoria, who had probably never heard or sung a round. At about the same time many of the clubs began to include women in their membership. This brought forth collections of a more "genteel" character. In them emphasis was on different aspects of nature, the joys of music, rewards of virtue and quite a few lugubrious rounds on war and death.

By the beginning of the 20th century, rounds had become the accepted way of teaching singing in schools. Some of the lovely music of Purcell and his contemporaries was introduced into schoolbooks of rounds with rigorously disinfected words. But through all the various changes in taste and fashion rounds managed to retain their vitality. Even when relegated to the bottom of pages in community sing books, they were always great favorites. In recent years they have gradually recovered their popularity and collections of them are being printed again.

Separating the rounds into chapters has been quite a game, particularly when faced with deciding where to place those that could fit equally well into several categories. Somewhere in Professor David Boyden's book, *An Introduction to Music*, I remember a lovely quip about avoiding "hardening of the categories" and that is what Carol Dyk and I have tried to do as we wrestled with those that defied classification.

There are those that cry out for special mention for one rea-son or another. In the two-part "Bartholomew Fair," for instance, the first section, "Here's That Will Challenge," is by Purcell and the second part, "Here Are the Rareties," is by his old teacher, Dr. Blow. Did they do them together ? Or what ? There are a dozen or more similarly written on different aspects of the same subject and by different composers. You will find them.

Purcell's "Jack Thou'rt a Toper" must have become very popular because Marella wrote "Jack Thou'rt a . . . ," which is obviously one man trying to sing Purcell's with the other singers trying to stop him. I can find no dates on Marella but he was one of several Italians who settled in England and, judging from his rounds, fit well into the Purcell era.

"Now Foot It As I Do," "Who'll Buy My Roses" and "Mingled Melodies" are notable for being "Quodlibets" (literal translation: "What You Please"), which is a sort of musical joke formed by the juxtaposition of different songs with each one maintaining its own individuality while becoming a part of a round.

Many of the rounds which seem meaningless to us today had very real meaning in their own time. The street cry "White Sand and Grey Sand" is an example. Blotters were not yet invented, so to dry the wet ink on a freshly written page, sand was sprinkled over it and then returned to a small container to be used again. White to begin with, it gradually became gray but the sand-sellers would buy it back and resell it very cheaply to others who could not afford the luxury of the pure white sand. Nearly all the street and market cries, and those referring to trades and crafts, are cheery skeletons of long dead customs some of which we can figure out, while the meaning of others eludes us.

There are two rebuses—a kind of puzzle popular at the time— one, "One Industrious Insect," which is on the name of Anthony Hall, with music by Purcell, and the other, "A Mate to a Cock," on Henry Purcell's name composed by John Lenton after Purcell's death, with the words to both written by one "Mr. Tomlinson," not otherwise identified. As apropos today as they were when written are "My Pocket's Low and Taxes High" and "Good Unexpected." And women's libbers may take a fancy to "Ye Heavens, If Innocence Deserves Your Care."

The bawdy and ribald ones get pretty boring in their insistent vulgarity but, by and large, their music is some of the best in the book and worthy of making up new words if you can't stomach the originals. At the other extreme, the cloying, mawkish "smuggery" of the late 19th- and early 20th-century words was repellent enough to throw rounds into the decline from which they have been recovering. In between these extremes there exists a staggering variety, to fit every mood.

An interesting sidelight on the tenacity of rounds' continuing grip on people is to be found in the "Contemporary" chapter. Thirty years ago I asked two musician friends to write some rounds for the collection I was then doing. Obligingly, and because she had become such an avid rounds singer, Louise Levinger promptly produced "What's Icumen In?" Shortly afterward Johan Franco presented me with "Elephants, or The Force of Habit" which, incidentally, he later incorporated as a movement in one of his string quartets. Then when I started putting this collection together I asked them for more. After all these years, and just as obligingly, they complied: Louise with her two saucy ones, "Trumpets" and "Crumpets," and Johan with the delicate "Water-Go-Round" for which his poet wife, Eloise, wrote the lovely words.

It was my English mother-in-law who sparked my interest in rounds, more than thirty-five years ago. A miserable, wet summer in Devon kept ten of us penned indoors most of the time. Trying to keep five small children from each other's throats became our principal occupation. Suddenly at tea-time one drenching day, when we were all rather snarly, Mother said, "Let's sing a round." We ran through the few old standbys we all knew and as our spirits rose she said, "Now let's learn a long one."

She began teaching us "A Southerly Wind." I can still hear us stumbling over those fast tongue-twisting words, rarely getting them in the right order but clued in to the tune so the words didn't matter too much. And when we reached the final part with its "Hark! Hark! Follow, Tally-ho, Tally-ho, Tally-ho!" even the youngest child, only eighteen months old, was wildly waving his arms in time and roaring with delight.

From that moment we were hooked. Mother pulled out from her memory, like balls of yarn from a big knitting bag, about a dozen more, all fairly long ones which we learned. When we returned to this country we immediately started gathering in friends to sing rounds with us. Their enthusiasm matched ours and inspired me to start collecting them. You can imagine my amazement as over the years I discovered how many there were to be dug out. We are still singing, and interest in rounds is now surfacing in some of our grandchildren.

The temptation is strong to go on and on, calling your attention to especially beautiful rounds or pointing out differences, similarities, inconsistencies, obscurities, double-meanings, puns, riddles, jokes, etc., but it is time to resist and allow you to make your own discoveries.

If many faultes in this book you fynde,
   Yet think not the correctors blynde;
If Argos heere hymselfe had beene
   He should perchance not all have seene.
   Richard Shacklock . . . 1565

So, please forgive the errors and enjoy ! Enjoy !!

Mary C. Taylor

HOW TO SING ROUNDS

To get the most out of singing rounds one must, first and last, sing softly. Consciously think of *blending* your voice. Round-singing is a co-operative endeavor and if anyone in your group shows a tendency toward "operatic" voice projection quell him or her at once. That sort of singing has no place in rounds. Rounds by definition take a group, not a soloist. Sung softly, they are ineffably beautiful, as well as exciting. Therefore be warned. It may mean warning yourself because enthusiasm sometimes makes one forget to listen to the other voices. Aim for a gentle, tuneful, natural delivery, singing from the head rather than the chest, and *never* forcing your voice.

The second requirement is to keep good time. For your first efforts choose short and simple rounds, with a firmly marked, even time, without rests. Begin by learning a tune all together in unison. That is what makes rounds so much easier and more fun than other kinds of part-singing. There are no soprano, alto, tenor or bass parts. Everyone learns the same tune in unison and then puts it together as indicated below and the round forms its own parts and harmony. You will soon get the feel of the rhythm and how to maintain it while singing your part. You will then want to tackle more intricate tunes. In these you will find broken rhythms with not all measures having the same number of notes. There are the same number of beats, however, and they do not vary.

In the beginning you may want to keep the group together by marking time with a hand or foot. However this upsets some people, understandably, so as soon as you can, start inwardly counting the time or wiggling a toe inside your shoe, giving careful attention to the rests. In complicated rounds rests become a most important part of the song's structure and can be very tricky. Sometimes you will come across a brief rest inserted between two syllables of a word, which may seem odd at first but careful observance of that little rest produces a cheerful lilt in the tune.

You may find that you want to change the key of some of the rounds. That is all right. Pitch them to suit the range of your voices. In the course of singing a round you may go flat. Do not worry if this happens. Everyone tends to do this at first. But as you are doing it all together you will only realize how *much* you have gone off key if you strike your starting note on the piano (or recorder) when you finish. You will discover how far you have slipped. Don't let the chorus of incredulous "Oh, no" deter you. Go back to the beginning of the round and sing it over again and notice how much you improve with practice.

When you come to the actual learning of an unknown tune, not everyone can sight-read, i.e. vocally pick out a tune from printed music, but almost anyone can pick out a tune with one finger on the piano or guitar, or can tootle it on a recorder. That will fix it in your mind sufficiently to enable you to start singing the round in unison. After you have done that a few times you are ready to sing it as a round. You are on your way. You will feel prodigiously proud of your music, believe me, and you'll want to go on singing it over and over. Of course at some time you must end the round. So how do you stop?

There are no hard and fast *rules* on ending a round. It is your own decision, really, and the length of the round usually has some bearing on what method you choose. If it is a very long one, a good way is to have the singer who enters last give a signal to stop when he comes to the end of his first-time round. Short ones you will want to sing through a half-dozen times or more, and it does not much matter who makes the signal to stop. It may well be whoever runs out of breath first.

You can also decide before you start how many times you want to go through a particular round. Then the first voice stops after having sung it the agreed upon times, with the succeeding voices dropping out in turn until only one voice is left at the end. Generally speaking this way seems rather dreary, although certain rounds do lend themselves to that treatment.

If you become a member of a group singing together regularly, it is good to appoint a conductor who then directs when and how to come to a close. Following a leader will make you feel professional and make you sound that way, too. You may want to rotate the role of conductor periodically.

I want to call your attention to the music notation. In the interests of page design and easy reading some of the songs are printed horizontally and others vertically. An example follows:

Oh, My love, lov'st thou me? Then
quick ly come and save him that dies for thee.

Oh, My love,
lov'st thou me? Then
quick ly come and save him that
dies for thee.

In the first version you see the numerals horizontally along the top of the staff, indicating the entrance points for the different voices. When Voice 1 reaches (2), Voice 2 enters at (1); Voice 3 enters when Voice 2 reaches (2), and so on.

In the second version, numerals are placed vertically against each line of the round. On the left they indicate the entrance of succeeding voices while those on the right tell you where to go next, from stave to stave. Thus, when you come to Number 1 in the lower right-hand corner, that tells you to go back to the beginning Number 1 in the upper left hand corner.

One more aid to singing is the "Movable Do" symbol (⊨), found just beside the time signature. Its little prongs embrace the line or space on which the "Do" is in each melody.

The key is determined by the last note. Where it is the same as the "Do," then the round is major. If it is one space or one line lower, then the round is minor.

"Do" is G, however last note is one line lower (E).
Therefore E minor.

"Do" is G and last note is G.
Therefore G major.

In either case, your ear should be able to decide. Major is generally bright and gay, whereas minor is morose and melancholy. If the tune does not start on "Do," count the lines and spaces to where it does start, then *think* your "Do" scale, up or down, to the starting note and there you are all ready to begin.

Quite often, just to make things interesting presumably, the composer wanders in and out of several keys in the course of a round, but there is no point in attempting to make a note of all those. Just be prepared, when you see "accidentals" looming ahead, to trust your ear and innate musical sense to "absorb" those into the tune and make it your own. It becomes easier every time you learn a new round.

It will not be long before these instructions are second nature and seem very simple indeed. I can already hear you snorting and saying, "Why! Everybody already *knows* how to sings rounds!" Having become addicted to them yourself you will forget that once upon a time the only ones you knew were "Row, Row, Row Your Boat," "Frère Jacques," "Oh, How Lovely Is the Evening" and a few others, learned long ago in primary school and camp or on picnics back in the days before TV gobbled up so much of our time that we almost gave up making our own music.

Today, a whole new generation of young people, turned off by pre-fabricated entertainment, is looking for ways to make its own music. Young people have turned to guitars, recorders, other instruments, folk songs and now rounds. Rounds open up a whole new world and, unlike many forms of music, can be enjoyed out of doors, traveling the turnpikes and freeways, as well as at home.

On these pages both new and old rounds-singers are going to find enough new and old rounds to suit every taste for years to come.

OLD FAMILIARS

Scotland's Burning

Maeder

Scot - land's burn - ing, Scot - land's burn - ing! Look out! Look out!

Fire! fire! fire! fire! Pour on wa - ter, pour on wa - ter!

Hello! Hello!

CANON: 2 VOICES

Wilson

Hel - lo! Hel - lo! Yes? Yes?

Here we come sing - ing, Our voi - ces are ring - ing with

All in a Fairy Ring

Wood

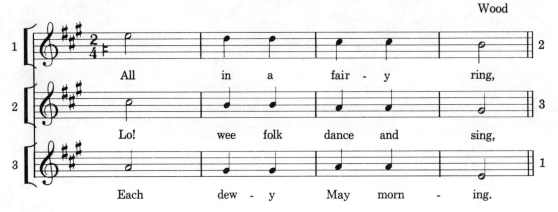

All in a fair - y ring,

Lo! wee folk dance and sing,

Each dew - y May morn - ing.

Wake and Sing

CANON: 4 VOICES

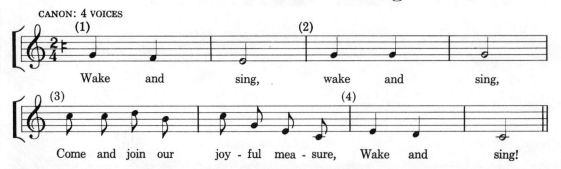

Wake and sing, wake and sing,

Come and join our joy - ful mea - sure, Wake and sing!

Morning Bells I Love to Hear I

CANON: 4 VOICES

(1) (2) (3) (4)

Morn - ing bells I love to hear, Ring - ing mer - ri - ly loud and clear.

Morning Bells I Love to Hear II

CANON: 4 VOICES

(1) (2)

Morn - ing bells I love to hear,

(3) (4)

Ring - ing mer - ri - ly, loud and clear.

½ doz X's.

1 - are you sleeping
2 - Toot - sing it together
3 - rounds
4 - ½ doz X's

Frère Jacques

E♭ Major — B♭ E♭ A♭

Old French

1 2

Frère___ Jacques Frère___ Jacques, Dor - mez vous? Dor - mez vous?

3 4

Sonnez les ma - tines,___ Sonnez les ma - tines,___ Din, din, don, Din, din, don.

English version:

Are you sleeping, are you sleeping,
Brother John, Brother John?
Morning bells are ringing, morning bells are ringing,
Ding, ding, dong, ding, ding, dong.

Spanish version:

Martinillo, Martinillo,
Quieres tú, quieres tú?
Toca la campana, toca la campana,
Din, din, don, din, din, don.

For the following Chinese version in translation we are indebted to Mr. George Kin Leung:

Eight, eight airplanes, eight, eight airplanes
Flying low, flying low,
Five of them have no gas, five of them have no gas,
Oh, how sad, just too bad.

Gently Flow

Hayes

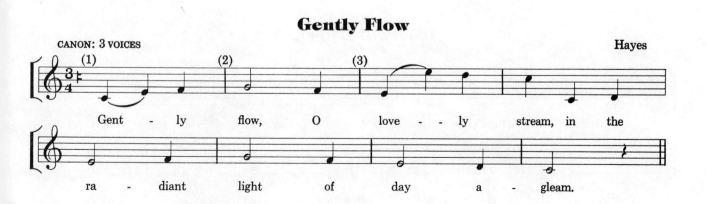

CANON: 3 VOICES

(1) (2) (3)

Gent - ly flow, O love - ly stream, in the

ra - diant light of day a - gleam.

Winter Days

CANON: 4 VOICES

Win - ter days a - gain are here, Slow - ly wanes the year.

O Render Thanks

CANON: 3 VOICES

O ren - der thanks to God a - bove, the Fount of love.

Come Let's Laugh

CANON: 4 VOICES

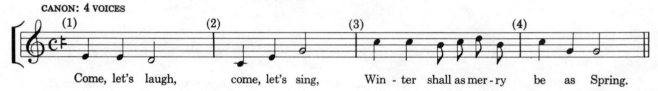

Come, let's laugh, come, let's sing, Win - ter shall as mer - ry be as Spring.

A Merry Roundelay

CANON: 3 VOICES

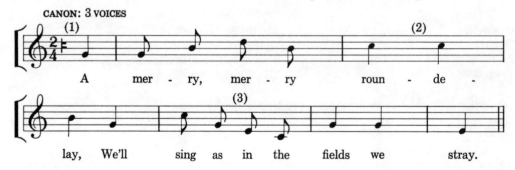

A mer - ry, mer - ry roun - de - lay, We'll sing as in the fields we stray.

Hurrah! Hurrah!

Briskly

Hur - rah! hur - rah! hur - rah! Hur - rah! hur - rah! hur - rah! Hur - rah! hur - rah! hur - rah!

Day Is Done

Day is done, Gone the sun from the lake, from the hills from the sky, Safe-ly rest, All is well, So good-night!

Flowers Are Dying

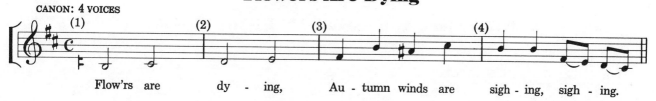

Flow'rs are dy-ing, Au-tumn winds are sigh-ing, sigh-ing.

Never Murmuring

Virtuously

Nev-er murm'-ring, Nev-er griev-ing, Meek and kind and pa-tient be.

Gone Is Autumn's Kindly Glow

With shivers

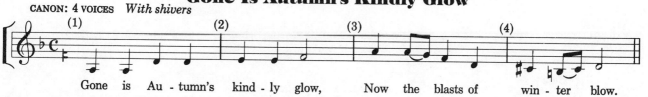

Gone is Au-tumn's kind-ly glow, Now the blasts of win-ter blow.

Now We Say Farewell

Same tune as "Whether you whisper low ..."

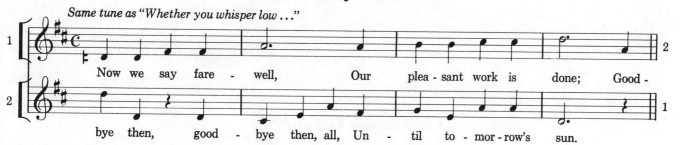

Now we say fare-well, Our plea-sant work is done; Good-bye then, good-bye then, all, Un-til to-mor-row's sun.

Now the Day Is Nearly Done

Now the day is near-ly done, Night is slow-ly com-ing on, Sweet-ly sleep till morn-ing light: Good-night! Good-night!

Heave and Ho, Rumbelow, or, Turn Again, Whittington

Rhythmically

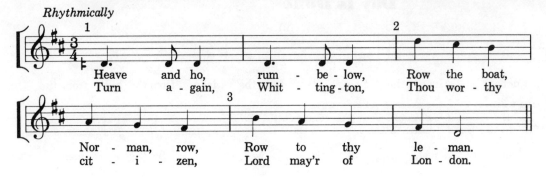

Heave and ho, rum - be - low, Row the boat,
Turn a - gain, Whit - ting - ton, Thou wor - thy

Nor - man, row, Row to thy le - man.
cit - i - zen, Lord may'r of Lon - don.

Where Are You Going, My Pretty Maid?

Purcell

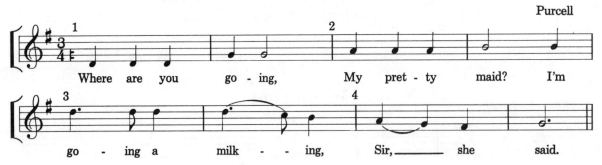

Where are you go - ing, My pret - ty maid? I'm

go - ing a milk - ing, Sir,_____ she said.

Here I Go

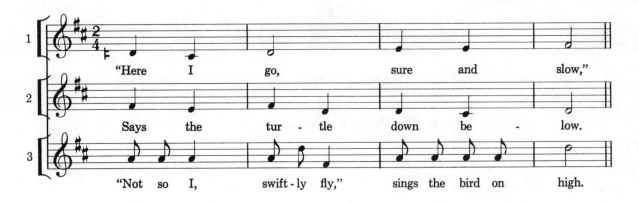

"Here I go, sure and slow,"

Says the tur - tle down be - low.

"Not so I, swift - ly fly," sings the bird on high.

Christmas Is Coming

Christ - mas is com - ing! The goose is get - ting fat;

Please to put a pen - ny in the old man's hat,

Please to put a pen - ny in the old man's hat.

See Those Poor Fellows

Purcell

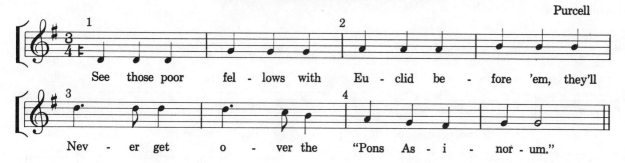

See those poor fel - lows with Eu - clid be - fore 'em, they'll

Nev - er get o - ver the "Pons As - i - nor - um."

Morning Is Come

Morn - ing is come, Night is a - way,

Rise with the sun_____ And__ wel - come the day.

Why Doesn't My Goose

Plaintively

Why doesn't my goose Sing as much as thy goose,

When I paid for my goose Twice as much as thou?

Wake Up! Wake Up!

Wachsmann

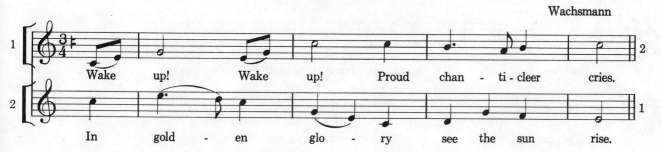

Wake up! Wake up! Proud chan - ti - cleer cries.

In gold - en glo - ry see the sun rise.

7

Will You Come into My Parlor?

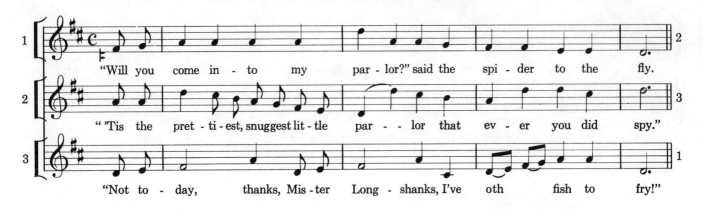

"Will you come in-to my par-lor?" said the spi-der to the fly.

"'Tis the pret-ti-est, snuggest lit-tle par-lor that ev-er you did spy."

"Not to-day, thanks, Mis-ter Long-shanks, I've oth fish to fry!"

Sleep, Sleep Well

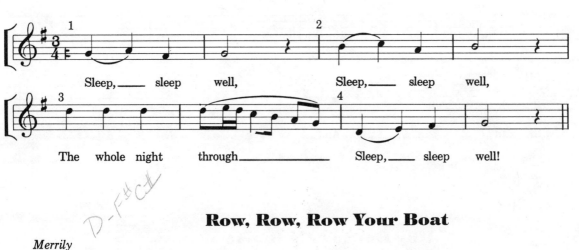

Sleep,___ sleep well, Sleep,___ sleep well,

The whole night through_____ Sleep,___ sleep well!

Row, Row, Row Your Boat

Merrily

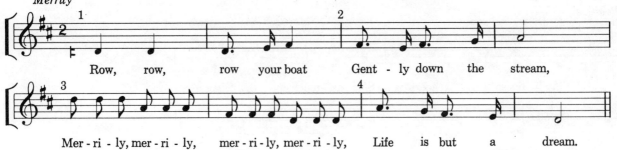

Row, row, row your boat Gent-ly down the stream,

Mer-ri-ly, mer-ri-ly, mer-ri-ly, mer-ri-ly, Life is but a dream.

Hey, Ho! Nobody at Home

Boisterously, with syncopation   Pammelia

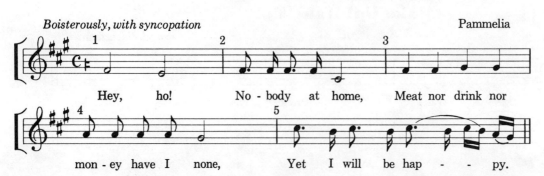

Hey, ho! No-body at home, Meat nor drink nor

mon-ey have I none, Yet I will be hap - py.

Now To All a Kind Goodnight

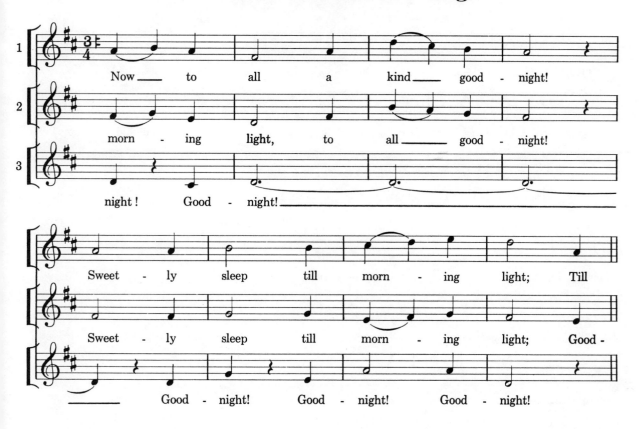

Now ___ to all a kind ___ good - night!

morn - ing light, to all ___ good - night!

night ! Good - night! ___

Sweet - ly sleep till morn - ing light; Till

Sweet - ly sleep till morn - ing light; Good -

___ Good - night! Good - night! Good - night!

Rose, Rose, Rose

Rose, rose, rose, rose, Shall I ev - er see thee red?

Aye, mar - ry, that thou wilt, If thou but stay.

It's Jolly To Sing

Wood

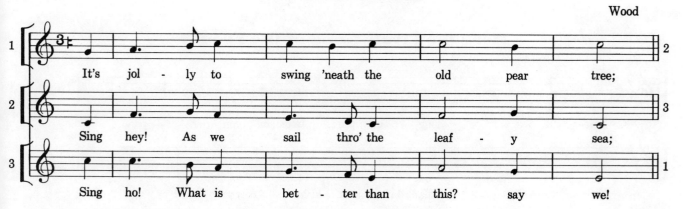

It's jol - ly to swing 'neath the old pear tree;

Sing hey! As we sail thro' the leaf - y sea;

Sing ho! What is bet - ter than this? say we!

9

Sing We Now Our Morning Song

Day is break - ing o'er the hills,

Rouse ye, broth - ers, sis - ters all, _____

morn - ing! Good morn - ing! Good

Dawn - ing on the lit - tle rills;

Cheer - i - ly to each oth - er call, Good

morn - ing! Good morn - ing! Good morn - ing!

Day Is Breaking

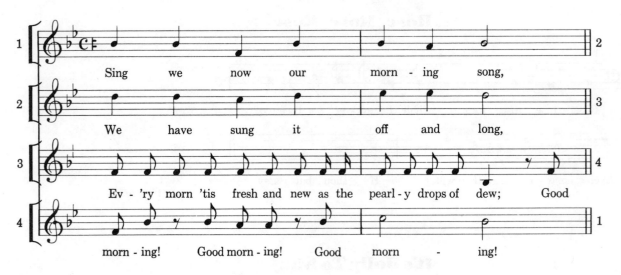

Sing we now our morn - ing song,

We have sung it off and long,

Ev - 'ry morn 'tis fresh and new as the pearl - y drops of dew; Good

morn - ing! Good morn - ing! Good morn - ing!

Hear the Lively Song of the Frogs

Hear the live - ly song of the frogs in yon - der pond:

Krik, krik, krik, krik, krik, krik, Brrrrr - - um!

10

Sweet, Goodnight

Sweet, good - night! We have sung our part - ing lay; The
stars are bright, To our homes we must a - way!
We have sung our part - ing lay; A - way! a - way!

Good Night, Good Night

Peacefully

Good night! Good night!
Time sends a warn - ing call, sweet rest de - scend on all,
Time sends its warn - ing call, sweet rest de - scend on all,
Good night, good night!

Little Bo-Peep

Lit - tle Bo - Peep has lost her sheep, and can - not tell where to find them,
Leave them a - lone and they'll come home, and bring their tails be - hind them.

Twelve Bright Elves

Wood

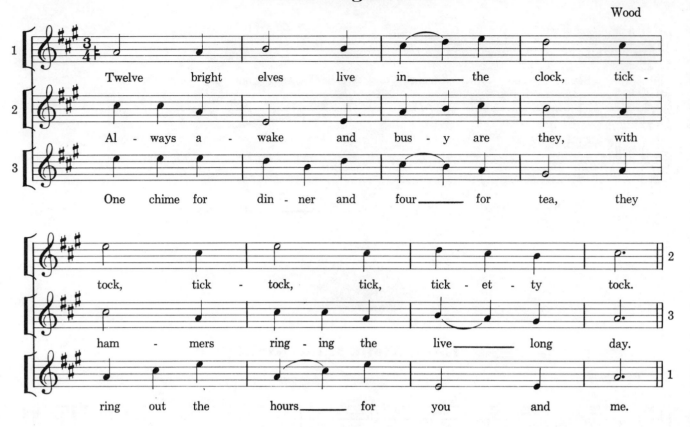

Twelve bright elves live in the clock, tick- tock, tick - tock, tick, tick - et - ty tock.

Al - ways a - wake and bus - y are they, with ham - mers ring - ing the live long day.

One chime for din - ner and four for tea, they ring out the hours for you and me.

Little Miss Muffet

Brightly

Nesbitt

Lit - tle Miss Muf - fet sat on a tuf - fet, Eat - ing her curds and whey; There

came a great spi - der, And sat down be - side her, And fright - end Miss Muf - fet a - way. How

hor - rid of the spi - der, That ver - y nas - ty spi - der, To fright - en Miss Muf - fet a - way! Oh!

Three Geese in Halberstoe

Three geese in Hal - ber - stoe; All were old and all were slow.

Hear the farm - er call - ing as the night is fall - ing.

Wer do? Wer do? Wer do? Wer do?

Where _____ did _____ those three geese go?

Halberstadt in Germany

Three Blind Mice I

Deuteromelia

Three blind mice,

See how they run!

They all ran af - ter the farm - er's wife, Who

Did ev - er you see such a thing in your life As

Three blind mice; _____

See, how they run! _____

chopp'd off their tails with a carv - ing knife;

three blind mice! _____

13

Three Blind Mice II-Dame Juliane

Deuteromelia - Melvill

Three blind mice, Three blind mice.

Dame Ju - li - ane. Dame Ju - li - ane. The

mill - er and his mer - ry old wife, She scrap'd her tripe, lick thou the knife.

Three Blind Mice III

Three blind mice, Three blind mice,

Ran a - round thrice, ran a - round thrice, The

mill - er and his mer - ry old wife Ne'er laughed so much in all their life.

Humpty Dumpty

Sweeting

Hump - ty Dump - ty sat,_____ Hump - ty Dump - ty sat,_____

Hump - ty Dump - ty had,_____ Hump - ty Dump - ty

All_____ the king's hor - - ses, and all_____ the king's men,_____

Hump - ty Dump - ty sat_____ on a wall,

had,_____ Hump - ty Dump - ty had_____ a great fall;

Couldn't put Hump - ty Dump - ty to - geth - er a - gain.

Jack and Jill I

Try It Fast!

Dr. Burney

Jack and Jill went up a hill, To fetch a pail of wa-ter;

Jack fell down and broke his crown, And Jill came tum-bling aft-er.

Jack and Jill II

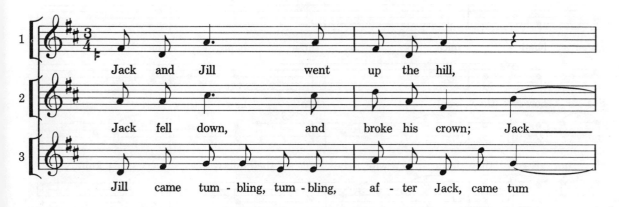

Jack and Jill went up the hill,

Jack fell down, and broke his crown; Jack

Jill came tum-bling, tum-bling, af-ter Jack, came tum

Jack and Jill went up the hill, Jack and Jill went

fell down, and broke his crown, Jack fell down, and

bling aft-er, Jill came tumbling, tumbling, af-ter, Jack came tumbling,

up the hill, To fetch a pail of wa-ter.

broke his crown. Jill came tumbling, tum-bling aft-er.

Jill aft-er Jack, came tumbling, aft-er Jack tumbling.

15

Are You Sleeping? – Three Blind Mice

Are you sleep - ing? Are you sleep - ing?

Broth - er John! Broth - er John!

Morn - ing bells are ring - ing, morn - ing bells are ring - ing

Ding, ding dong! Ding, ding, dong!

Three blind mice, three blind mice;

See how they run! See how they run They

all ran aft - er the farm - er's wife, she cut off their tails with a carv - ing knife, you

nev - er saw such a sight in your life as three blind mice.

Mingled Melodies ... A Quod Libet

BELLS

The Little Bell At Westminster

The lit - tle bell at West - min - ster goes Ding, ding, ding - a - dong.

Oh, How Lovely Is the Evening

Sonorously

Oh, how love - ly is the

When the bells are sweet - ly

Ding, dong, ding,

eve - ning, is the eve - ning,

ring - ing, sweet - ly ring - ing,

dong, ding, dong.

The Great Bells of Oseney

Merrily   Deuteromelia Melvill

The great bells of Ose - ney They ring, they jing, they

ring, they jing. The ten - or of them goes mer - ri - ly.

All in to Service

Merrily   Pammelia

All in to ser - vice, Let us ring mer - ri -

ly to - geth - er, Ding, dong, ding, dong bell.

List to the Sound

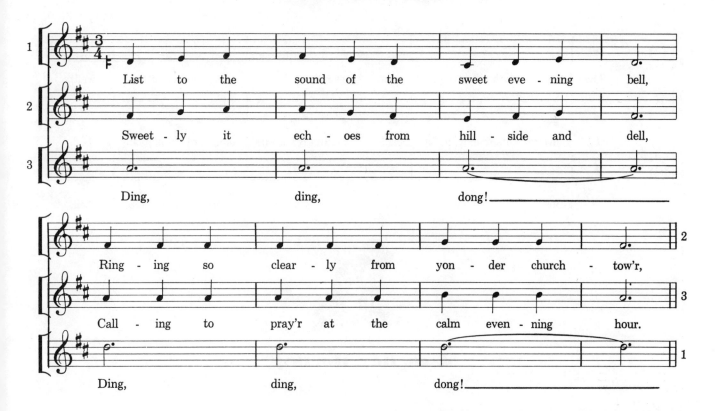

1. List to the sound of the sweet eve-ning bell,
2. Sweet-ly it ech-oes from hill-side and dell,
3. Ding, ding, dong!

Ring-ing so clear-ly from yon-der church-tow'r,
Call-ing to pray'r at the calm eve-ning hour.
Ding, ding, dong!

Great Tom Is Cast

With resonance   Henry Aldrich

Great Tom is cast and Christ-Church bells ring
one, two, three, four, five, six, and Tom comes last.

All in to Service the Bells Toll

CANON: 3 VOICES   Melvill Pammelia

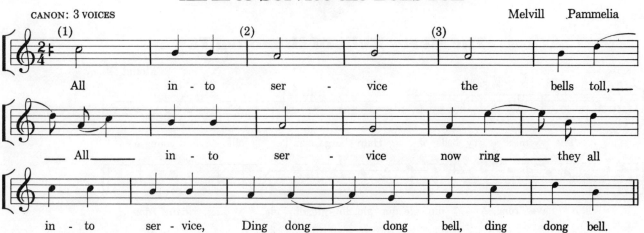

All in-to ser - vice the bells toll,

All into ser - vice now ring they all

in - to ser - vice, Ding dong dong bell, ding dong bell.

The Bell Doth Toll

1. The bell doth toll, its ech - oes roll, I know the sound full well;

2. I love its ringing, for it calls to singing with its bim, bim, bim, bom, bell.

3. Bom, Bom, Bom; bim, bome, bell.

Jack, Boy, Ho, Boy

Spiritedly   Pammelia

Jack, boy, ho, boy, news! news! The
cat is in the well! Let us ring now for her
knell, ding, dong, ding, dong, bell.

The Merry Bells of Hamburg Town

Moffat

The mer - ry bells of Ham - burg town, To old and young a -
like have rung, A din - gle, din - gle, din - gle, din - gle, ding, dang, dong.

Those Evening Bells

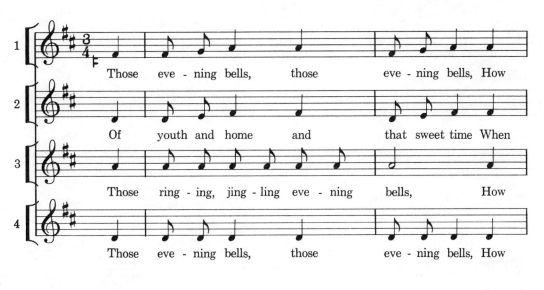

Those eve-ning bells, those eve-ning bells, How

Of youth and home and that sweet time When

Those ring-ing, jing-ling eve-ning bells, How

Those eve-ning bells, those eve-ning bells, How

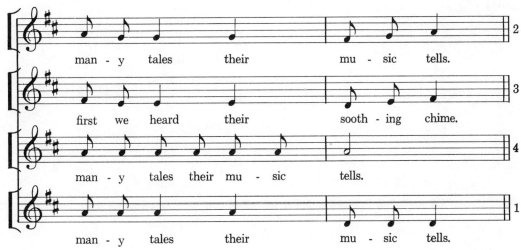

man-y tales their mu-sic tells.

first we heard their sooth-ing chime.

man-y tales their mu-sic tells.

man-y tales their mu-sic tells.

I Love to Hear the Pealing Bells

Sonorously

I love to hear the peal-ing bells, the peal-ing bells,

The mer-ry lit-tle chiming bells, the mer-ry little chiming bells, the mer-ry lit-tle chiming bells,

The clang-ing, wran-gling, bang-ing bells,

The big, low, slow, bells.

And See'st Thou My Cow

Melismata

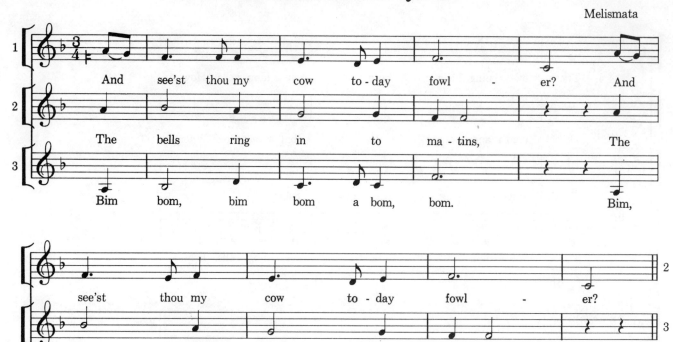

Hark! The Bell Is Ringing

Rhythmically

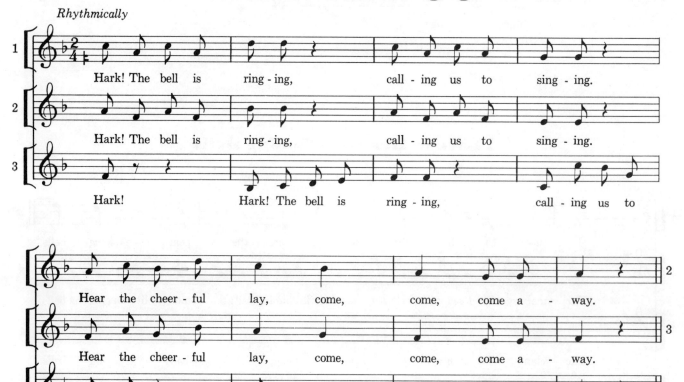

Sing You Now After Me

Fairly slow

Pammelia - Melvill

Sing you now aft - er me.

And as I sing, sing ye, So shall we well a - gree;

Five parts in u - - ni - ty, Ding - dong, ding-dong, ding-dong, ding-dong bell!

Let's Have a Peal for John Cooke's Soul

Pammelia - Melvill

Let's have_____ a peal for John Cooke's

With bells all in an or - der, the cruse with the black

And I mine own self will ring the tre - ble

Stand fast now my mates, ring mer - ri - ly and

soul, for he was an hon - est man,

bowl, The tan - kard like - wise with the can,

bell, And drink to you ev - er - y one.

well Till all this good ale is_____ gone.

May the Queen Live Long

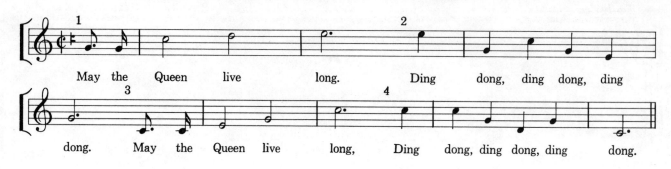

May the Queen live long. Ding dong, ding dong, ding

dong. May the Queen live long, Ding dong, ding dong, ding dong.

STREET CRIES
AND PROFESSIONS

Buy My Primroses

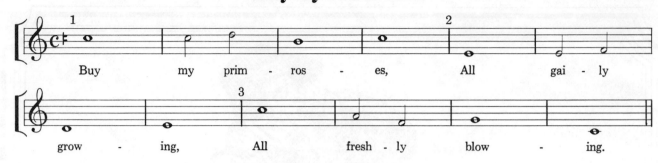

Buy my prim-ros-es, All gai-ly grow-ing, All fresh-ly blow-ing.

White Sand and Grey Sand

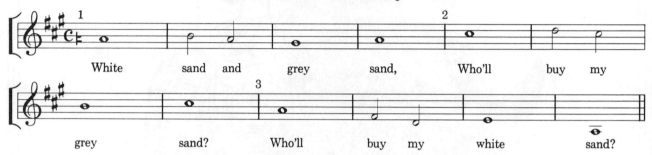

White sand and grey sand, Who'll buy my grey sand? Who'll buy my white sand?

Past Ten O'Clock

Past ten o'-clock, Fair is the night; Past ten o'-clock, stars shin-ing bright.

Morning Papers

Raucously

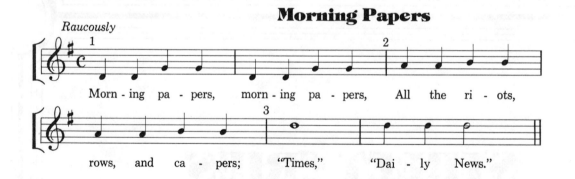

Morn-ing pa-pers, morn-ing pa-pers, All the ri-ots, rows, and ca-pers; "Times," "Dai-ly News."

Who'll Buy My Posies

Who'll buy my po-sies of Li-lies and ro-ses, of Cow-slips and prim-ro-ses? Come, la-dies, buy them.

Have You Any Work for a Tinker

Brightly

Nelham

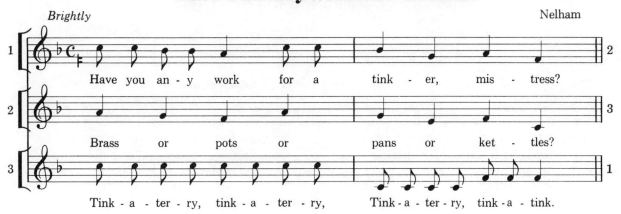

1. Have you an - y work for a tink - er, mis - tress?
2. Brass or pots or pans or ket - tles?
3. Tink - a - ter - ry, tink - a - ter - ry, Tink - a - ter - ry, tink - a - tink.

Now the Blacksmith's Arm

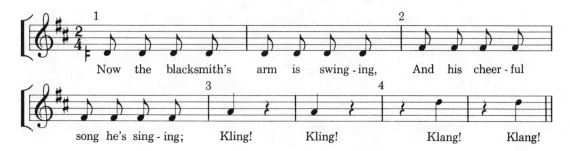

Now the blacksmith's arm is swing - ing, And his cheer - ful
song he's sing - ing; Kling! Kling! Klang! Klang!

A Miller, A Miller

Pammelia   Melvill

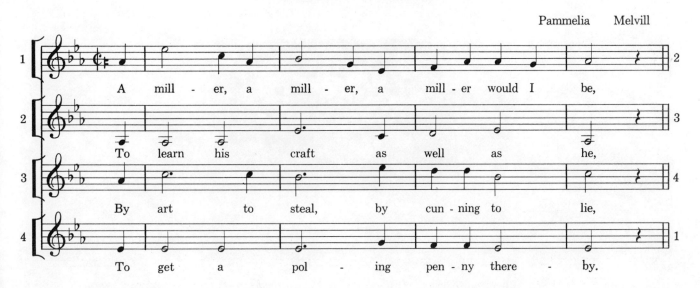

1. A mill - er, a mill - er, a mill - er would I be,
2. To learn his craft as well as he,
3. By art to steal, by cun - ning to lie,
4. To get a pol - ing pen - ny there - by.

He That Will an Alehouse Keep

Melismata

He that will an ale-house keep, Must have three things in store: A
cham - ber and a feath - er bed; A chim - ney and a Hey nonny, non-ny,
Hey nonny, non - ny, Hey non - ny no, Hey non - ny no, Hey non - ny no.

In Darkness

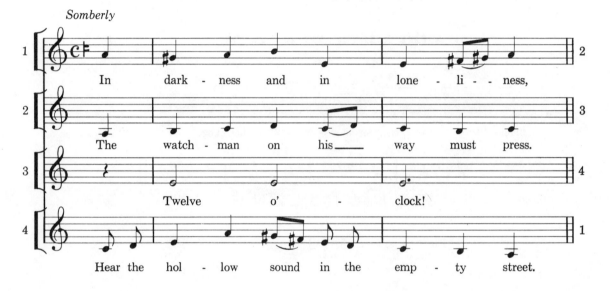

Somberly

In dark - ness and in lone - li - - ness,
The watch - man on his____ way must press.
Twelve o' - clock!
Hear the hol - low sound in the emp - ty street.

28

Buy My Dainty Fine Beans

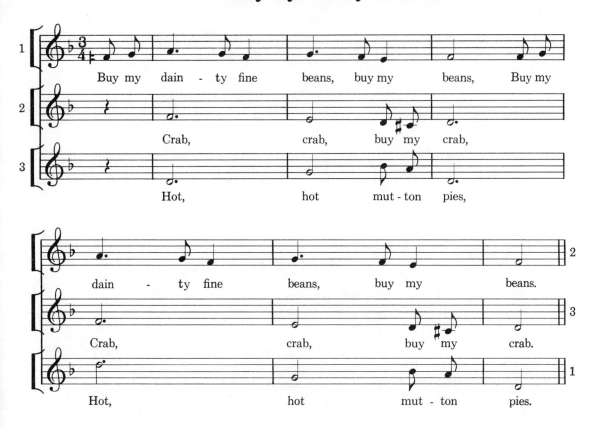

Pray Remember

Alcock

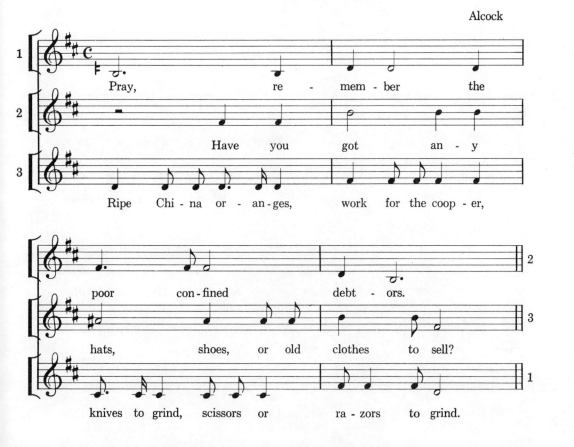

Chairs To Mend

Hayes

With marked rhythm

Chairs to mend, old chairs to mend,

mack - er - el, new mack - er - el,

Old rags, an - y old bones, Take

Rush or cane-bottomed old chairs to mend, old chairs to mend. New

New mack - er - el, new mack - er - el,

mon-ey for your old rags, an - y hare - skins or rab - bit skins.

New Oysters

Pammelia

New oys - ters, New oys -

Have you an - y wood to cleave? Have you an - y wood to

What kit - chen stuff have you, maids? What kit - chen stuff have you,

ters, New oys - ters, New!

cleave? Have you an - y wood to cleave?

maids? What kit - chen stuff have you, maids?

Half an Hour Past 12 O'Clock

Marella

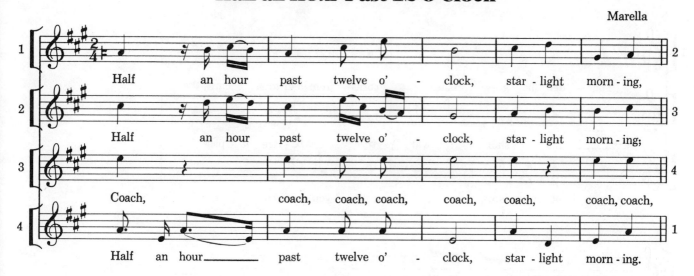

Hot Spice Ginger Bread

Yonder He Goes

Nelham

Yon - der he goes, takes corns from your toes, cures the

his skill I will try be - fore he pass

ports of your fame, sir, calls you a - gain, sir.

gout and all___ woes. Call him hith - er,___

by, or sure I shall die this weath - er. The re -

Show your skill or shame_____ your face ev - er.

Come Pretty Maidens

Brewer

Come pret - ty maid - ens, what will you buy?

Here be la - ces and masks for your fa - ces,

cham - ber. Come and buy, come

See what do you lack? If you can find a toy to your

cor - al, jet and am - ber; gloves made of thread, and

buy for your lov - ing hon - ey, some pret - ty toy

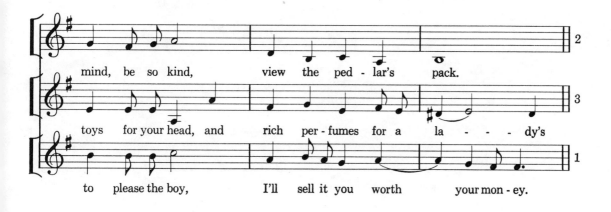

mind, be so kind, view the ped - lar's pack.

toys for your head, and rich per - fumes for a la - - - dy's

to please the boy, I'll sell it you worth your mon - ey.

These Are the Cries of London Town

Cobb

These are the cries of Lon - don town,

Now if you will but wait_____ a - while,

guile. To hear each one with sing - ing cry their

by. I have hot pip - pin pies,

Some go_ up street and some go down.

Sweet - - ly it will, sweet - ly it will the hour be -

sev - - 'ral things as_ they_____ pass

hot. Will you have an - y milk?_ Buy a brush!

33

Have You Observed

Holmes

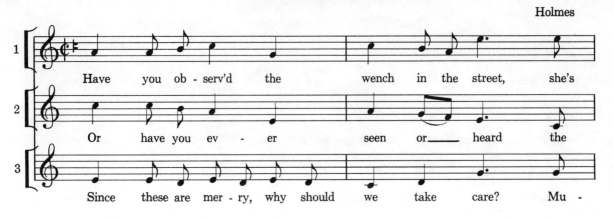

1. Have you ob - serv'd the wench in the street, she's
2. Or have you ev - er seen or heard the
3. Since these are mer - ry, why should we take care? Mu -

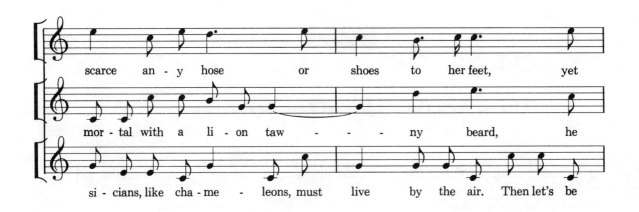

scarce an - y hose or shoes to her feet, yet
mor - tal with a li - on taw - - - ny beard, he
si - cians, like cha - me - leons, must live by the air. Then let's be

she is ver - y mer - ry, and when she cries she sings: I ha'
lives as mer - ri - ly as an - y heart can wish, and still he
blithe and bon - ny, and no good meeting balk, for

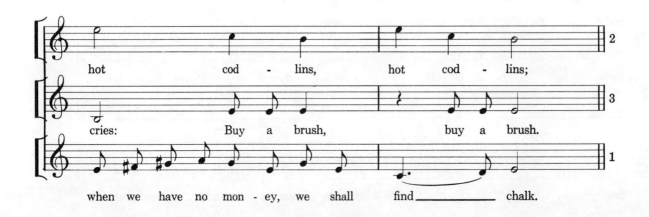

hot cod - lins, hot cod - lins;
cries: Buy a brush, buy a brush.
when we have no mon - ey, we shall find chalk.

Who'll Buy My Roses

A QUODLIBET OF THREE FOREIGN FOLK SONGS

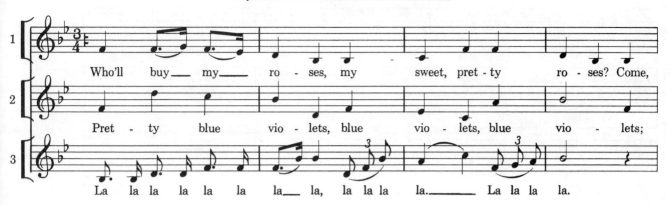

1 Who'll buy__ my__ ro - ses, my sweet, pret - ty ro - ses? Come,

2 Pret - ty blue vio - lets, blue vio - lets, blue vio - lets;

3 La la la la la la la__ la, la la la la.__ La la la la.

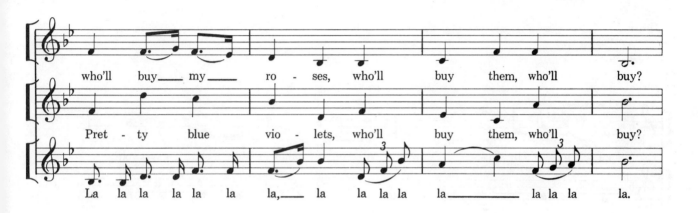

who'll buy__ my__ ro - ses, who'll buy them, who'll buy?

Pret - ty blue vio - lets, who'll buy them, who'll buy?

La la la la la la la,__ la la la la la__ la la la la.

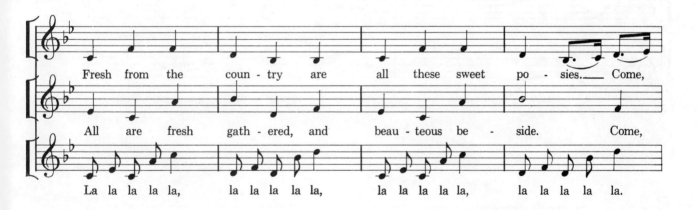

Fresh from the coun - try are all these sweet po - sies.__ Come,

All are fresh gath - ered, and beau - teous be - side. Come,

La la la la la, la la la la la, la la la la la, la la la la la.

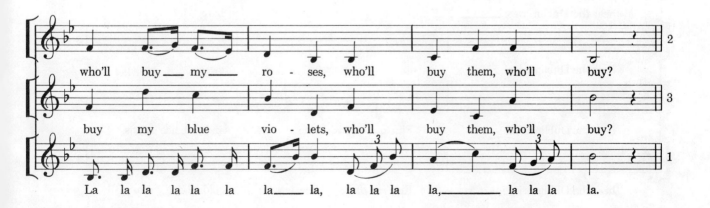

who'll buy__ my__ ro - ses, who'll buy them, who'll buy? 2

buy my blue vio - lets, who'll buy them, who'll buy? 3

La la la la la la la__ la, la la la la,__ la la la la. 1

Come, Buy My Cherries

Stevenson

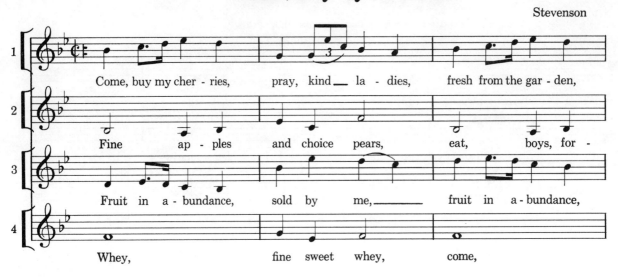

Come, buy my cher - ries, pray, kind __ la - dies, fresh from the gar - den,

Fine ap - ples and choice pears, eat, boys, for -

Fruit in a - bundance, sold by me, __ fruit in a - bundance,

Whey, fine sweet whey, come,

ga - - - ther'd by me. All on a summer's day, so __ gay you

get your cares. All on a summer's day so gay you

here you see. All on a summer's day so __ gay you

taste my whey. All on a summer's day, so __ gay you

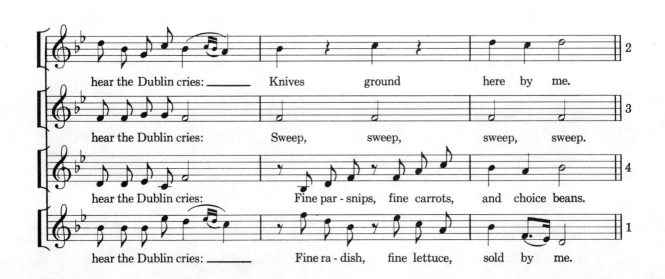

hear the Dublin cries: __ Knives ground here by me.

hear the Dublin cries: Sweep, sweep, sweep, sweep.

hear the Dublin cries: Fine par - snips, fine carrots, and choice beans.

hear the Dublin cries: __ Fine ra - dish, fine lettuce, sold by me.

36

Have You Any Work for a Tinker

Hilton

Plaintively

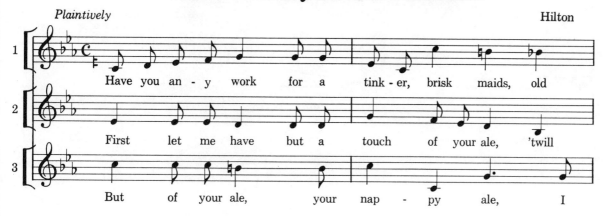

1. Have you an-y work for a tink-er, brisk maids, old
2. First let me have but a touch of your ale, 'twill
3. But of your ale, your nap - py ale, I

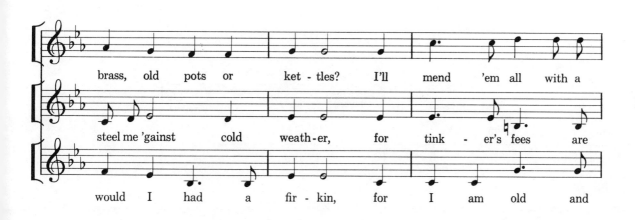

brass, old pots or ket-tles? I'll mend 'em all with a

steel me 'gainst cold weath-er, for tink - er's fees are

would I had a fir - kin, for I am old and

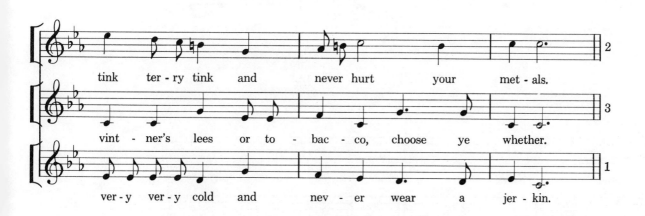

tink ter - ry tink and never hurt your met - als.

vint - ner's lees or to - bac - co, choose ye whether.

ver - y ver - y cold and nev - er wear a jer - kin.

37

Sweep, Sweep

Arne

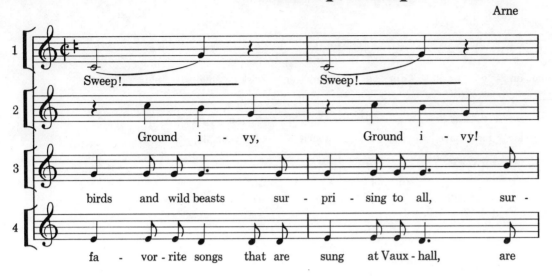

1. Sweep!_____ Sweep!_____
2. Ground i - vy, Ground i - vy!
3. birds and wild beasts sur - pri - sing to all, sur -
4. fa - vor - rite songs that are sung at Vaux - hall, are

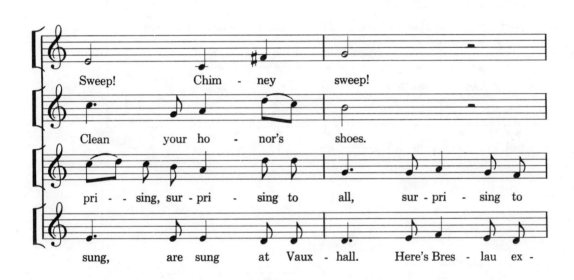

Sweep! Chim - ney sweep!
Clean your ho - nor's shoes.
pri - - sing, sur - pri - - sing to all, sur - pri - - sing to
sung, are sung at Vaux - hall. Here's Bres - lau ex -

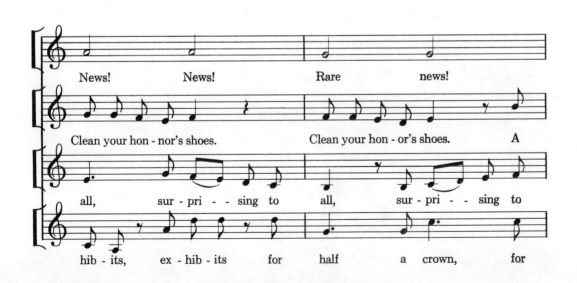

News! News! Rare news!
Clean your hon - nor's shoes. Clean your hon - or's shoes. A
all, sur - pri - - sing to all, sur - pri - - sing to
hib - its, ex - hib - its for half a crown, for

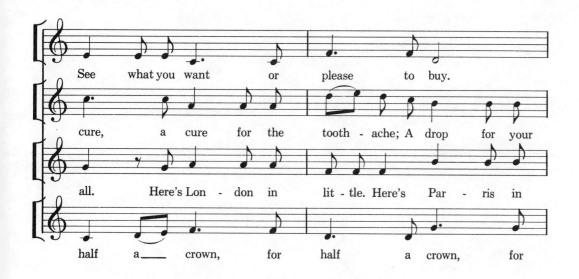

See   what you want   or   please   to   buy.

cure,   a   cure   for   the   tooth - ache; A   drop   for   your

all.   Here's Lon - don   in   lit - tle. Here's   Par - ris   in

half   a   crown,   for   half   a   crown,   for

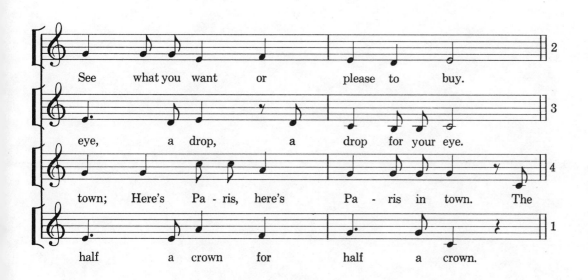

See   what you want   or   please   to   buy.   2

eye,   a   drop,   a   drop   for   your   eye.   3

town;   Here's   Pa - ris,   here's   Pa - ris   in   town.   The   4

half   a   crown   for   half   a   crown.   1

SACRED AND PIOUS

For Health & Strength

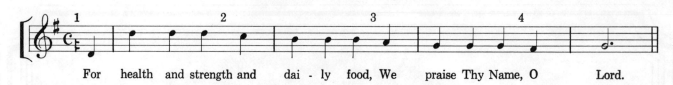

For health and strength and dai - ly food, We praise Thy Name, O Lord.

Conditor Kirie

Pammelia - Melvill

Con - di - tor Ki - ri - e Om - ni - um qui vi - vum Ki - rie lei - son.

Hosannah

Ho - san - nah! Let the earth and skies re - peat the joy - ful sound.

We Thank Thee

Wilson

We thank Thee for our dai - ly bread,

For bless - ings on this ta - ble spread

Our Fa - ther we thank Thee.

Join in Singing Hallelujah

Join in sing - ing Hal - le - lu - jah! Hal - le - lu - jah! A - men,

A - men, Hal - le - lu - jah! Hal - le - lu - jah! A - men.

O, Give Thanks

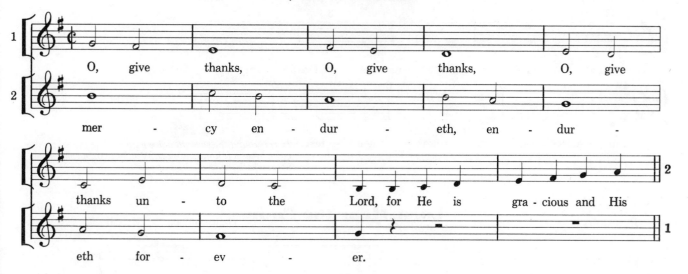

O, give thanks, O, give thanks, O, give
mer - cy en - dur - eth, en - dur -

thanks un - to the Lord, for He is gra - cious and His
eth for - ev - er.

Adiuva Nos Deus

Pammelia

CANON: 4 VOICES

A - div - ra nos De - - - - - us.

Donec A Boire

Old French   Pammelia

CANON: 4 VOICES

Do - nec a boire al - le bon com - pan - i -
on Al - le - lu - ia, Al - le - lu - ia.

Attend My People

Pammelia - Melvill

At - tend my peo - ple and give ear,
I am thy Sov - er'n Lord and God,

Of fer - ly'* things I shall thee tell.
Which have thee brought I from care - ful thrall,

See that my words in mind thou bear,
And ere re - claim'd from Phar - oah's rod.

And to my pre - cepts lis - ten well.
Make thee no gods on them to call.

*ferly = wondrous

43

Laudate Nomen

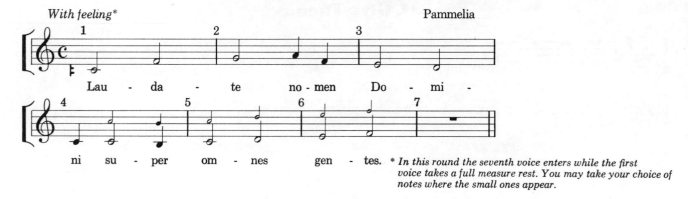

With feeling* Pammelia

Lau - da - te no - men Do - mi - ni su - per om - nes gen - tes.

* *In this round the seventh voice enters while the first voice takes a full measure rest. You may take your choice of notes where the small ones appear.*

Lord, Hear the Poor

Plaintively Deuteromelia - Melvill

Lord, hear the poor that cry, they which do live in pain and mi - ser - y, Son of God, show some pit - y.

Joy in the Gates

CANON: 6 VOICES Pammelia - Melvill

Joy in the gates of Je - ru - sa - lem, Peace be in Si - on.

O Lord, on Whom I Do Depend

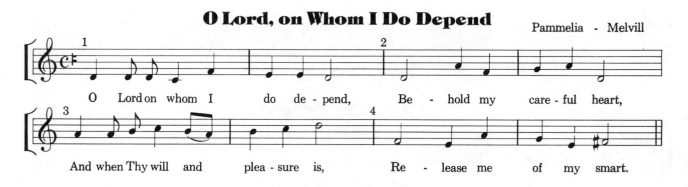

Pammelia - Melvill

O Lord on whom I do de - pend, Be - hold my care - ful heart, And when Thy will and plea - sure is, Re - lease me of my smart.

Praise the Lord, O Ye Servants

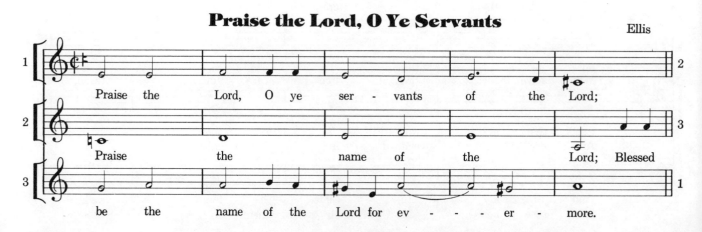

Ellis

Praise the Lord, O ye ser - vants of the Lord; Praise the name of the Lord; Blessed be the name of the Lord for ev - er - more.

O Lord, in Thee Is all My Trust

Pammelia - Melvill

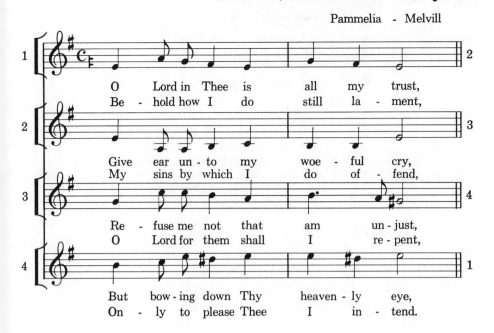

O Lord in Thee is all my trust,
Be - hold how I do still la - ment,

Give ear un - to my woe - ful cry,
My sins by which I do of - fend,

Re - fuse me not that am un - just,
O Lord for them shall I re - pent,

But bow - ing down Thy heaven - ly eye,
On - ly to please Thee I in - tend.

I Wept and Chastened Myself

Lawes

CANON: 3 VOICES

I wept and cha - sten'd my -

self with fast - ing, and

that was turn'd to my re - proof.

Hear Thou My Prayer

Hayes

Slowly

Hear Thou my pray'r, O Lord,

And aid Thy ser - vant in this hour of need;

Hear me, O Lord, hear my pray'r, O Lord.

45

O, My Fearful Dreams

Pammelia - Melvill

O my fear-ful dreams nev - er for-get shall
I; Me-thought I
demn'd to die, Whose name was Je -

I, nev - - er for - get shall
heard a maid - en's child con -
sus, Whose name was Je - - sus.

Oh, Praise The Lord

Pammelia

With dignity

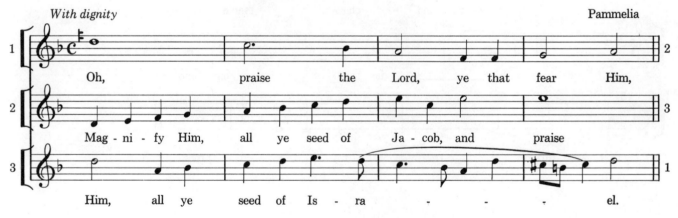

Oh, praise the Lord, ye that fear Him,
Mag - ni - fy Him, all ye seed of Ja - cob, and praise
Him, all ye seed of Is - ra - - - - el.

Miserere Nostri Domine Secundum

Pammelia

Mi - se - re - re no - stri Do - mi - ne, se - cun - dum
mi - se - ri - cor - di - am tu - - am.

Miserere Nostri Domine Viventium

Pammelia - Mevill

Mi - se - re - re nos - tri Do - mi - ne vi - ven - ti -

um et mor - tu - o - - - - rum.

Haleluia, Haleluia

Cobb

Ha - le - lu - ia, Ha - le - lu - -

ia, Ha - le - lu - ia, Ha - le - lu - - ia.

Emitte Lucem Tuam

Pammelia

CANON: 4 VOICES

E - mit - te lu - cem tu - am et ve - ri - ta - - -

tem ip - sa me de - du - cant et ad -

du - cant in mon - tem sanc - tum tu - um et in ta - ber - na - cu - la.

Pietas Omnias Virtutum

Pammelia - Melvill

Pi - e - tas om - ni - um vir - tu -

tum, pa - rens et fun - da - men -

tum, pa - rens et fun - da - men - - tum.

C'est Benir Ton Nom

Celebrons Sans Cesse

Pammelia

Quicavid Petieritis Patrem

Pammelia

CANON: 4 VOICES

Vias Tuas, Domine

Pammelia

Vi - as tu - as, Do - mi - ne, de - mon - stra mi - hi, et se - mi - tas tu - as e - do - ce me, e - do - ce - me.

Benedic, Domine, Nobis His

Pammelia

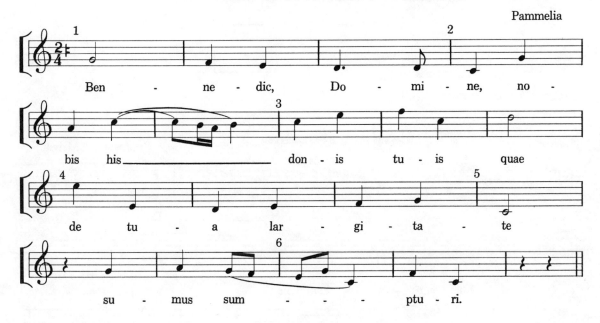

Ben - ne - dic, Do - mi - ne, no - bis his _____ don - is tu - is quae de tu - a lar - gi - ta - te su - mus sum - - - ptu - ri.

Domine Fili Dei Vivi

Pammelia

Do - mi - ne Fi - li De - i vi - - - - - vi, mi - ser - e - re no - stri, qui tol - lis qui _____ tol - lis pec - ca - ta _____ mun - di.

Exaudi Domine (I)

Pammelia

Ex - au - di Do - mi - ne or - a - - - ti - o - - - nem me - am.

Exaudi Domine (II)

CANON: 3 VOICES

Hilton

Ex - au - di Do - mi - ne_____ o - ra - ti - o - nem me - - - - - - - um.

Cantate Domino

CANON: 4 VOICES

Pammelia - Melvill

Can - ta - - - - - te_____ Do - - - - mi - no, can - ti - cum no - - - - vum, can - ti - - - cum no - vum, no - vum, no - - vum.

I Am so Weary

CANON: 3 VOICES

Ford

I am so wear - - - ry of this ling - - 'ring grief;

Some speed-y help, I__ faint and die; Some speed-y

help, I__ faint and die;_____ in brief to live and

lan - - - guish thus with - out_____ re - lief.

Dona Nobis Pacem (I)

With deep feeling

Attributed to Palestrina

Fides Et Animae Vita (I)

CANON: 4 VOICES

Pammelia

Fides Et Animae Vita (II)

Pammelia

Mane Nobiscum

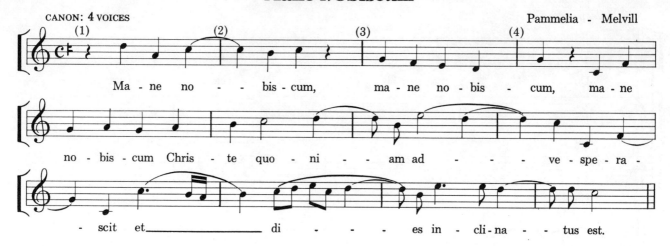

Haec Est Vita Aeterna

Inte Domine Speravi

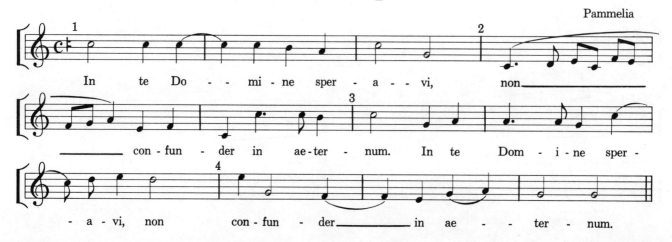

Intende Voci Orationis Meae

CANON: 3 VOICES

Pammelia - Melvill

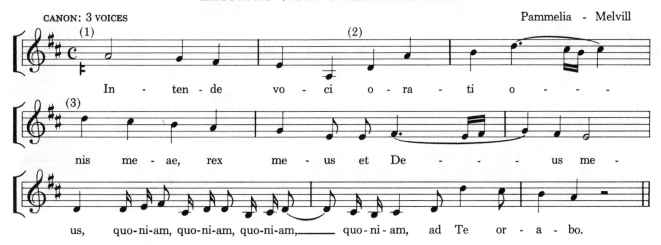

In - ten - de vo - ci o - ra - ti - o - -

nis me - ae, rex me - us et De - - - us me -

us, quo-ni-am, quo-ni-am, quo-ni-am,_____ quo - ni - am, ad Te or - a - bo.

Libera Me Domine

Pammelia

Li - be - ra me Do - mi - ne a per - se - quen -

ti - bus_____ me qui - a_____ com - - for - ta - ti

sunt_____ su - - - - per_____ me.

Verbum Domine Manet

Pammelia

Ver - - - - - - - bum Do - mi - ni_____

_____ ma - net_____

in_____ ae - ter - num, in ae - ter - - - num.

53

Oh; Absalom, My Son

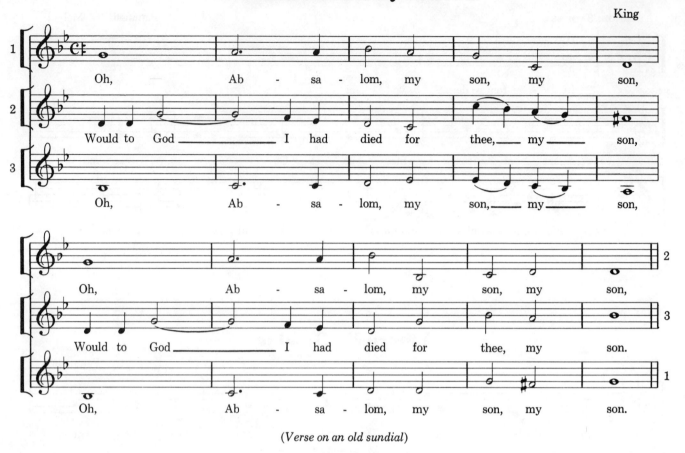

Oh, — Ab - sa - lom, my son, my son,

Would to God _____ I had died for thee,— my _____ son,

Oh, Ab - sa - lom, my son,— my _____ son,

Oh, — Ab - sa - lom, my son, my son,

Would to God _____ I had died for thee, my son.

Oh, Ab - sa - lom, my son, my son.

(Verse on an old sundial)

With Warning Hand

Piously

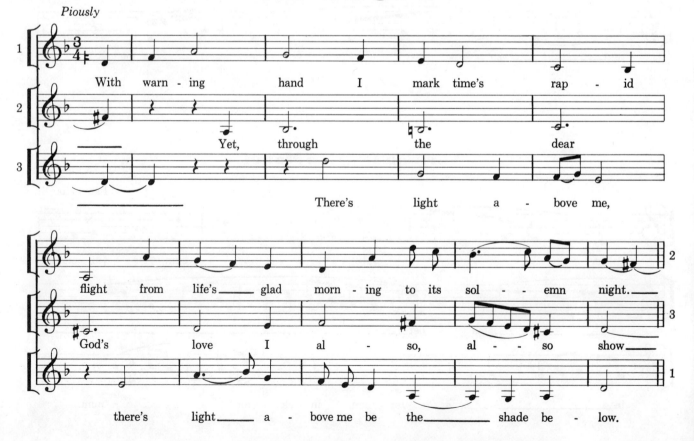

With warn - ing hand I mark time's rap - id

Yet, through the dear

There's light a - bove me,

flight from life's _____ glad morn - ing to its sol - emn night.—

God's love I al - so, al - so show—

there's light _____ a - bove me be the _____ shade be - low.

54

I Charge Ye, O Daughters of Jerusalem

Hilton

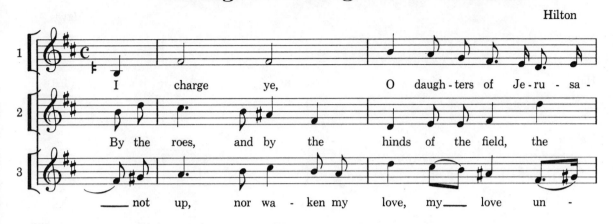

I charge ye, O daugh-ters of Je-ru-sa-
By the roes, and by the hinds of the field, the
—— not up, nor wa-ken my love, my—— love un-

lem,———————— Jer-ru-sa-lem,
field, That ye stir————
til———————————— she please.

Bless Them That Curse You

Hilton

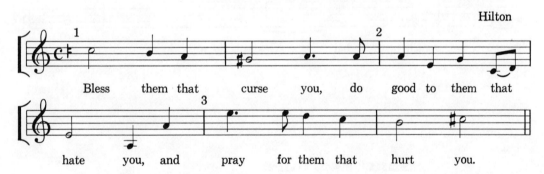

Bless them that curse you, do good to them that
hate you, and pray for them that hurt you.

Laudate Nomen Domini

Pammelia

Lau-da-te no-men Do-mi-ni, Lau-da-te ser-vi———— Do-mi-
num qui———— sta-tis in do-mo Do-mi-ni.

Hallelujah

Hayes

Hal - - le - - lu - - jah, hal -
Hal - - le - - lu - - jah, hal -
Hal - le - lu - jah, hal - le - lu - jah, hal -
Hal - le - lu - jah, hal - le - lu - jah, hal -

le - - lu - jah, hal - le - lu - jah!
- le - - lu - jah, hal - le - lu - jah!
le - - lu - jah, hal - le - lu - jah!
le - lu - jah, hal - - le - lu - jah!

Sanct Escriture

CANON: 4 VOICES

Pammelia

Sanct es - cri - ture te pro - po - se, Si tu

ven - i a com - pler la loy, D'a - mer ton

dieu sour tou - te chose, Et ton pro - chain au - tant_____ que toy.

56

CYNICAL

Seven Great Towns

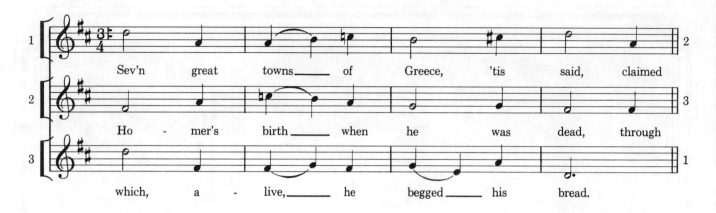

Sev'n great towns___ of Greece, 'tis said, claimed
Ho - mer's birth___ when he was dead, through
which, a - live,___ he begged___ his bread.

By Shady Woods

J. S. Smith

By sha - dy woods and pur - ling streams, I
And would not for the world be taught, to
For who, a - las! can hap - py be,___ that

spend my life in pleas - ing dreams,
change my false de - light - ful thought;
does the truth of all___ things see?

Now I Am Married

Webbe

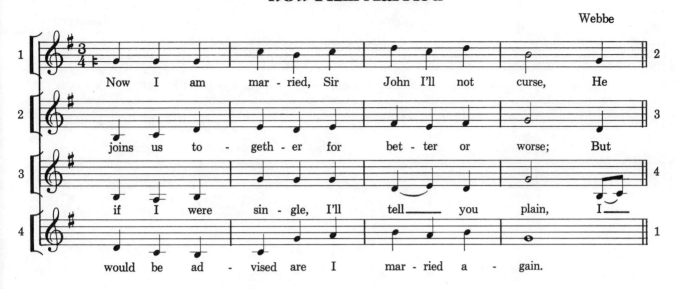

Now I am mar-ried, Sir John I'll not curse, He joins us to-geth-er for bet-ter or worse; But if I were sin-gle, I'll tell____ you plain, I____ would be ad - vised are I mar-ried a - gain.

She That Will Eat

Hilton

She that will eat her break-fast in her bed, And sit at din-ner____ like __ a __ maid - en bride, And Jove of his mer - cy may do much to save her; But____

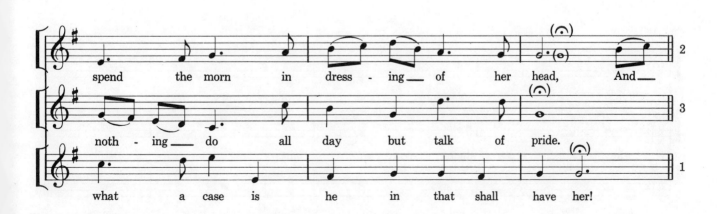

spend the morn in dress-ing ____ of her head, And____ noth - ing ____ do all day but talk of pride. what a case is he in that shall have her!

Come, Where Shall We Walk

Harrington

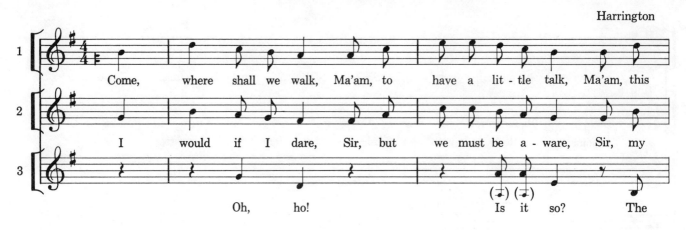

1. Come, where shall we walk, Ma'am, to have a lit-tle talk, Ma'am, this
2. I would if I dare, Sir, but we must be a-ware, Sir, my
3. Oh, ho! Is it so? The

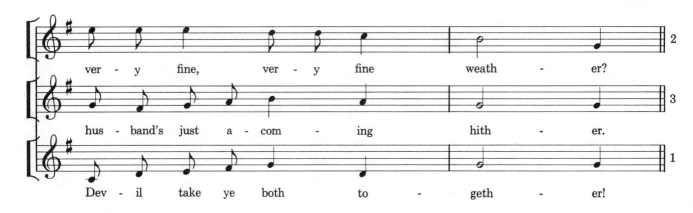

ver-y fine, ver-y fine weath - er?
hus - band's just a-com - ing hith - er.
Dev - il take ye both to - geth - er!

Here Pleasures Are Few

Purcell

1. Here plea - sures are few, and we few - er en - joy; Like
2. We strive hard to grasp it_ and_ with our best skill, Still,
3. When seiz'd at the last, com - pute your real gains. What

quick - sil - ver, plea-sure is bright and is coy:
still it_ e - ludes us, it_ glit - ters_ on_ still.
is it? Poi - son must rank in your veins.

A Woman's Rule

A wom-an's rule should be in such a her o-be-dience nev-er out of sea-son, So fares the hap-less fam-i-ly that shows, A cock that's si-lent, know not which live more un-na-tur-al lives, O -

fash-ion On - - ly to guide her long, so long as ei-ther be - dient hus - bands, or com-mand - ing, a cock that's si - lent, long, so long as ei - ther be - dient hus - bands, or com-mand - ing,

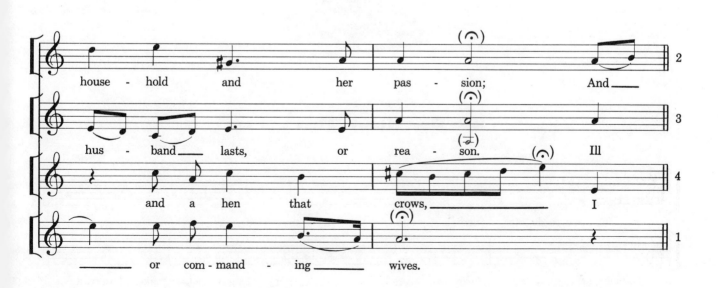

house - hold and her pas - sion; And hus - band lasts, or rea - son. Ill and a hen that crows, I or com-mand - ing wives.

While Adam Slept

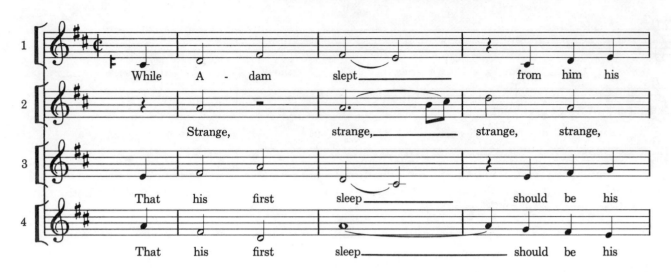

1. While A - dam slept_____ from him his
2. Strange, strange,_____ strange, strange,
3. That his first sleep_____ should be his
4. That his first sleep_____ should be his

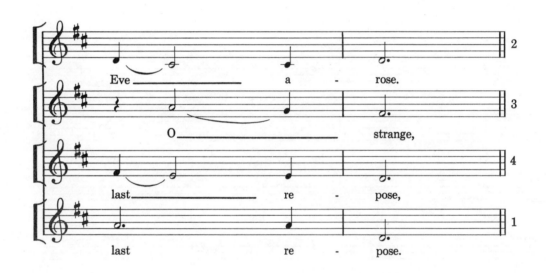

Eve_____ a - rose.
O_____ strange,
last_____ re - pose,
last re - pose.

He That Reads This Verse

Webbe

He_ that reads this verse_ now, per - haps may have a_ low - 'ring sow, whose
looks are no - thing near so bad, as is_ her tongue that makes him mad.

Give Me the Sweet Delight of Love

Harrington

Give me the sweet delights of love, let not anxious

Pure are the blessings love bestowing, peace and harmony,

A smoky house, a

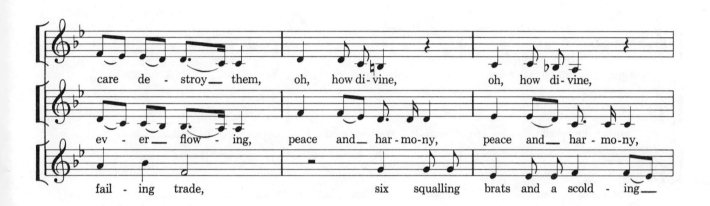

care destroy them, oh, how divine, oh, how divine,

ever flowing, peace and harmony, peace and harmony,

failing trade, six squalling brats and a scolding

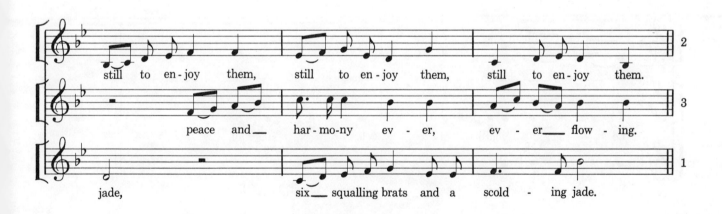

still to enjoy them, still to enjoy them, still to enjoy them.

peace and harmony ever, ever flowing.

jade, six squalling brats and a scolding jade.

63

Mortals Learn Your Lives to Measure

Greene

1. Mor - tals learn your lives to mea - sure, Not by length of

2. Soon your Spring must have a Fall, Los - ing youth is

3. Then you'll ask, but none will give, You may ling - er

time, but plea - sure; Mor - tals learn your lives to mea - sure,

los - ing all; Soon your Spring must have a Fall,

but not live; Then you'll ask, but none will give,

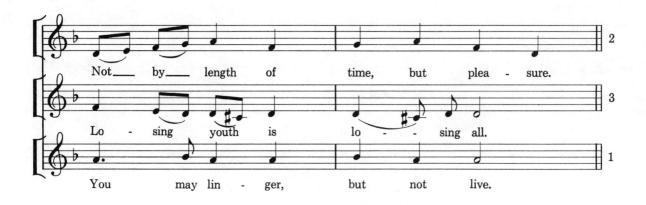

Not by length of time, but plea - sure.

Lo - sing youth is lo - sing all.

You may lin - ger, but not live.

I Have No Hopes

Alcock

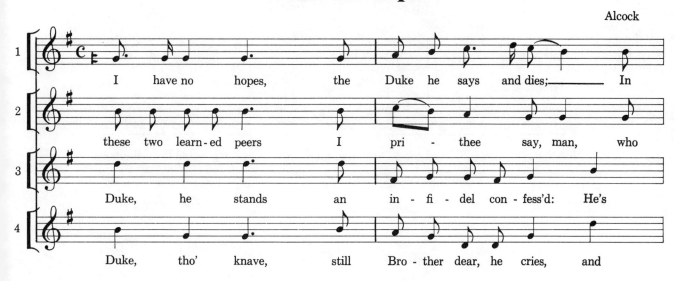

I have no hopes, the Duke he says and dies;_____ In

these two learn-ed peers I pri - thee say, man, who

Duke, he stands an in - fi - del con - fess'd: He's

Duke, tho' knave, still Bro - ther dear, he cries, and

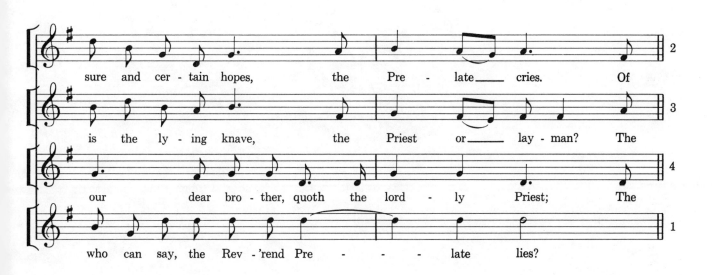

sure and cer - tain hopes, the Pre - late_____ cries. Of

is the ly - ing knave, the Priest or_____ lay - man? The

our dear bro - ther, quoth the lord - ly Priest; The

who can say, the Rev - 'rend Pre - - - late lies?

Whenever I Marry

Lawes

When - ev - er I mar - ry, I'll mar - ry a maid, I'll mar - ry a maid, for

wid - ows are wil - ful, For wid - ows are wil - ful and will be o - beyed.

Ill Fares the Family

Ill fares the fam - i - ly that shews, A si - lent cock and

hen that crows, And a wife that pulls the hus-band by the nose.

EPITAPHS
AND DIRGES

Mourn Anglia

Mourn, mourn, An - glia, mourn, For thy he - ro__ Lost and gone.__

Calm He Rests

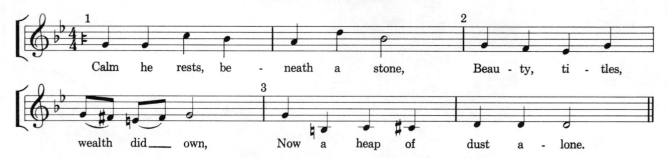

Calm he rests, be - neath a stone, Beau - ty, ti - tles,

wealth did__ own, Now a heap of dust a - lone.

Old Abram Brown

Old A - bram Brown is dead and gone, You'll ne - ver see him more; He

used to wear a long brown coat, That but - toned down be - fore.

Here Lies Poor Teague

Here lies, here lies poor

that Death, his friend,

Death, his friend, has sav'd his life, that

Teague; Pray tell his wife

Has sav'd his life;

Death, his friend, has sav'd his life.

I Am Weary of My Groaning

Nelham

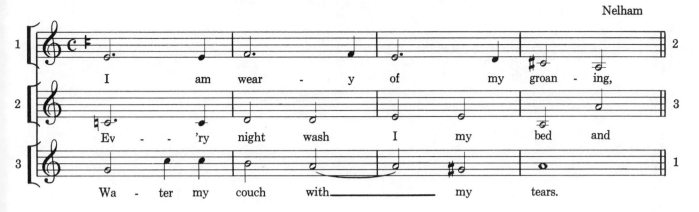

I am wear - y of my groan - ing,

Ev - - 'ry night wash I my bed and

Wa - ter my couch with_____ my tears.

Let's Have a Peal, etc./(Short Version)

Slowly

Pammelia Melvill

Let's have a peal for_____ John Cooke's

soul, For he was a ver - y, ver - y hon - est

man, An hon - est man.

Look, Neighbors, Look

Harrington

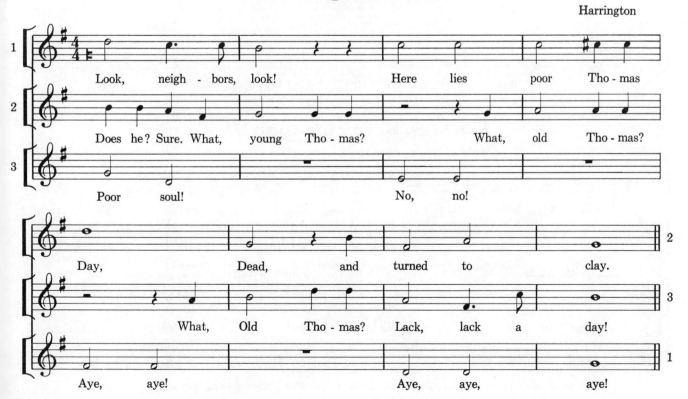

Look, neigh - bors, look! Here lies poor Tho - mas

Does he? Sure. What, young Tho - mas? What, old Tho - mas?

Poor soul! No, no!

Day, Dead, and turned to clay.

What, Old Tho - mas? Lack, lack a day!

Aye, aye! Aye, aye, aye!

Mourn for the Thousands Slain

Slowly and solemnly

Mourn for the thou - sands slain, the youth - ful and the strong,

Mourn for the ty - rant's fa - tal reign, and — the de - lud - ed throng!

Mourn, mourn, mourn, Mourn for the thou-sands slain.

So Peaceful Rests

Greene

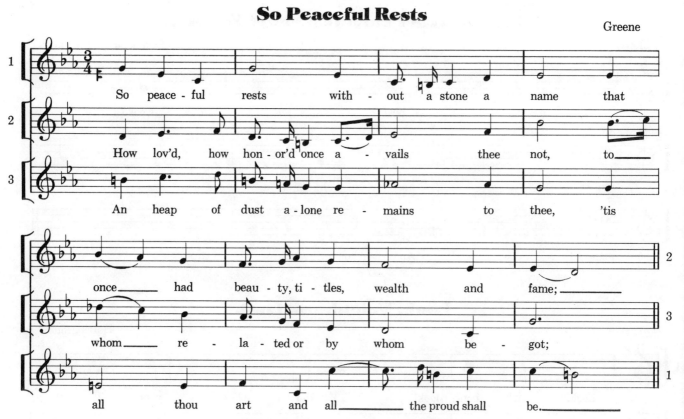

So peace - ful rests with - out a stone a name that

How lov'd, how hon - or'd once a - vails thee not, to —

An heap of dust a - lone re - mains to thee, 'tis

once — had beau - ty, ti - tles, wealth and fame; —

whom — re - la - ted or by whom be - got;

all thou art and all — the proud shall be. —

Uds Nigs, Here Ligs John Digs

Uds nigs, here ligs John Digs and Rich - - ard Dig - ger, and to say —

— the truth, to say the truth none knows which was — the big - ger.

They far - ed well and liv - - ed eas - y, and now —

they're dead, and now they're dead, and now they're dead and shall please ye.

70

To Thee 'Tis Given to Live

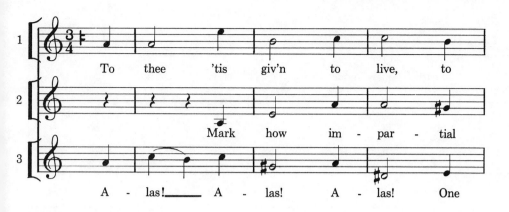

1. To thee 'tis giv'n to live, to me 'twas giv-en to die.

2. Mark how im - par - tial is the will of Heav'n.

3. A - las!___ A - las! A - las! One mo - ment sets us ev'n.

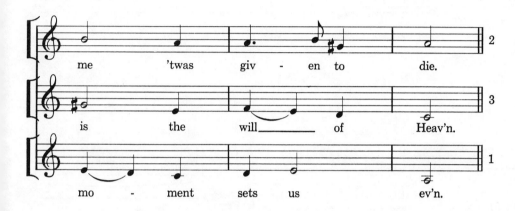

Under This Stone Lies Gabriel John

Purcell

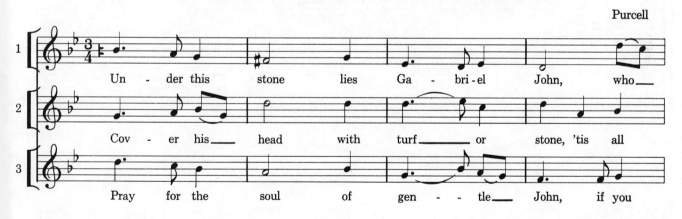

1. Un - der this stone lies Ga - bri - el John, who___ died in the year one thou - sand and one.

2. Cov - er his___ head with turf___ or stone, 'tis all one, 'tis all one, with turf or stone, 'tis all one.

3. Pray for the soul of gen - tle___ John, if you please, you may, or let___ it a - lone, 'tis all one.

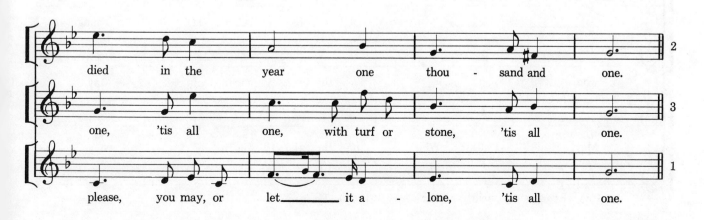

Underneath This Mound'ring Clay

Webbe

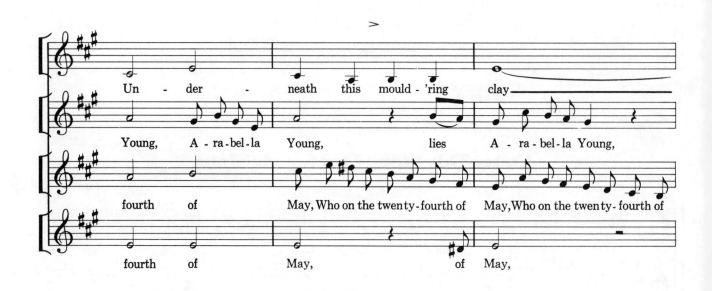

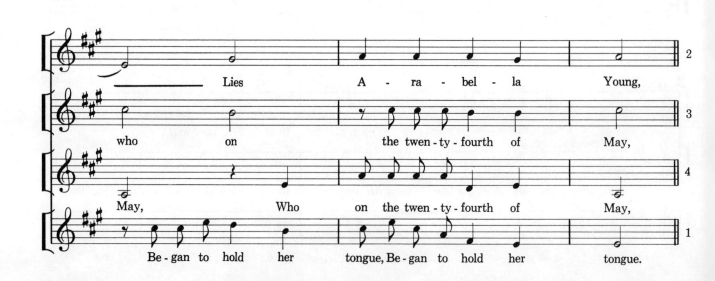

Under A Green Elm

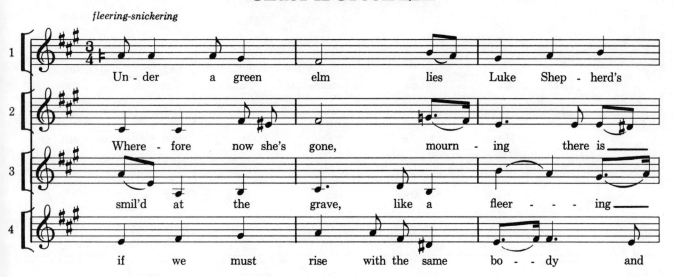

fleering-snickering

Un - der a green elm lies Luke Shep - herd's

Where - fore now she's gone, mourn - ing there is____

smil'd at the grave, like a fleer - - - ing____

if we must rise with the same bo - - dy and

Helm, that____ steer'd____ him ev - - - 'ry way;

none, he____ fol - low'd her corpse____ in gray. He

knave, she'll tell him on't at the last____ day, For

eyes,____ she'll____ have the same tongue,____ folks say.

She Weepeth Sore

Lawes

She weep - eth sore in the night, and her

tears____ are on____ her cheeks;____ Her priests sigh____

____ and her vir - - - gins are af - flict - ed, and a - mong____

all her lov - ers she__ hath none__ to__ com - fort her.

73

Here Innocence & Beauty Lies

Travers

Here In - no - cence and Beau - ty

Hence did she go just as she

Death, that does sin and sor - row

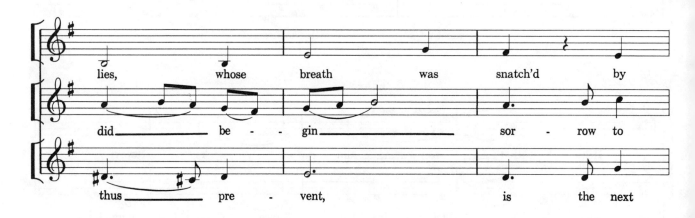

lies, whose breath was snatch'd by

did____ be - gin____ sor - row to

thus____ pre - vent, is the next

ear - ly, not____ un - time - ly Death;

know be - fore____ she knew to sin.

bless - ing to a life well spent.

Oh, That My Head Were Waters

Holmes

Oh, that my head were wa - ters,____ and my

weep, that I might weep, that I might

slain of the daugh - ters, of the daugh - ters of my peo - -

74

eyes a foun - tain of tears, that I might

weep day___ and___ night for the slain, for the

ple, the slain___ of the daughters of my peo - ple.

Poor Ralpho

Savage

Poor Ralph - o

rood, and sure he must be blest; For

best. Think of your souls, ye guilt - y

ye guilt-y throng, who, know-ing what is right, who,

lies be - - neath this

tho' he could do nothing good, he meant to___ do his

throng, think of your souls___

knowing what is right, do wrong, do wrong.

'Mongst Other Folks

J. S. Smith

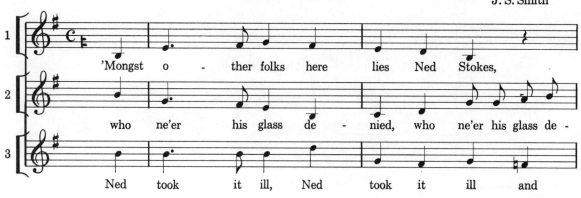

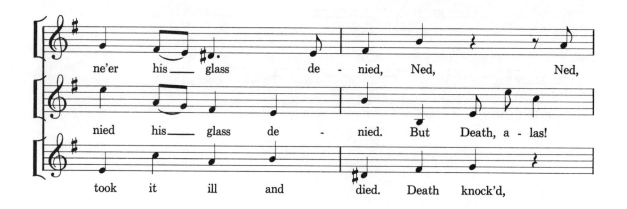

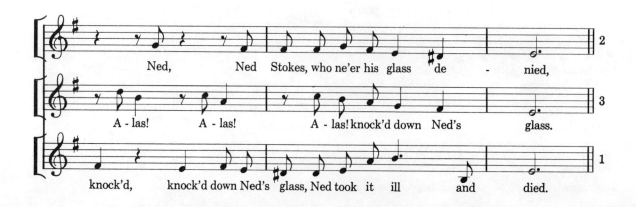

Lost He Wanders

Cocchi

Lost, he wan - - - ders

Now this way, now that way,

grow - ing drifts have bound him, the____ drear - y winds howl round him, the____

He stops, he sinks,

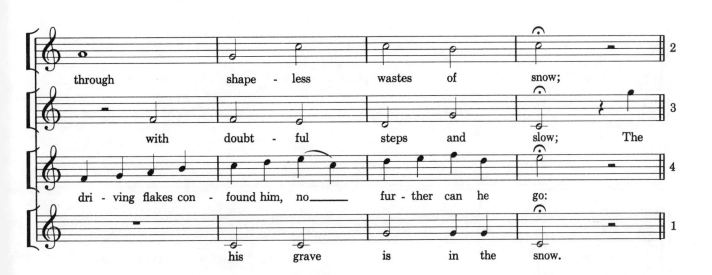

through shape - less wastes of snow;

with doubt - ful steps and slow; The

dri - ving flakes con - found him, no____ fur - ther can he go:

his grave is in the snow.

Here Lies a Woman

Hilton

Here lies a wo - man. Who can de - ny it? She died in peace tho' lived un - quiet.

Her husband prays if o'er her grave you walk, you would tread soft, you would tread

soft, for if she wakes, for if she wakes, she'll talk, tread soft, for if she wakes, she'll talk.

I, Thomas of Bedford

Browne

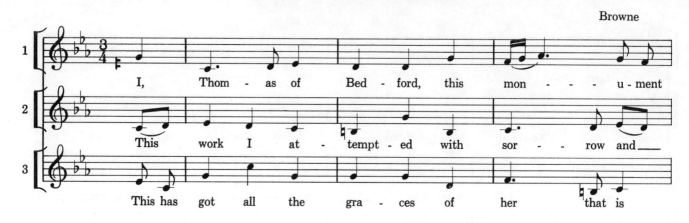

I, Thom - as of Bed - ford, this mon - - - u - ment

This work I at - tempt - ed with sor - - row and__

This has got all the gra - ces of her that is

made for a pair of good__ wives, tho' but one of 'em's

woe: 'cause one wife was__ dead, and the o - ther not__

gone, and o'er and a - bove 'em some few of her__

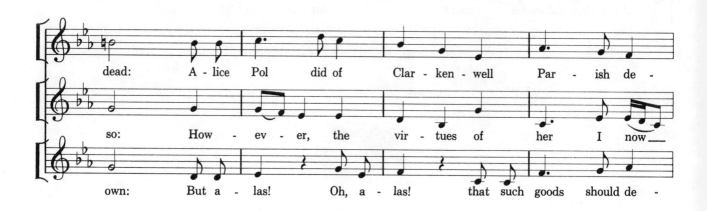

dead: A - lice Pol did of Clar - ken - well Par - ish de -

so: How - ev - er, the vir - tues of her I now__

own: But a - las! Oh, a - las! that such goods should de -

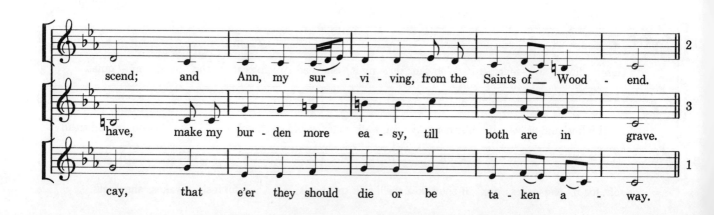

scend; and Ann, my sur - - vi - ving, from the Saints of__ Wood - end.

have, make my bur - den more ea - sy, till both are in grave.

cay, that e'er they should die or be ta - ken a - way.

Intombed Here Lies Good Sir Harry

Browne

1. In - tomb - ed here_____ lies good_____ Sir Har - ry, be -

2. When he_____ did live,_____ and had_____ his feel - - ing,

3. But_ now he's dead,_____ and lost_____ his_ feel - - ing,

lov'd full well_____ but would_____ not mar - ry.

she_____ did lie_____ and he was kneel - - ing.

he_____ doth lie, and she_____ is kneel - - ing.

Ask Me Why I Do Not Sing

Webbe

1. Ask me why I_ do_ not_ sing to the

2. did, as I did not long a - go, when my numbers, when my num - -

3. _____ ah me_____, hath struck my lute and my tongue, and my

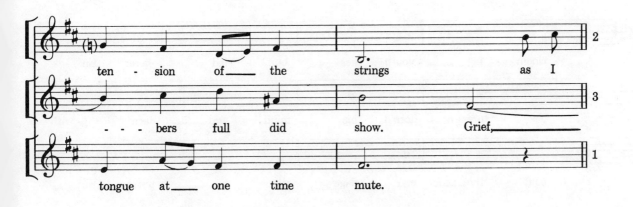

ten - sion of_____ the strings as I

- - - bers full did show. Grief,_____

tongue at_ one time mute.

Beneath in the Dust

Fairly quickly

Cooke

Beneath in the dust, the mould - y old crust of Nell

Having lived long e - nough, she made her last puff, a

Now here doth she lie, to make a dirt pie, in

Batch - e - lor late - ly was shoven; She was skilled in the arts of pies,

puff by her hus - band much praised; A puff, a puff, she

hopes that her crust will be raised, her crust will be raised, her

cus - tards and tarts, and knew ev - ry trick of the ov - en;

made her last puff, a puff by her hus - band much praised.

crust will be raised, in hopes that her crust will be raised.

A Blooming Youth Lies Buried

Boyce

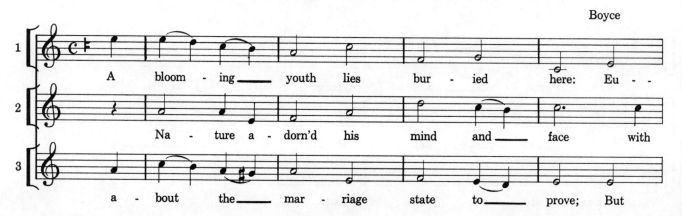

A bloom - ing youth lies bur - ied here: Eu - -

Na - ture a - dorn'd his mind and face with

a - bout the mar - riage state to prove; But

phe - - mius, to_____ his coun - try_____ dear.

ev - - - 'ry charm_____ and ev - 'ry grace

Death had quick - er quick - er, wings than Love.

Ding, Ding, Ding Dong Bell

Stoner

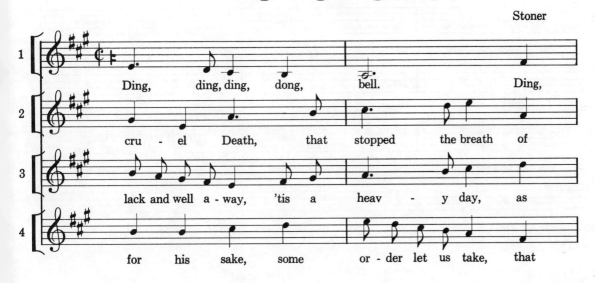

Ding, ding, ding, dong, bell. Ding,

cru - el Death, that stopped the breath of

lack and well a - way, 'tis a heav - y day, as

for his sake, some or - der let us take, that

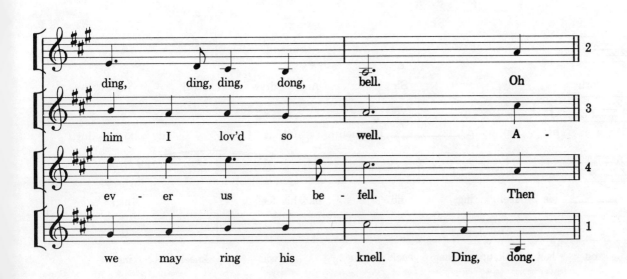

ding, ding, ding, dong, bell. Oh

him I lov'd so well. A -

ev - er us be - fell. Then

we may ring his knell. Ding, dong.

81

Here on His Back Doth Lay

Battishill

82

Here in Sweet Sleep

Horsley

Here Lies, Here Lies

Yates

Tread Soft My Friend

Danby

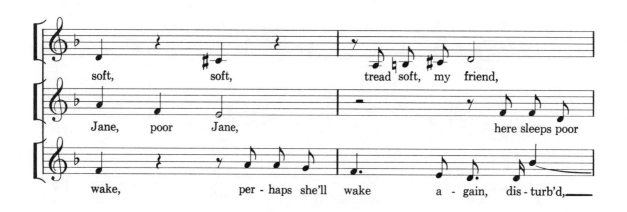

'Tis Thus, Thus, & Thus Farewell

Boyce

1. 'Tis thus, thus, and thus fare-well to
2. The rest an an-gel's pen must tell, long,_____
3. Those bless-ings which we___ high - - est___ prize are

1. all vain mor-tals do per-fec-tion call; to
2. _____ long_____ be - lov - ed Dust fare - well,
3. soon-est ra - - vish'd from our___ eyes; those

1. Beaut - y, to Good - ness, to Mod - es - ty,
2. fare - well, fare - well, fare - well, be -
3. bless - ings, those bless - ings which we prize are

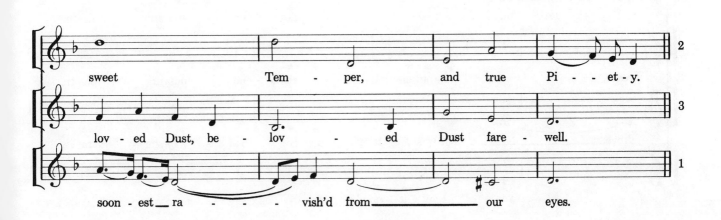

1. sweet Tem - per, and true Pi - et - y.
2. lov - ed Dust, be - lov - ed Dust fare - well.
3. soon-est___ ra - - vish'd from_____ our eyes.

Here Flat on her Back

Smith

1. Here flat on her back but un - ac - tive at last, _____ poor
2. Thro' the course of her vi - ces she gal - lop'd so fast, no
3. To the goal of her pleasures she drove ve - ry hard, but was
4. And tho ev - 'ry one fan - cy'd her life was a yard, yet it

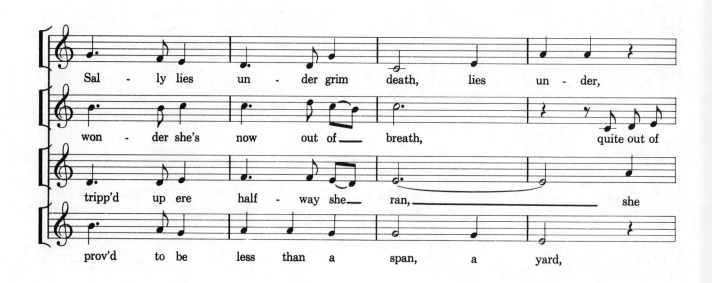

Sal - ly lies un - der grim death, lies un - der,
won - der she's now out of _____ breath, quite out of
tripp'd up ere half - way she _____ ran, _____ she
prov'd to be less than a span, a yard,

lies un - der, lies un - der grim death.
breath, quite out of breath, she's now out of breath.
drove, _____ but was tripp'd up ere half - way she ran.
a yard, yet it prov'd to be less than a span.

Come, Lay Aside Your Sighing

Banteringly

Come, lay a - side, your sigh - - ing, Nor ev - er - more be cry - - - ing.

Never Till Tomorrow Leave

Heavily

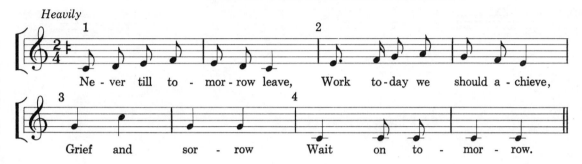

Ne - ver till to - mor - row leave, Work to - day we should a - chieve,

Grief and sor - row Wait on to - mor - row.

Keep to the Work

Keep to the work you best can do, and let all oth - er bus 'ness go, and

hold this home - ly pro - verb fast, "Good cob - bler, ne'er for - sake your last."

If a Hard and Weary Task

If a hard and weary task you find it, just per - se - vere, yes,

per - se - vere, don't mind it; Go on, go on, nev - er mind it.

He Who'd Lead a Happy Life

Lampe

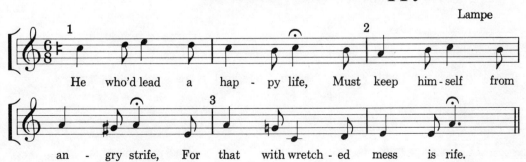

He who'd lead a hap - py life, Must keep him - self from

an - gry strife, For that with wretch - ed mess is rife.

Early to Bed and Early to Rise

Words attributed to Benjamin Franklin

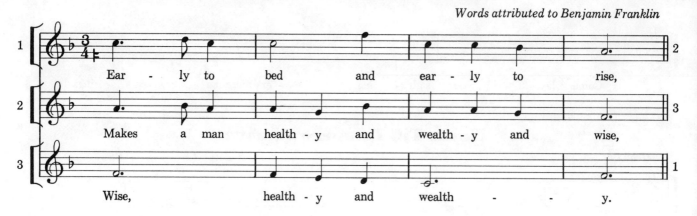

1. Ear - ly to bed and ear - ly to rise,
2. Makes a man health - y and wealth - y and wise,
3. Wise, health - y and wealth - - - y.

Go Learn of the Ant

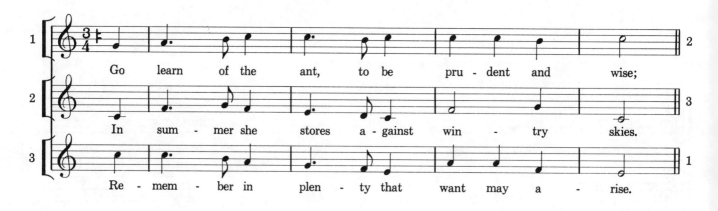

1. Go learn of the ant, to be pru - dent and wise;
2. In sum - mer she stores a - gainst win - try skies.
3. Re - mem - ber in plen - ty that want may a - rise.

Whether You Whisper Low

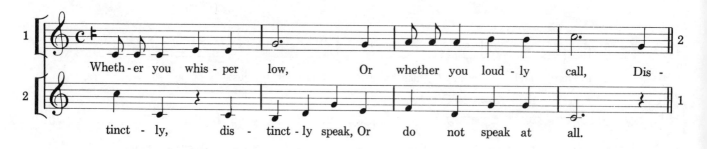

1. Wheth - er you whis - per low, Or whether you loud - ly call, Dis -
2. tinct - ly, dis - tinct - ly speak, Or do not speak at all.

When a Weary Task You Find It

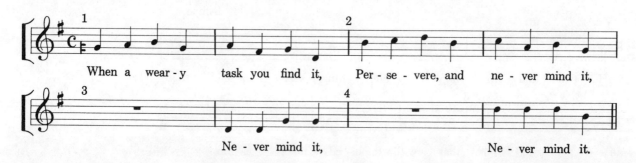

When a wear - y task you find it, Per - se - vere, and ne - ver mind it,
Ne - ver mind it, Ne - ver mind it.

Busy, Curious, Thirsty Fly

Cocchi

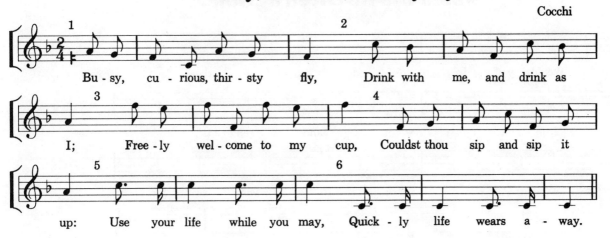

Bu - sy, cu - rious, thir - sty fly, Drink with me, and drink as
I; Free - ly wel - come to my cup, Couldst thou sip and sip it
up: Use your life while you may, Quick - ly life wears a - way.

Up and Down This World Goes Round

M. Locke

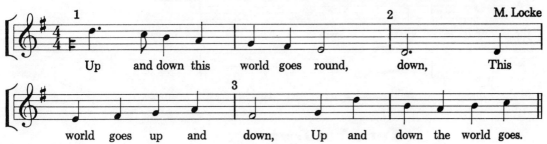

Up and down this world goes round, down, This
world goes up and down, Up and down the world goes.

Time and Tide

Sententiously

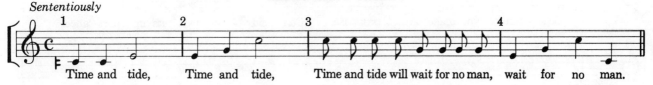

Time and tide, Time and tide, Time and tide will wait for no man, wait for no man.

Uncurb'd Tongues

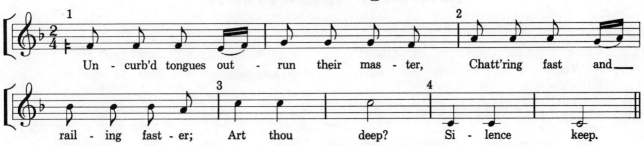

Un - curb'd tongues out - run their mas - ter, Chatt'ring fast and___
rail - ing fast - er; Art thou deep? Si - lence keep.

Whene'er a Nobel Deed is Wrought

CANON: 2 VOICES

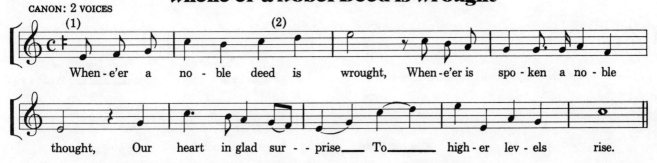

When - e'er a no - ble deed is wrought, When - e'er is spo - ken a no - ble
thought, Our heart in glad sur - - prise___ To___ high - er lev - els rise.

Would You Be Loved by Others

Would you be lov-ed by o-thers,

True must your words be and gen-tle,

Ev - er wise as the

o - thers you first must love,

not those that wrath will move.

ser - pent, and mild____ as the dove.

Turn Not from

Shield

Be - fore you make a____ prom-ise, Con-sid - er well its im - port - ance;

And when made, En - grave it up - on your heart.

Before You Make a Promise

Lawes

Turn not from sad sor - row, You may help to bear the weight.

Gen - tle words and kind com - pas - sion, May the woe a - bate.

Merrily We Shepherds Live

Mer - ri - ly we shep - herds live up - on the sun - ny down;____ What-

e'er is sent we take with con - tent and so we fear not for - tune's frown.

I Envy Not the Mighty Great

Lidarti

I en - vy not the might - y great, Those

Who set - tle na - tions as ___ they please, And

Great I'll be ___ by be - ing good, To

pow'r - ful ru - lers of ___ the state

gov - ern at th'ex - pense ___ of ease.

guide my - self ___ is all I would.

Let Us Now Be Up and Doing

Let us now be up and do - ing, With a heart for a - ny fate; Still a -

chiev - ing, still pur - su - ing, Learn to la - bor, and to wait.

'Tis Women

Purcell

'Tis wo - men makes us love, ___ 'Tis love that makes us sad, ___ 'Tis

sad - ness makes us drink, ___ And drink - ing makes us mad. ___

91

Nor Love Thy Life

John Milton/Shield

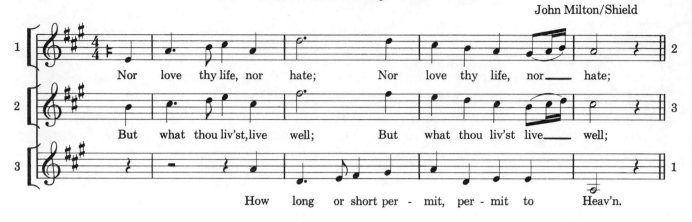

Nor love thy life, nor hate; Nor love thy life, nor____ hate;

But what thou liv'st, live well; But what thou liv'st live____ well;

How long or short per - mit, per - mit to Heav'n.

Life Is a Jest

Travers

Life is a jest, and all things show it: I

thought so once, but now I know____ it.

Life is a jest, and all____ things show____ it!

I thought so once, but now I know____ it!

What You Would Not Have Done to Yourself

Shield

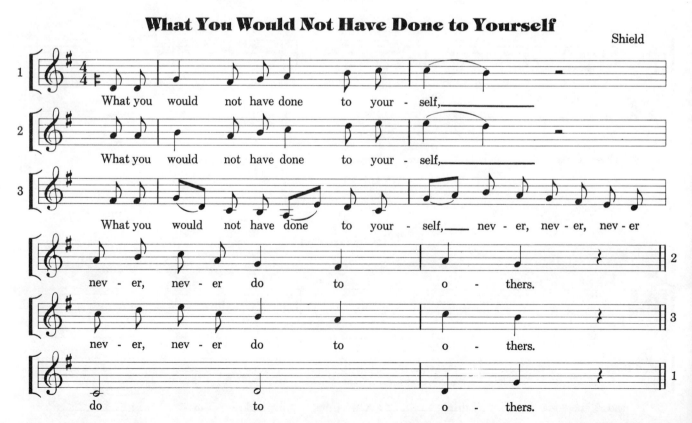

What you would not have done to your - self,____

What you would not have done to your - self,____

What you would not have done to your - self,____ nev - er, nev - er, nev - er

nev - er, nev - er do to o - thers.

nev - er, nev - er do to o - thers.

do to o - thers.

92

Never Let a Man

Advisingly Lawes

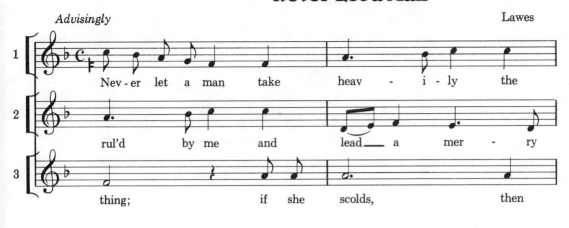

1. Nev-er let a man take heav-i-ly the

2. rul'd by me and lead a mer-ry

3. thing; if she scolds, then

clam-or of his wife; but be

life. Let her have her will in ev-'ry-

laugh and sing, hey der-ry, der-ry, der-ry ding.

Hold Thy Peace

Shakespeare (in *Twelfth Night*) Melvill – Deuteromelia

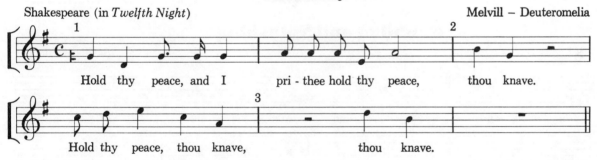

Hold thy peace, and I pri-thee hold thy peace, thou knave.

Hold thy peace, thou knave, thou knave.

Let Simon's Beard Alone

John Hilton

1. Let Si-mon's beard a-lone, a-lone, let Si-mon's beard a-lone,

2. 'Tis no dis-grace to Si-mon's face for he had nev-er one;

3. Then mock not, nor scoff not, nor jeer not, nor sneer not, but ra-ther him be-moan.

93

Good Unexpected

Arnold

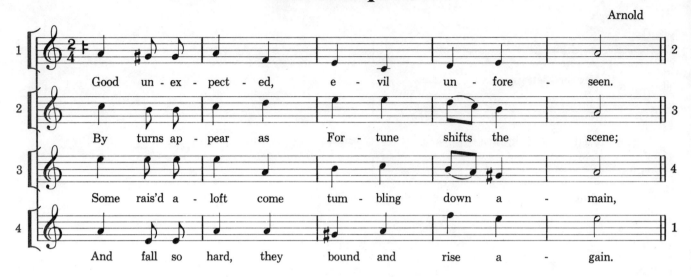

1. Good un-ex-pect-ed, e-vil un-fore-seen.

2. By turns ap-pear as For-tune shifts the scene;

3. Some rais'd a-loft come tum-bling down a-main,

4. And fall so hard, they bound and rise a-gain.

I, Poor and Well

Hilton

Smugly

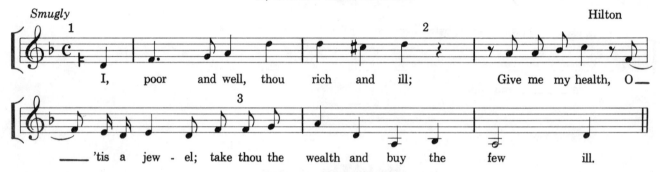

I, poor and well, thou rich and ill; Give me my health, O—

—— 'tis a jew-el; take thou the wealth and buy the few ill.

Bubbling and Splashing

Saville or Purcell

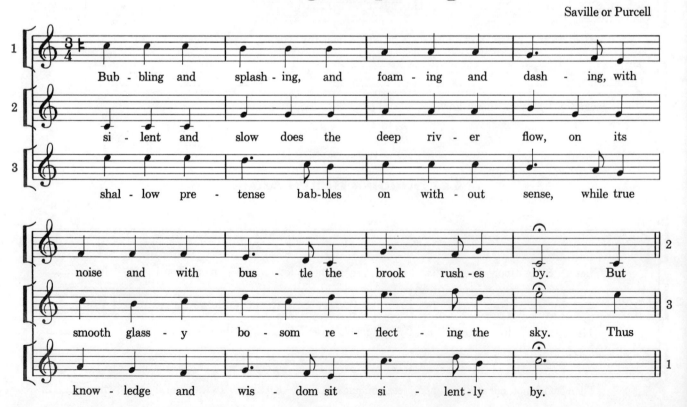

1. Bub-bling and splash-ing, and foam-ing and dash-ing, with

2. si-lent and slow does the deep riv-er flow, on its

3. shal-low pre-tense bab-bles on with-out sense, while true

noise and with bus-tle the brook rush-es by. But

smooth glass-y bo-som re-flect-ing the sky. Thus

know-ledge and wis-dom sit si-lent-ly by.

The Macedon Youth

Purcell

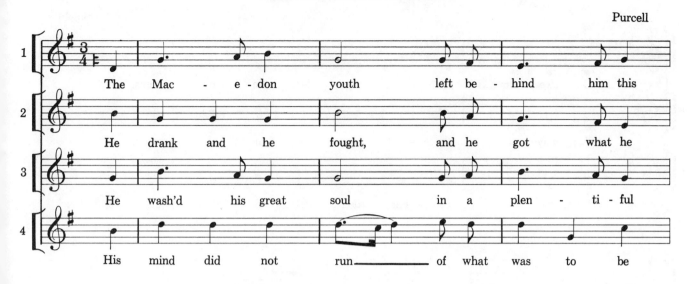

The Mac - e - don youth left be - hind him this

He drank and he fought, and he got what he

He wash'd his great soul in a plen - ti - ful

His mind did not run_____ of what was to be

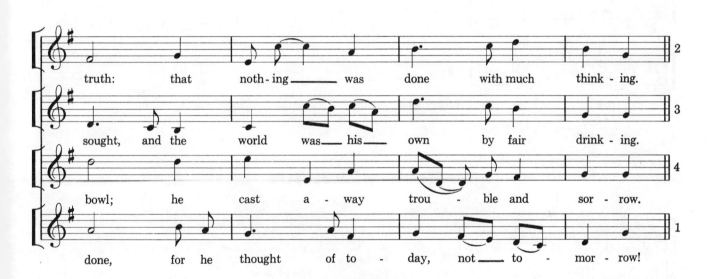

truth: that noth-ing_____ was done with much think - ing.

sought, and the world was_____ his_____ own by fair drink - ing.

bowl; he cast a - way trou - ble and sor - row.

done, for he thought of to - day, not_____ to - mor - row!

Smoothly Glide

CANON: 3 VOICES

Hayes

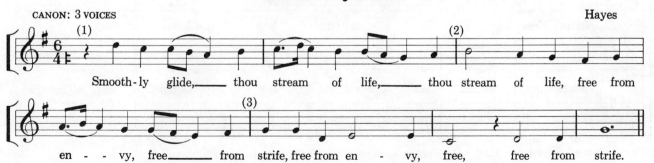

(1) (2)

Smooth - ly glide,_____ thou stream of life,_____ thou stream of life, free from

(3)

en - - vy, free_____ from strife, free from en - - vy, free, free from strife.

95

O Sweet Simplicity

Shield

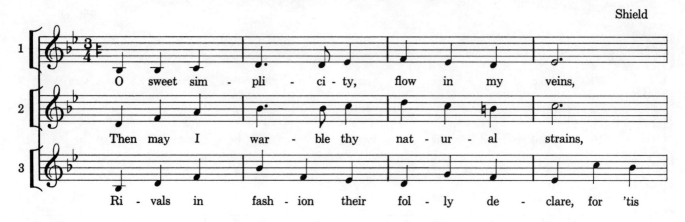

O sweet sim - pli - ci - ty, flow in my veins,

Then may I war - ble thy nat - ur - al strains,

Ri - vals in fash - ion their fol - ly de - clare, for 'tis

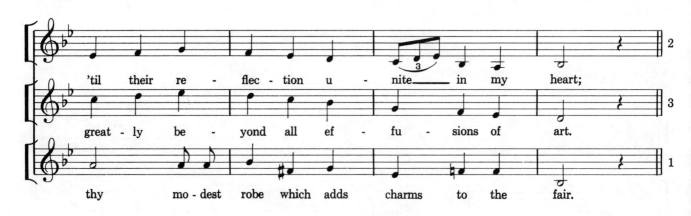

'til their re - flec - tion u - nite___ in my heart;

great - ly be - yond all ef - fu - sions of art.

thy mo - dest robe which adds charms to the fair.

Boldly with Mettle

Blow

Bold - ly___ with met - tle, if you seize a net - tle, then

But if you lin - ger, and touch with slow fin - ger, its

bold daunt - less heart, it will scarce feel the smart of

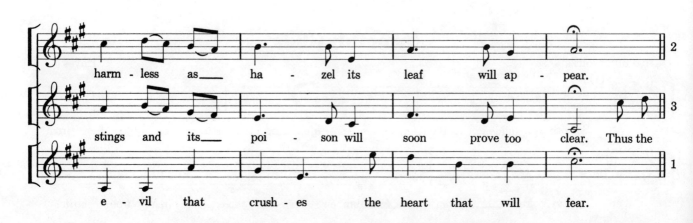

harm - less as___ ha - zel its leaf will ap - pear.

stings and its___ poi - son will soon prove too clear. Thus the

e - vil that crush - es the heart that will fear.

Blest, Blest Is He

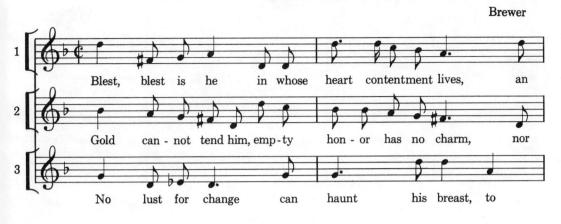

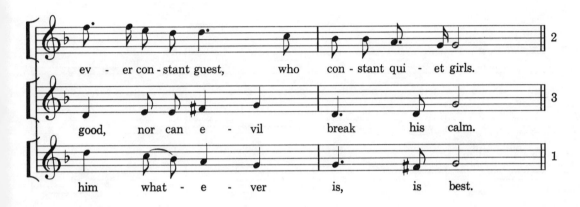

A Friend, a Friend

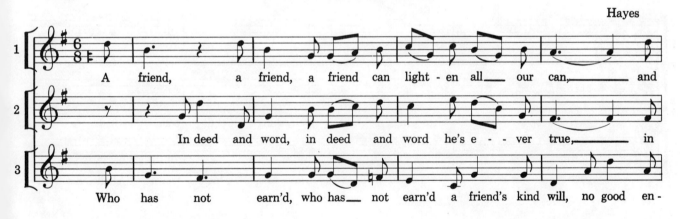

97

I've Seen the Smiling

Giardini

1. I've seen the__ smi-ling of For-tune be-guil-ing. I've tast-ed her
2. Sweet, sweet is her bless - ing, and kind her ca-
3. Should she seem my pro-tect - - or, should she

fa - vors and felt her de - cay. And felt__ her de-
ress - ing. But soon it is fled, fled far,__ far a-
seem my pro-tect - or, still, still I'll sus - pect her, sus-

cay,_____ felt her de-
way. Sweet is her bless - ing, her bless-ing, but soon fled a-
pect her. No smile shall e - late me, no frown shall dis-

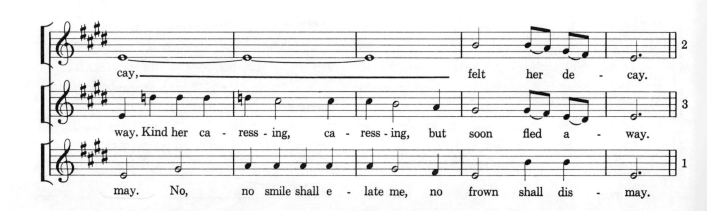

cay,_____ felt her de - cay.
way. Kind her ca - ress - ing, ca - ress-ing, but soon fled a - way.
may. No, no smile shall e - late me, no frown shall dis - may.

98

Hard Is the Fate

Atterbury

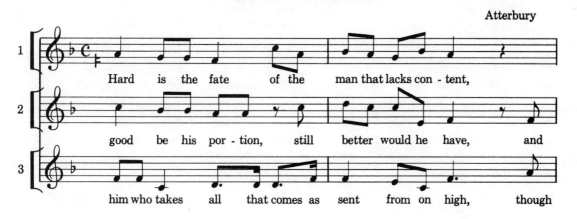

1. Hard is the fate of the man that lacks con - tent,

2. good be his por - tion, still better would he have, and

3. him who takes all that comes as sent from on high, though

whose heart on what is ___ not ___ is for - e - ver bent.

bet - ter when gain'd, why bet - ter still he'd crave.

bit - ter it may seem, whis - pers Hope, "Ne - ver sigh,

Hard is his fate, hard is his fate,

"Hard is my fate, hard is my fate,

nay, nev - er sigh, nay, nev - er

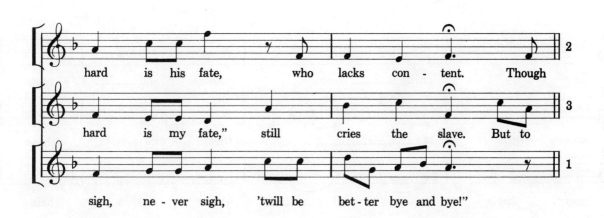

hard is his fate, who lacks con - tent. Though

hard is my fate," still cries the slave. But to

sigh, ne - ver sigh, 'twill be bet - ter bye and bye!"

99

The Silver Swan

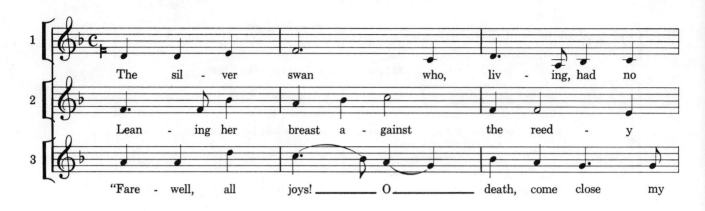

1. The sil - ver swan who, liv - ing, had no
2. Lean - ing her breast a - gainst the reed - y
3. "Fare - well, all joys! O death, come close my

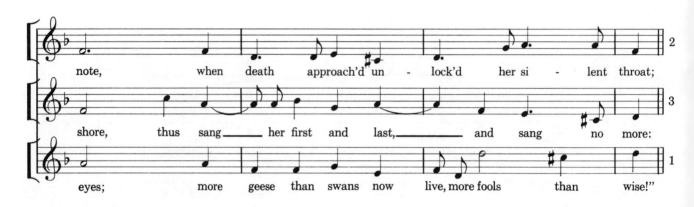

1. note, when death approach'd un - lock'd her si - lent throat;
2. shore, thus sang her first and last, and sang no more:
3. eyes; more geese than swans now live, more fools than wise!"

'Tis Providence Alone Secures

Boyce

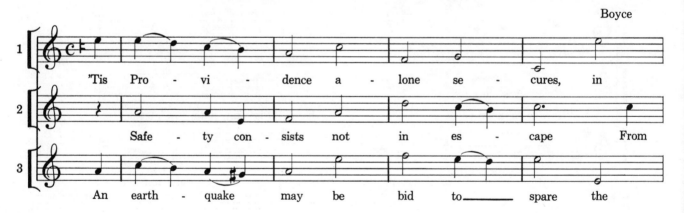

1. 'Tis Pro - vi - dence a - lone se - cures, in
2. Safe - ty con - sists not in es - cape From
3. An earth - quake may be bid to spare the

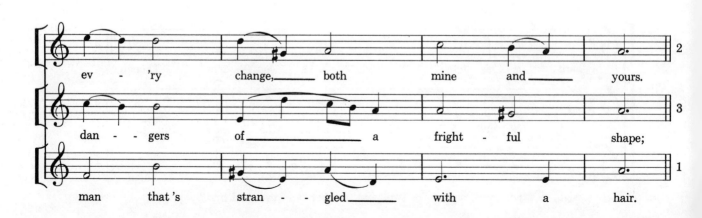

1. ev - 'ry change, both mine and yours.
2. dan - gers of a fright - ful shape;
3. man that's stran - gled with a hair.

Pri'thee Why So Sad

Purcell

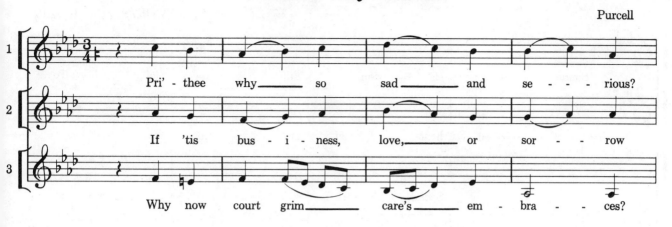

1 Pri' - thee why____ so sad____ and se - - - rious?

2 If 'tis bus - i - ness, love,____ or sor - - row

3 Why now court grim____ care's____ em - bra - - ces?

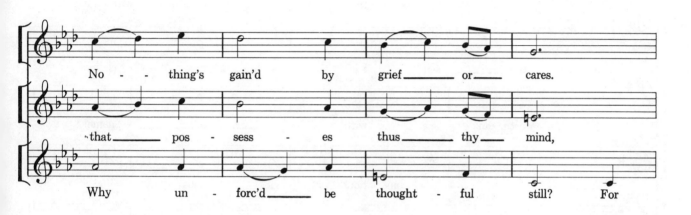

No - - thing's gain'd by grief____ or____ cares.

'that____ pos - sess - es thus____ thy____ mind,

Why un - forc'd____ be thought - ful still? For

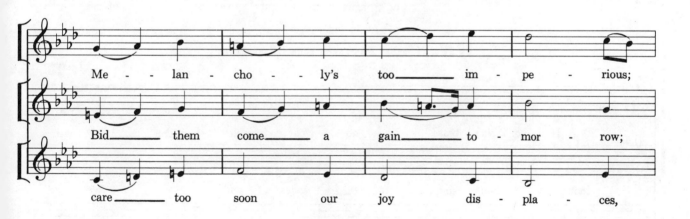

Me - lan - cho - ly's too____ im - pe - rious;

Bid____ them come____ a gain____ to - mor - row;

care____ too soon our joy dis - pla - ces,

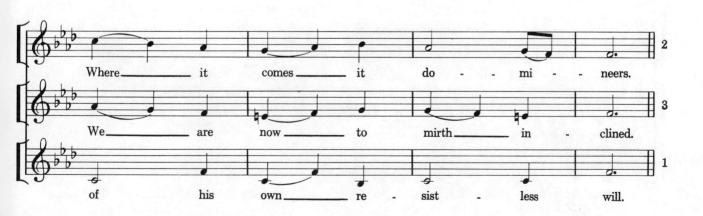

2 Where____ it comes____ it do - mi - neers.

3 We____ are now____ to mirth____ in - clined.

1 of his own____ re - sist - less will.

101

Sound the Clarion!

Sir Walter Scott   Hogarth

1. Sound, sound the cla - rion! Fill the fife! To

2. One crowd - ed hour of glo - rious life

3. Sound, cla - rion, sound! One ___ crowd - ed

4. is worth an age, an age with - out a

all the ___ sen - sual world ___ pro - claim:

Is worth an age with - out ___ a ___ name!

hour, one hour of glo - rious life,

name, an age with - out a name!

If Neither Brass no Marble

Hayes

1. If nei - ther brass nor mar - ble can ___ with -

2. moun - tains sink ___ to ___ vales, and ci - ties

3. When my old cas - sock, says a Welsh Di -

stand the might - y force ___ of time's de - struc - tive hand, If

die, and less - 'ning ri - ers mourn their foun - - - tains dry;

vine, is out at el - bows, why should I ___ re - pine? ___

102

HUMOROUS

I Faint! I Die!

I faint! I die! And so do I! The
world then must know you both lie, To - ge - ther, to - ge - ther, Oh Fie!

John Ran

Arnold

John ran so long and ran so fast,

That he ran out his all at last.

He ran in debt, and then to pay,

Took to his heels and ran a - way!

Sandy McNab

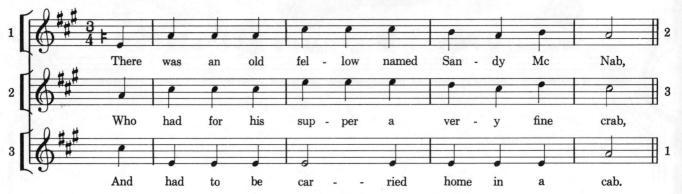

There was an old fel - low named San - dy Mc Nab,

Who had for his sup - per a ver - y fine crab,

And had to be car - - ried home in a cab.

Joy and Temperance

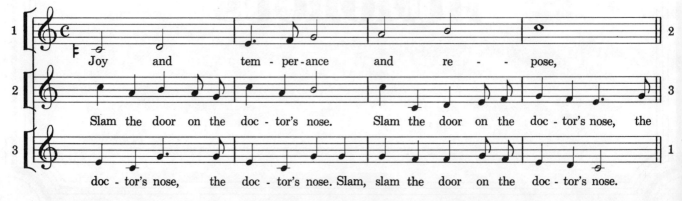

Joy and tem - per - ance and re - - pose,

Slam the door on the doc - tor's nose. Slam the door on the doc - tor's nose, the

doc - tor's nose, the doc - tor's nose. Slam, slam the door on the doc - tor's nose.

104

Laughter Makes the World Go Round

Wilson

Laugh - ter makes the world go round, so the wise men say.

Laugh - ter is the re - ci - pe to make us all feel gay:

Ha, ha, ha, ha, ha, ha, ha, ha, ho, ho, ho, ho, ho, ho, ho.

Well Fare the Nightingale

Pammelia

Well fare the night - in - gale,

Fare fall the thrush - cock too, But foul

fare the fil - thy fowl that sing - eth cuck - oo!

Where Is John?

Smetana

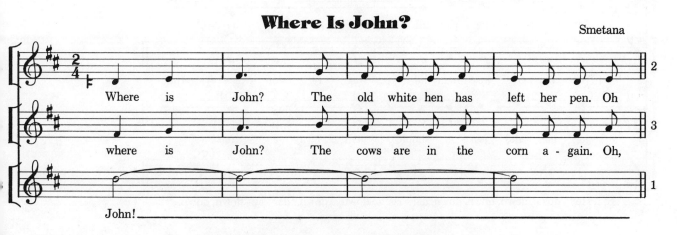

Where is John? The old white hen has left her pen. Oh

where is John? The cows are in the corn a - gain. Oh,

John! _____

The Maid She Went a-Milking

Melvill - Deuteromelia

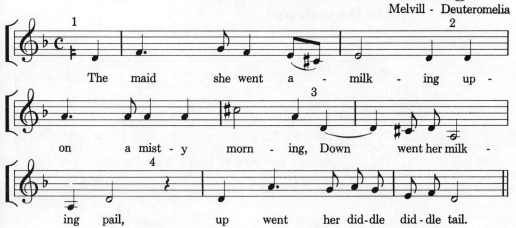

The maid she went a - milk - ing up -

on a mist - y morn - ing, Down went her milk -

ing pail, up went her did - dle did - dle tail.

On Mules We Find

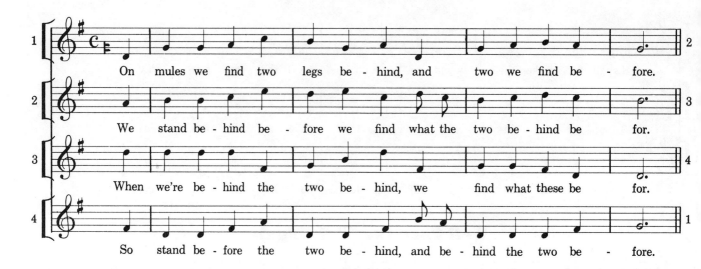

On mules we find two legs be-hind, and two we find be-fore.

We stand be-hind be-fore we find what the two be-hind be for.

When we're be-hind the two be-hind, we find what these be for.

So stand be-fore the two be-hind, and be-hind the two be for.

Jinkin the Jester

Pammelia

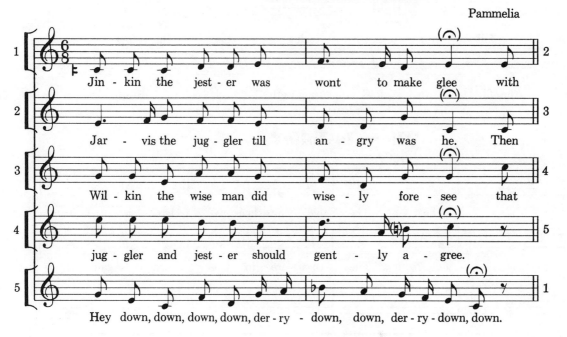

Jin-kin the jest-er was wont to make glee with

Jar-vis the jug-gler till an-gry was he. Then

Wil-kin the wise man did wise-ly fore-see that

jug-gler and jest-er should gent-ly a-gree.

Hey down, down, down, down, der-ry-down, down, der-ry-down, down.

'Tis Humdrum

Harrington

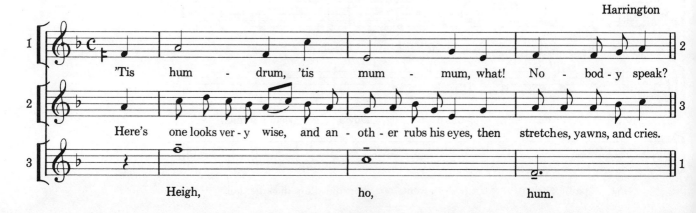

'Tis hum-drum, 'tis mum-mum, what! No-bod-y speak?

Here's one looks ver-y wise, and an-oth-er rubs his eyes, then stretches, yawns, and cries.

Heigh, ho, hum.

Margery, Serve Well the Black Sow

Melvill Deuteromelia

Mar - ger - y, serve well the black sow, all in a mist - y morn - ing.

Come to thy dinner, sow, come, come, come, or else thou shalt have nev - er a crumb.

Timothy Tippen's Horse

Moffat

Tim - o - thy Tip - pen's horse was blind, be - cause he could - n't see, O!

Two legs in front and two be - hind, that's just one more than three, O!

Tho' if two "be - four" and be - hind two more, it looks like six to me, O!

Not a Day More Than Thirty

Berg

Not a day more than thir - ty, dear Sir, on my

By my troth, cries a wag, that must sure - ly be

By my troth, cries a wag, that must sure - ly be

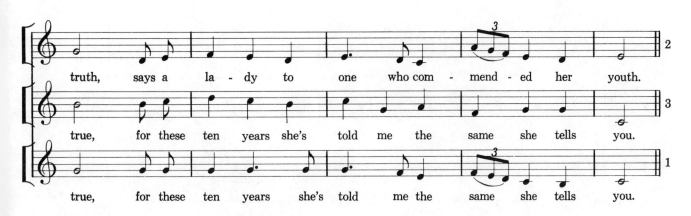

truth, says a la - dy to one who com - mend - ed her youth.

true, for these ten years she's told me the same she tells you.

true, for these ten years she's told me the same she tells you.

Peter White I

Burney

Pe - ter White, who nev - er goes right, would you

fol - lows his nose wher - ev - er he goes, and

fol - lows his nose wher - ev - er he goes, and

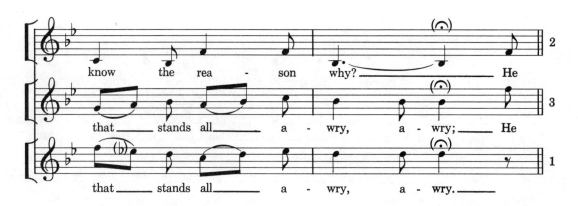

know the rea - son why? He

that stands all a - wry, a - wry; He

that stands all a - wry, a - wry.

Peter White II

Brown

Pe - ter White, that nev - er goes right, would you

know the rea - son why? He

that stands all a - wry, a - wry, and

know the rea - son why? Would you

fol - lows his nose, wher - ev - er he goes, and

that stands all a - wry.

There Was Three Cooks in Colebrook

Hilton

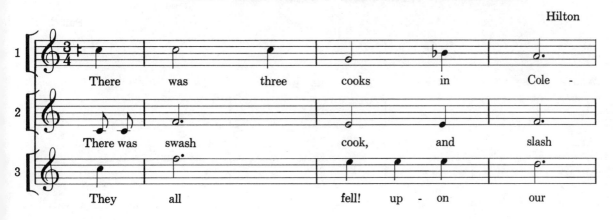

There was three cooks in Cole -

There was swash cook, and slash

They all fell! up - on our

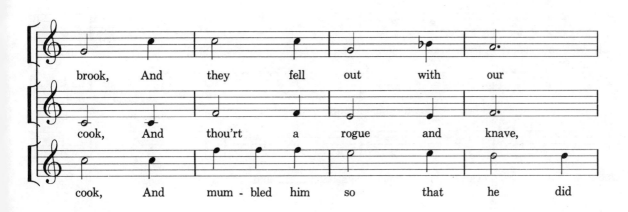

brook, And they fell out with our

cook, And thou'rt a rogue and knave,

cook, And mum - bled him so that he did

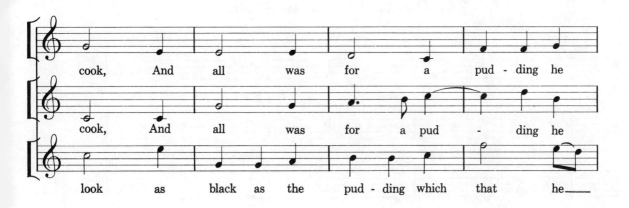

cook, And all was for a pud - ding he

cook, And all was for a pud - ding he

look as black as the pud - ding which that he

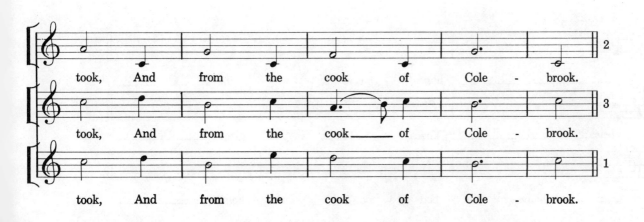

took, And from the cook of Cole - brook.

took, And from the cook of Cole - brook.

took, And from the cook of Cole - brook.

"Who Can Swim?"

H. Purcell

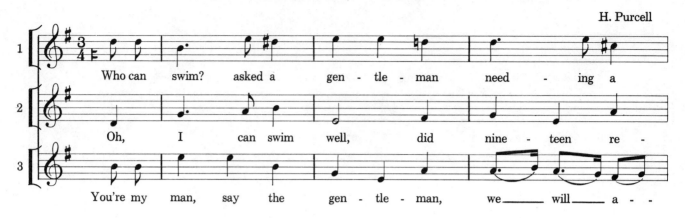

1. Who can swim? asked a gen-tle-man need-ing a
2. Oh, I can swim well, did nine-teen re-
3. You're my man, say the gen-tle-man, we____ will____ a -

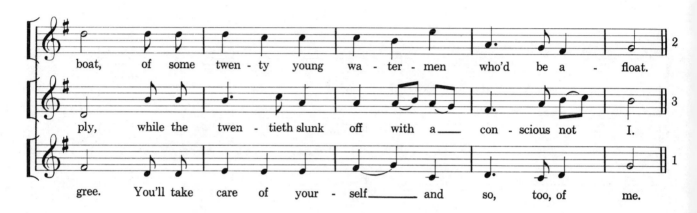

boat, of some twen-ty young wa-ter-men who'd be a - float.
ply, while the twen-tieth slunk off with a____ con - scious not I.
gree. You'll take care of your - self____ and so, too, of me.

You Beat, Beat Your Pate

Hayes

1. You beat, beat your pate,____ you beat, you beat your
2. Knock, knock as you please,____ knock, knock as you
3. There's no - bod -y home,____ at home, no - bod - y at home,____

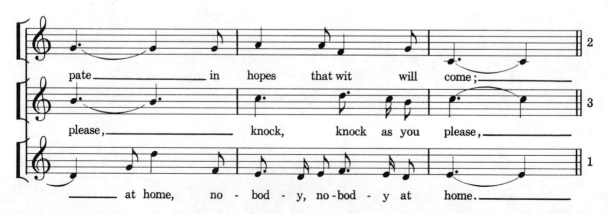

pate____ in hopes that wit will come;____
please,____ knock, knock as you please,____
____ at home, no - bod - y, no - bod - y at home.____

110

Have You Sir John Hawkins' Hist'ry?

Callcott

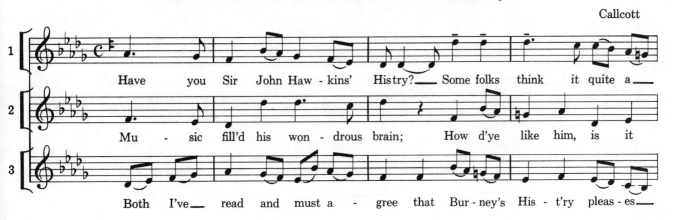

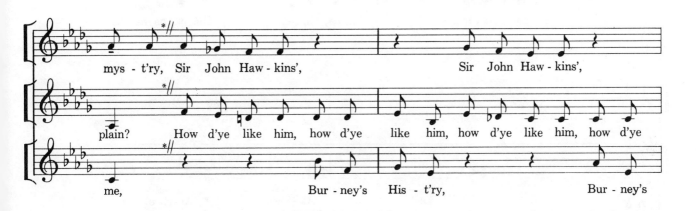

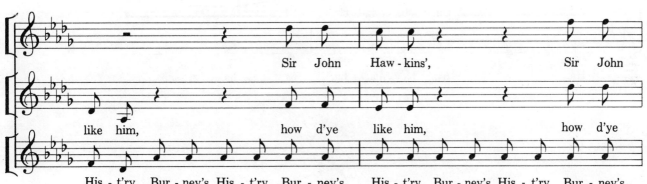

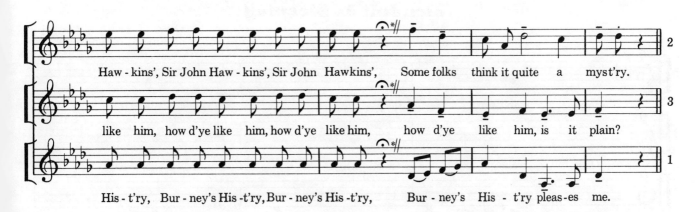

*"Leave out the bars [measures] between the **[⫽ ⫼] till the Third Voice comes in, then go on." – Callcott's note.

Yah-Atchee-Oh-Ha-Ha

Giles Jolt As Sleeping

Stephenson

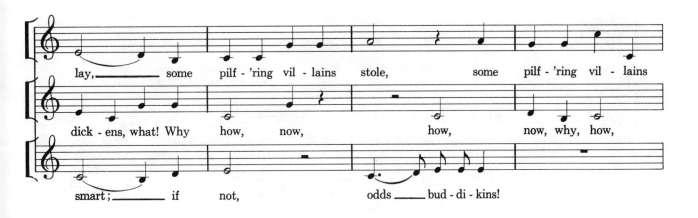

lay,_____ some pilf - 'ring vil - lains stole, some pilf - 'ring vil - lains

dick - ens, what! Why how, now, how, now, why, how,

smart;_____ if not, odds ____ bud - di - kins!

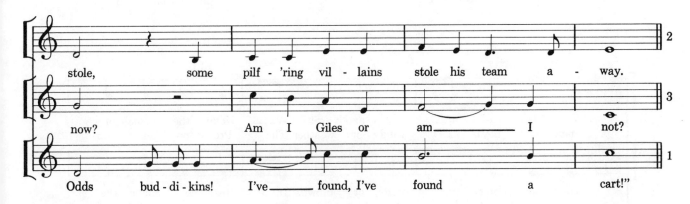

stole, some pilf - 'ring vil - lains stole his team a - way. 2

now? Am I Giles or am_____ I not? 3

Odds bud - di - kins! I've_____ found, I've found a cart!" 1

As There Be Three Blewe Beans

Milton

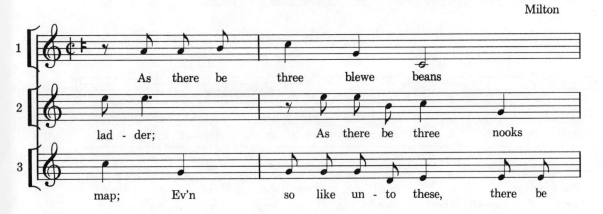

As there be three blewe beans

lad - der; As there be three nooks

map; Ev'n so like un - to these, there be

in a blewe blad - der, and thrice three rounds in a long 2

in a corn - er cap, and three corn - ers and one in a 3

three un - i - ver - si - ties: Ox - ford, Cam - bridge and James._____ 1

Three Little Words

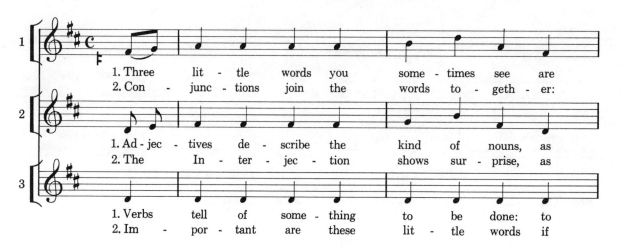

1. Three lit - tle words you some - times see are
2. Con - junc - tions join the words to - geth - er:

1. Ad - jec - tives de - scribe the kind of nouns, as
2. The In - ter - jec - tion shows sur - prise, as

1. Verbs tell of some - thing to be done: to
2. Im - por - tant are these lit - tle words if

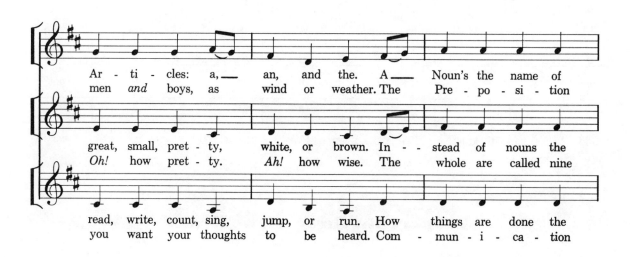

Ar - ti - cles: a, an, and the. A Noun's the name of
men *and* boys, as wind or weather. The Pre - po - si - tion

great, small, pret - ty, white, or brown. In - stead of nouns the
Oh! how pret - ty. *Ah!* how wise. The whole are called nine

read, write, count, sing, jump, or run. How things are done the
you want your thoughts to be heard. Com - mun - i - ca - tion

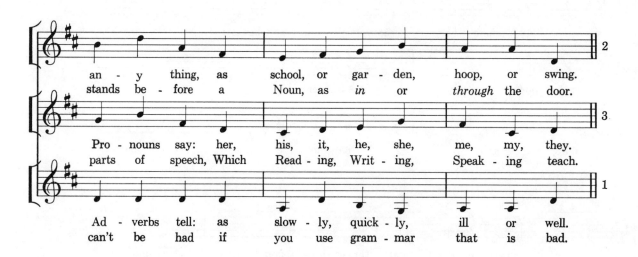

an - y thing, as school, or gar - den, hoop, or swing.
stands be - fore a Noun, as *in* or *through* the door.

Pro - nouns say: her, his, it, he, she, me, my, they.
parts of speech, Which Read - ing, Writ - ing, Speak - ing teach.

Ad - verbs tell: as slow - ly, quick - ly, ill or well.
can't be had if you use gram - mar that is bad.

114

Quoth Roger to Nelly

Woodward

Quoth Ro - ger to Nel - ly, "Sup -

get an - oth - er, would you get an -

"Yes, that I would, Ro - ger, would Ro - ger, would

Would you have me hug_____ pill - ow and

pose_____ I were dead,_____ sup -

oth - - er good man in my

Ro - ger. Pray, man, do not stare, do not

bol - - ster, my dear?_____ Would you

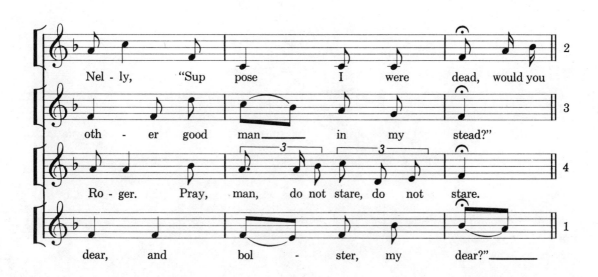

Nel - ly, "Sup pose I were dead, would you

oth - er good man_____ in my stead?"

Ro - ger. Pray, man, do not stare, do not stare.

dear, and bol - ster, my dear?"_____

pose I were dead." Quoth Ro - ger to

stead, in my stead?_____ Would you get an -

stare, do not stare; Yes, that I would Ro - ger, would Ro - ger, would

have me hug___ pill - ow and bol - ster, my

I've Lost My Mistress, Horse, and Wife

Greene

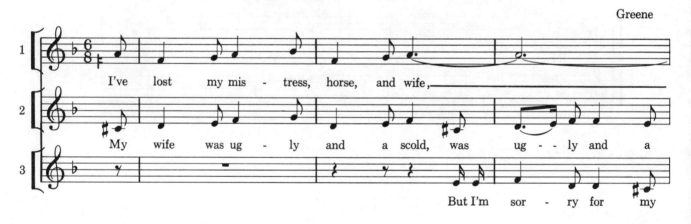

I've lost my mis - tress, horse, and wife,_____

My wife was ug - ly and a scold, was ug - ly and a

But I'm sor - ry for my

_____ I've lost my mis - tress, horse, and wife,_____

scold, a scold; My mis - tress was grown lean and old, grown

horse, my horse, I'm

I've lost my mis - tress,
lean,_____ lean and old, and old; My wife was ug - ly
sor - ry for my horse, my horse;

horse, and wife,_____ but when I think on
and a scold, was ug - ly and a scold, a scold; My mis - tress
I'm sor - ry for my horse, my horse, I'm sor - ry, sor - ry

hu - man_____ life, I'm glad_____ it is no worse.____ 2
was grown lean, grown lean,____ lean and old.____ 3
for my horse, I'm sor - ry for my horse.____ 1

Two Lawyers, Two Lawyers

Cuzens

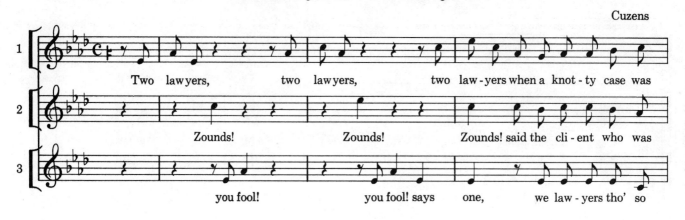

Two lawyers, two lawyers, two law-yers when a knot-ty case was

Zounds! Zounds! Zounds! said the cli-ent who was

you fool! you fool! says one, we law-yers tho' so

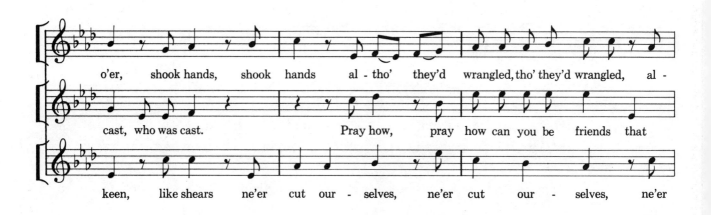

o'er, shook hands, shook hands al-tho' they'd wrangled, tho' they'd wrangled, al-

cast, who was cast. Pray how, pray how can you be friends that

keen, like shears ne'er cut our-selves, ne'er cut our-selves, ne'er

tho' they'd wrangled, al-tho' they'd wrangled, tho' they'd wrangled hard be-fore.

were such foes just now, just now, that were such foes just now?

cut our-selves, but what's be-tween, but what's be-tween.

ROUNDS ABOUT ROUNDS

Now We'll Make the Rafters Ring

Now we'll make the raft-ers ring, while we all this round will sing.

Now We Are Met

Samuel Webbe

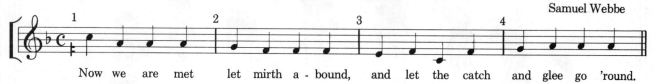

Now we are met let mirth a-bound, and let the catch and glee go 'round.

Pleasant Is It

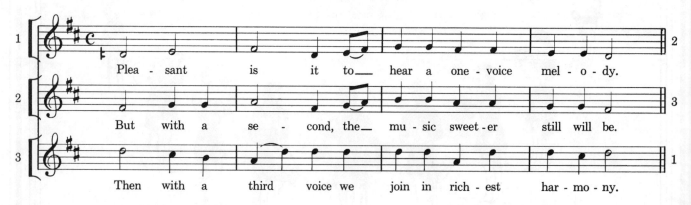

Plea - sant is it to__ hear a one - voice mel - o - dy.

But with a se - cond, the__ mu - sic sweet - er still will be.

Then with a third voice we join in rich - est har - mo - ny.

A Round! A Round!

A round! A round! A mer - ry, laugh - ing round,__

A mer - ry, laugh - ing, mer - ry, laugh - ing round we sing.__

A round!__

Come, Let's Sing a Merry Round

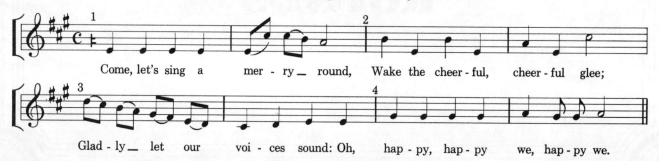

Come, let's sing a mer - ry__ round, Wake the cheer - ful, cheer - ful glee;

Glad - ly__ let our voi - ces sound: Oh, hap - py, hap - py we, hap - py we.

Come; Follow Me, Follow Me in This Round

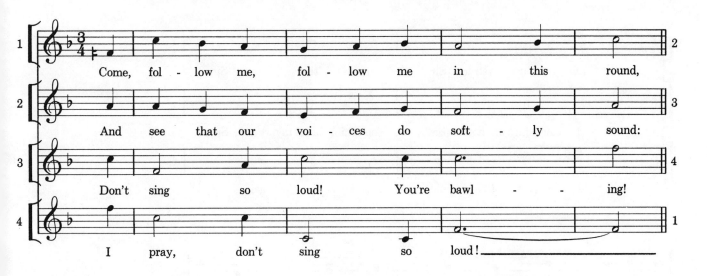

Come, fol - low me, fol - low me in this round,

And see that our voi - ces do soft - ly sound:

Don't sing so loud! You're bawl - ing!

I pray, don't sing so loud! _____

If Thou Art an Honest Friend

William Webbe

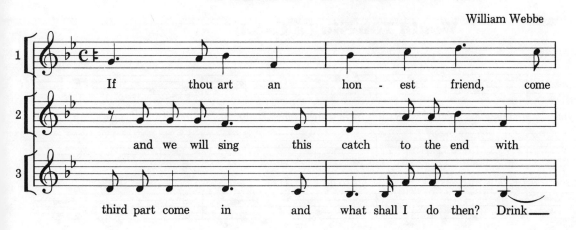

If thou art an hon - est friend, come

and we will sing this catch to the end with

third part come in and what shall I do then? Drink ___

fol - low, fol - low me, come fol - low, fol - low me,

mirth and mer - ry glee, with mirth and mer - ry glee. But

___ thy liq - uor off and come in a - gain.

I'm Not Strong, Sir!

With squeaks

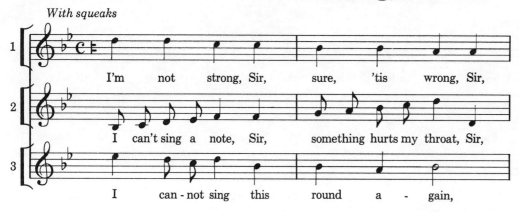

I'm not strong, Sir, sure, 'tis wrong, Sir,

I can't sing a note, Sir, something hurts my throat, Sir,

I can-not sing this round a - gain,

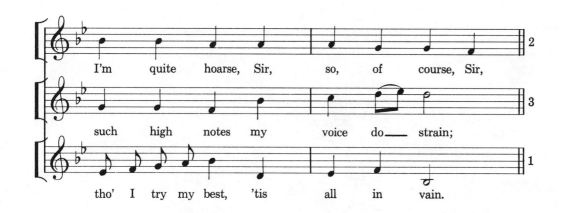

I'm quite hoarse, Sir, so, of course, Sir,

such high notes my voice do__ strain;

tho' I try my best, 'tis all in vain.

Would You Sing a Catch

Hayes

Would you sing a catch with plea - sure, just - ly mark, just - ly

Ne - ver strain with bog - gling throat,__ Do,__ Re,__

bold - ly__ lead or glib - ly fol - low, bold - ly__ lead, bold - ly__

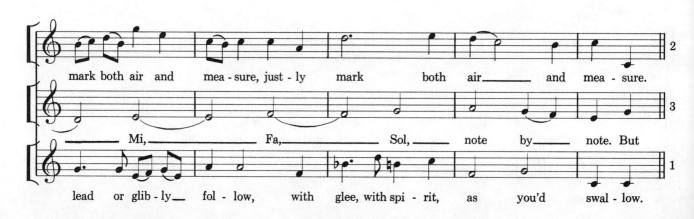

mark both air and mea - sure, just - ly mark both air__ and mea - sure.

__ Mi,__ Fa,__ Sol,__ note by__ note. But

lead or glib - ly__ fol - low, with glee, with spi - rit, as you'd swal - low.

Come, Honest Friends

Ives

1. Come, hon-est friends and jo - - vial boys,
2. Jo - - vial boys and hon - est friends, fol - low,
3. Hon - est friends, come fol - - low me,

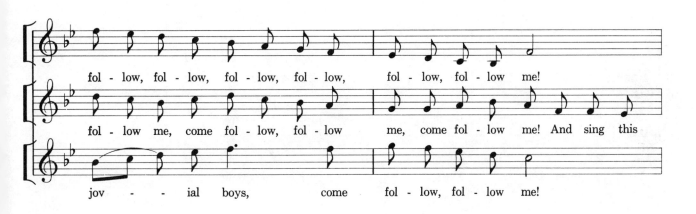

fol - low, fol - low, fol - low, fol - low, fol - low, fol - low me!
fol - low me, come fol - low, fol - low me, come fol - low me! And sing this
jov - ial boys, come fol - low, fol - low me!

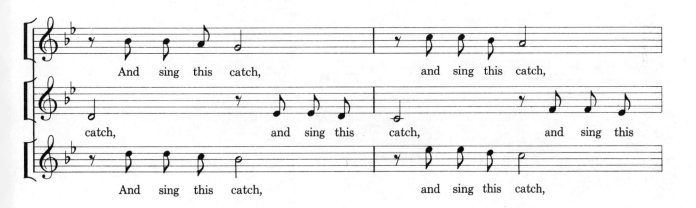

And sing this catch, and sing this catch,
catch, and sing this catch, and sing this
And sing this catch, and sing this catch,

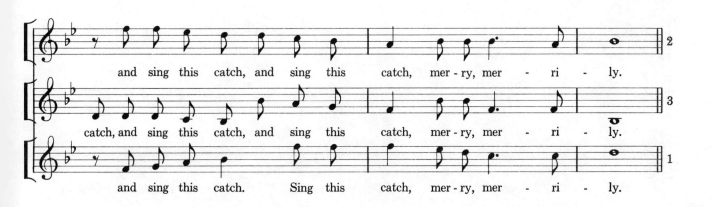

and sing this catch, and sing this catch, mer - ry, mer - ri - ly.
catch, and sing this catch, and sing this catch, mer - ry, mer - ri - ly.
and sing this catch. Sing this catch, mer - ry, mer - ri - ly.

Come Hither, Tom

Cranford

Come hith-er, Tom, and make up three and

So now comes in my no - ble Jack, keep

Now list - en to the bass, for

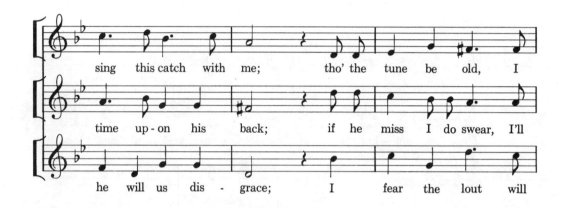

sing this catch with me; tho' the tune be old, I

time up - on his back; if he miss I do swear, I'll

he will us dis - grace; I fear the lout will

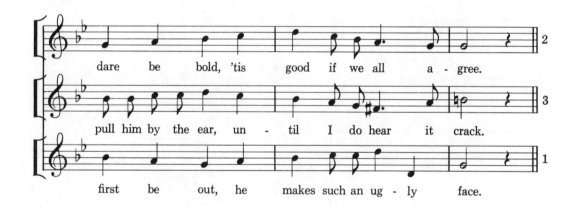

dare be bold, 'tis good if we all a - gree.

pull him by the ear, un - til I do hear it crack.

first be out, he makes such an ug - ly face.

One, Two, Three

Purcell

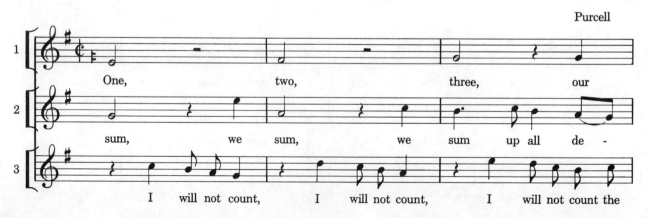

One, two, three, our

sum, we sum, we sum up all de -

I will not count, I will not count, I will not count the

num - ber is right. Let's sing_____

lights, de - lights in one. In sweet_____

care times bring. I'll on - ly, I'll

_____ and__ cheer our__ hearts to - night. We   2

_____ de - light of time and tune I will not count,   3

on - ly count my__ time to__ sing.   1

I Cannot Sing This Catch

Harrington

1   I can - not sing this catch, I shall laugh, I shall laugh_____

2   For shame, you sil - ly calf, don't you laugh, don't you laugh, don't you

3   Look at his face! Ha ha ha ha! Look!

__ ha ha ha ha! I shall laugh, shall laugh, ha ha ha

laugh! You will not sing it half, but make us all to

Look at his face! Ha ha ha! When he sings the

125

ha! O____ dear! I shall laugh____ ha ha ha!

laugh, make us all, all to laugh____ ha ha ha ha ha!

bass, look! Look! at his face! Ha ha ha ha ha ha ha ha ha!

A Catch That Is Merry

Hayes

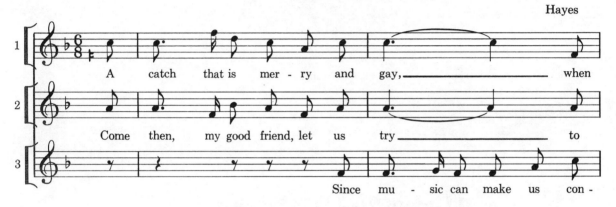

A catch that is mer-ry and gay,____ when

Come then, my good friend, let us try____ to

Since mu-sic can make us con-

voi-ces are right-ly in tune,____ will cheer up the most gloomy

ba-nish all sor-row and care,____ let no one for trouble now

tent,____ leave gold to the yel-low Na-bob; we're rich-er and

day,____ and turn a No-vem-ber to June.____

cry,____ and say it is too much to bear.____

hap-pier than he, who thus in a catch bear a bob.____

Hey, Down a Down, Behold and See

CANON: 3 VOICES: AT THE 5TH, 9TH

Melvill

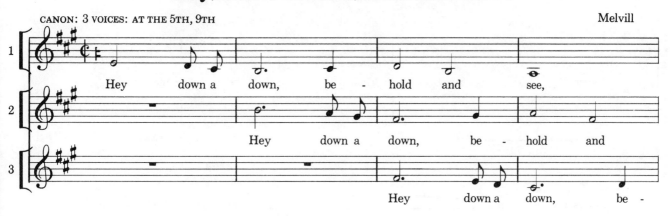

1 — Hey down a down, be - hold and see,

2 — Hey down a down, be - hold and

3 — Hey down a down, be -

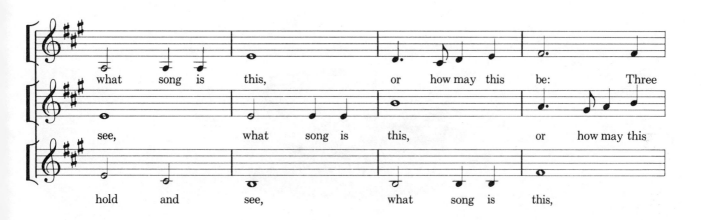

what song is this, or how may this be: Three

see, what song is this, or how may this

hold and see, what song is this,

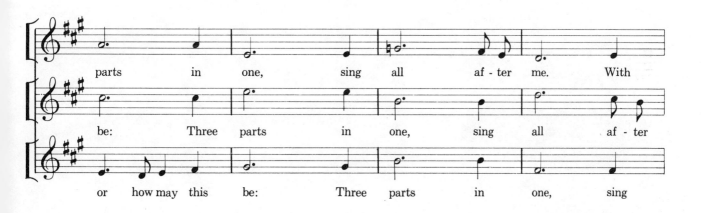

parts in one, sing all af - ter me. With

be: Three parts in one, sing all af - ter

or how may this be: Three parts in one, sing

hey down down a____ down a, troll____ the____

me. With hey down down a____ down a, troll____

all af - ter me. With hey down down a____

127

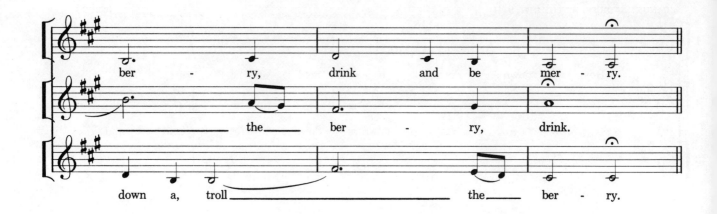

ber - ry, drink and be mer - ry.

_____ the ___ ber - ry, drink.

down a, troll _____ the ___ ber - ry.

HUNTING

Come; Merry Men

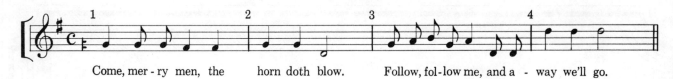

Come, mer - ry men, the horn doth blow. Follow, fol-low me, and a - way we'll go.

Hark! I Hear the Hunters

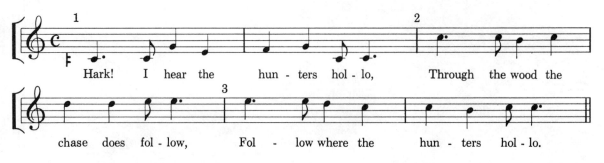

Hark! I hear the hun - ters hol - lo, Through the wood the

chase does fol - low, Fol - low where the hun - ters hol - lo.

NOTE: SAME TUNE AS "UXOR MEA."

We List to the Sound

Birch

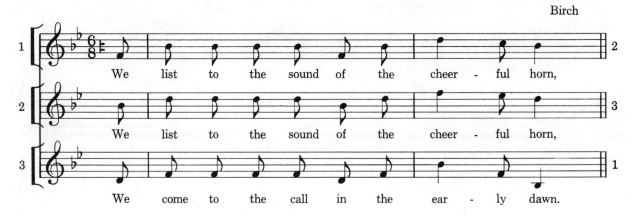

We list to the sound of the cheer - ful horn,

We list to the sound of the cheer - ful horn,

We come to the call in the ear - ly dawn.

Huntsman Sound the Winding Horn

W. W. Pearson

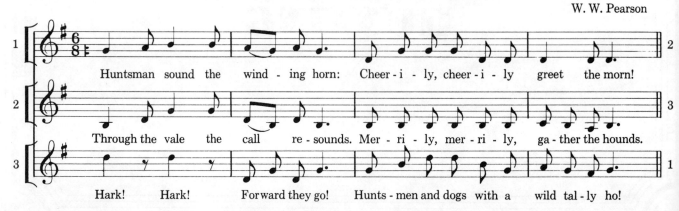

Huntsman sound the wind - ing horn: Cheer - i - ly, cheer - i - ly greet the morn!

Through the vale the call re - sounds. Mer - ri - ly, mer - ri - ly, ga - ther the hounds.

Hark! Hark! For ward they go! Hunts - men and dogs with a wild tal - ly ho!

Merrily, Merrily Greet the Morn

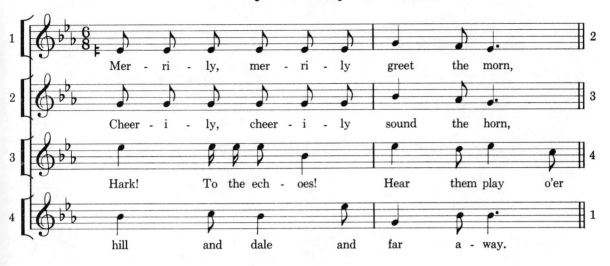

Mer - ri - ly, mer - ri - ly greet the morn,

Cheer - i - ly, cheer - i - ly sound the horn,

Hark! To the ech - oes! Hear them play o'er

hill and dale and far a - way.

With Deep-Toned Horn

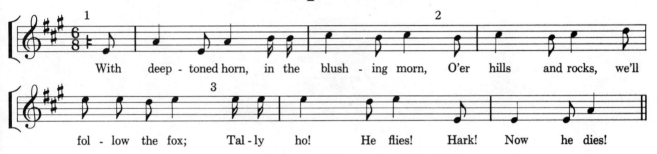

With deep - toned horn, in the blush - ing morn, O'er hills and rocks, we'll

fol - low the fox; Tal - ly ho! He flies! Hark! Now he dies!

O! The Wily, Wily Fox with His Many Wily Mocks

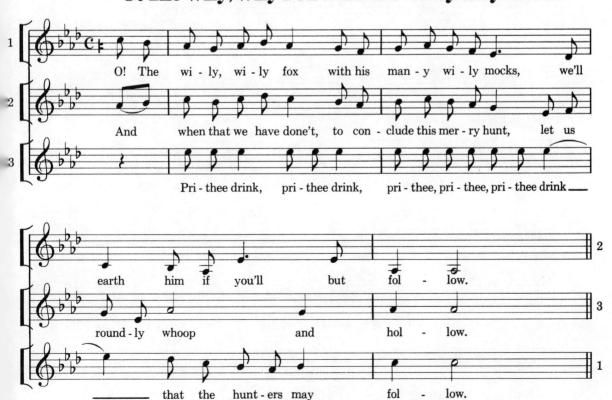

O! The wi - ly, wi - ly fox with his man - y wi - ly mocks, we'll

And when that we have done't, to con - clude this mer - ry hunt, let us

Pri - thee drink, pri - thee drink, pri - thee, pri - thee, pri - thee drink —

earth him if you'll but fol - low.

round - ly whoop and hol - low.

— that the hunt - ers may fol - low.

Come Follow Me with Merry Glee

CANON: 4 VOICES

Bates

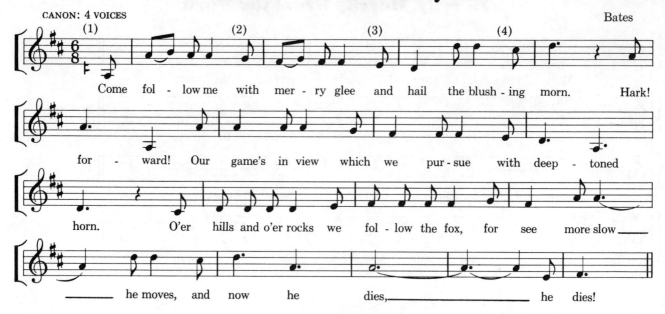

Come fol - low me with mer - ry glee and hail the blush - ing morn. Hark!

for - ward! Our game's in view which we pur - sue with deep - toned

horn. O'er hills and o'er rocks we fol - low the fox, for see more slow

—— he moves, and now he dies, —————————— he dies!

Come Follow Me to the Greenwood Tree

CANON: 3 VOICES

Hayes

Come fol - - - low me — to the green - wood tree, where the

well - toned horn sounds sweet in the morn, while the stag is in view and the

hunt - ers pur - sue with a tal - li - hoo, and our hor - ses dart fire from their eyes. O'er

hills and o'er dales their ar - dor, their ar - dor pre - vails. What

con - cert can vie with the hounds in full cry whilst we hol - low and fol - low the game till it pants, till it

dies, till it pants, pants, till it dies, ———— till it dies?

A Southerly Wind

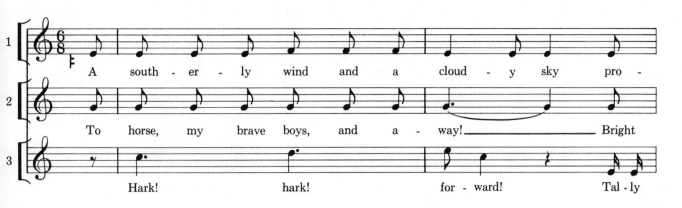

1. A south-er-ly wind and a cloud-y sky pro-

2. To horse, my brave boys, and a-way!_____ Bright

3. Hark! hark! for-ward! Tal-ly

claim it a hunt-ing morn-ing. Be-fore the sun ris-es, a-

Phoebus the hills is a-dorn-ing. The face of all na-ture looks

ho, tal-ly ho, tal-ly ho!_____ Hark! Hark!

way we'll fly, dull sleep in her down-y bed scorn-ing.

gay. 'tis a beau-ti-ful hunt-ing morn-ing.

For-ward! Tal-ly ho, tal-ly ho, tal-ly ho!_____

Hark, How the Woods

White

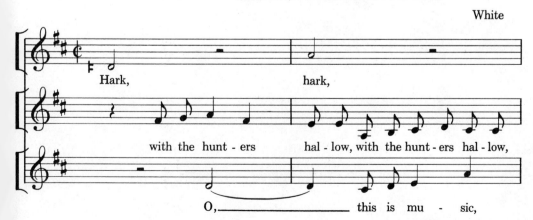

Hark, hark,

with the hunt-ers hal-low, with the hunt-ers hal-low,

O,_____ this is mu-sic,

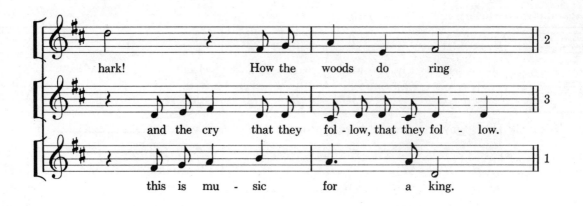

hark! How the woods do ring

and the cry that they fol - low, that they fol - low.

this is mu - sic for a king.

GREAT MASTERS, SO-CALLED

I Ask You

English translation: Carol Dyk

Beethoven

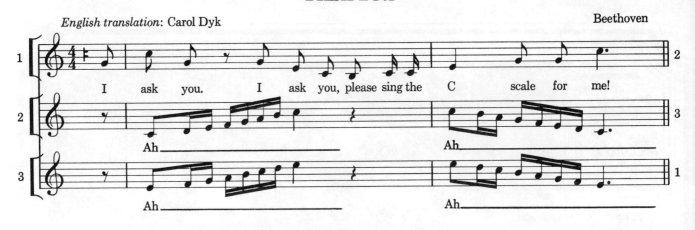

Hoffmann, Hoffmann

English translation: Carol Dyk

Beethoven

Kühl, Nicht Lau (COLD, NOT WARM)

Beethoven

Signor Abbate

Beethoven

Signor Ab - ba - te, I suf - fer. I

May St. Pe - ter come down and bring to me his

The de - vil take you if you don't come soon, the de - vil

suf - fer, I suf - fer with a tooth - ache.

be - ne - dic - tion, bring to me his be - ne - dic - tion.

take you if you don't come soon, if you don't come soon!

O! Come Sweet Slumber

Beethoven

O come sweet slum - ber, down - y

Our eye - lids close, to wear - ry limbs bring sweet re -

While twink - ling star - lets on us

sleep, down - y sleep, down - y sleep,

pose, to wea - ry limbs, bring sweet re - pose,

peep, an - gels' eyes, fires di - vine.

Tock Tick Tock . . . Dear Old Mälzel

Beethoven

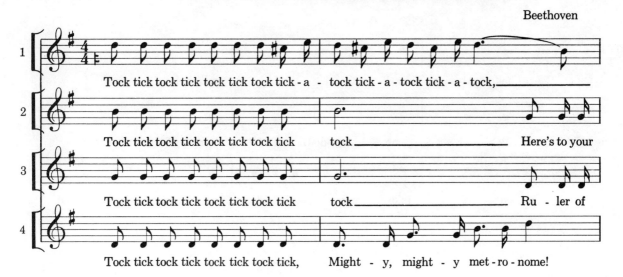

Tock tick tock tick tock tick tock tick - a - tock tick - a - tock tick - a - tock,

Tock tick tock tick tock tick tock tick tock Here's to your

Tock tick tock tick tock tick tock tick tock Ru - ler of

Tock tick tock tick tock tick tock tick, Might - y, might - y met - ro - nome!

dear, old dear, old Mal - zel.

health: long life!

time, ru - ler of time! Tick - a - tock, Tick - a -

Might - y met - ro - nome! Tick - a - tock, Tick - a -

It Must Be

English Translation: Carol Dyk

Beethoven

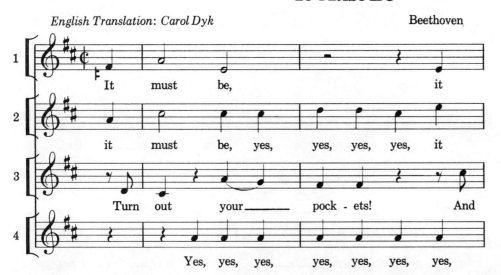

It must be, it

it must be, yes, yes, yes, yes, it

Turn out your pock - ets! And

Yes, yes, yes, yes, yes, yes, yes,

138

must be, yes, yes, yes, yes,

must be, yes, yes, yes, yes!

pay! And pay! It must be!

yes, yes, yes, it must be!

Falstafferel

Beethoven

Fal - staf - fe - rel, Fal - staf - fe - rel, Fal - staf - fe - rel, Fal - staf - fe - rel, Fal -

Fal - staf - fe - rel, Fal - staf - fe - rel, Fal - staf - fe - rel, Fal - staf - fe - rel, Fal -

Fal - staf - fe - rel, Fal - staf - fe - rel, Fal - staf - fe - rel, Fal -

Fal - staf - fe - rel, Fal - staf - fe - rel, Fal -

Fal - staf - fe - rel, Fal -

staf - - - - - - staf - fe - rel,

- - staff, Fal - staff, Fal - staff show your - self now!

- - staff, Fal - staff, Fal - staff show your - self now!

- - staff, Fal - staff, Fal - staff show your - self now!

- - staff, Fal - staff, Fal - staff show your - self now!

Short, Short Is the Pain

English translation: Carol Dyk

Beethoven

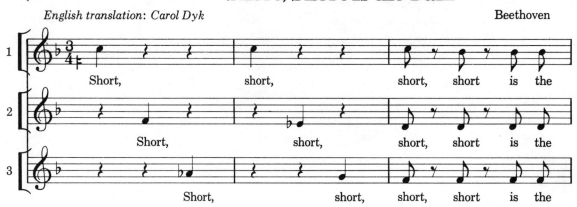

Short, short, short, short is the

Short, short, short, short is the

Short, short, short, short is the

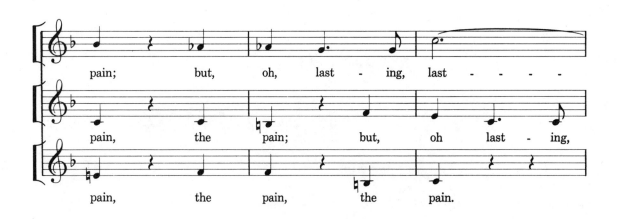

pain; but, oh, last - ing, last - - -

pain, the pain; but, oh last - ing,

pain, the pain, the pain.

- ing is the joy,_____ is the joy,_____ is the

last - - - - ing is the joy,_____ is the

Last - ing, last - - - - - ing is the

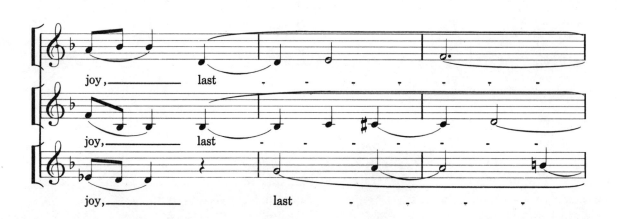

joy,_____ last - - - - - - -

joy,_____ last - - - - - - - -

joy,_____ last - - - -

- - ing is the joy_____
- - ing is the joy, last - - - - ing,
- - ing is the joy_____

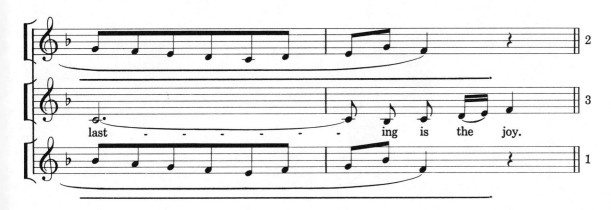

last - - - - - - ing is the joy.

So Come! So Come!

Cherubini

So come! So come!

come! Tra la la, tra la la!

come! Tra la la, tra la la!

Let's be - guile the day with dan - cing, so come! Then

Let's be - gin, let us be - gin,_____ so come, so

Let's be - gin our danc - ing! Bra - vo!

Ich Weiss Nicht (I KNOW NOT)

Brahms

Ich weiss nicht, was im Hahn die

Ob sie be - . trübt wie

des Freun - des, der von

Des Freun - des, der von ihr sich

Tau - be gir - ret!

mei - ne See - le har - ret

ihr sich hat ver - ir - ret?

hat ver - ir - ret?

Maiden Fair and Slender

CANNON: 2 VOICES

Cherubini

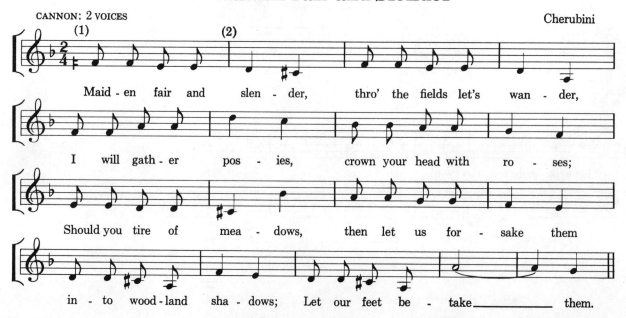

(1)   (2)

Maid - en fair and slen - der, thro' the fields let's wan - der,

I will gath - er pos - ies, crown your head with ro - ses;

Should you tire of mea - dows, then let us for - sake them

in - to wood - land sha - dows; Let our feet be - take them.

Louis Charles Zenobie Salvador Maria

CANON: 2 VOICES

Cherubini

Lou - is Char - les Ze - no - bi - e Sal - va - dor Ma - ri - a Cher - u - bi - ni, a - men, a - men, a - men.

Like As a Father

Cherubini

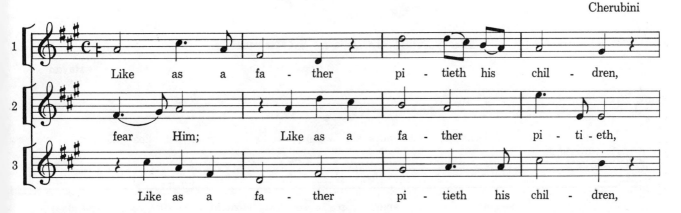

1. Like as a fa - ther pi - tieth his chil - dren,

2. fear Him; Like as a fa - ther pi - ti - eth,

3. Like as a fa - ther pi - tieth his chil - dren,

so the Lord has mer - cy, so the Lord has mer - cy,

pi - tieth his chil - dren, the Lord has mer - cy,

so the Lord hath mer - cy, the Lord hath

so the Lord has mer - cy on them that fear, on them that

the Lord has mer - cy on them that fear Him;

mer - cy on them that fear Him.

143

Death Is a Long, Long Sleep

Haydn

Death is a long,_____ long sleep; Sleep is a short re-treat from life that soothes our cares as death brings still-ness af-ter strife; Death is a long, long sleep.

Beware! Dearest Comrades

Haydn

Be-ware! Dear-est com-rades all, when words from your lips do fall, gov-ern and rea-son well, guard what your tongue does tell. Show pru-dence wis-dom, care, of rash speech e'er be-ware!

The Jolly Month of May

Haydn

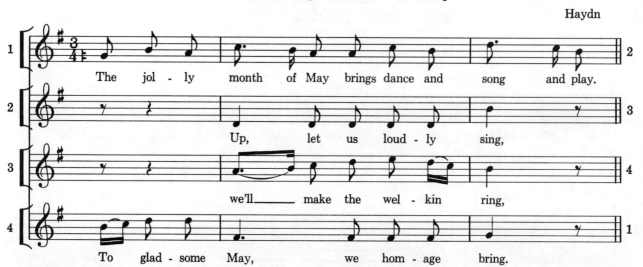

The jol-ly month of May brings dance and song and play.
Up, let us loud-ly sing,
we'll_____ make the wel-kin ring,
To glad-some May, we hom-age bring.

144

Ah, the Songs of Cherubini

English translation: Carol Dyk

Kuhlau

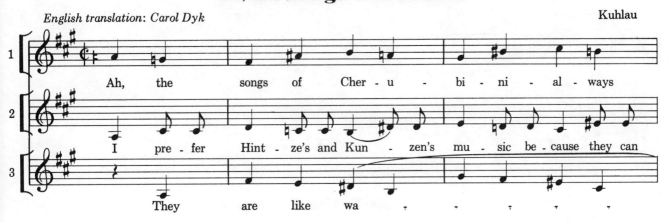

1 Ah, the songs of Cher-u-bi-ni al-ways

2 I pre-fer Hint-ze's and Kun-zen's mu-sic be-cause they can

3 They are like wa - - - - -

are_____ too chro-mat - ic! There-fore I pre-fer Hint-ze's and

write just as clear as a book. I'd ra - ther sing

- - - ter falls:_____ La la la_____ la la la la

Kun-zen's songs_____ be - cause they sound clear as a brook.

Hint - ze's and Kun - zen's sweet songs_____

la,_____ la la la_____ la la la_____ la_____ la.

Faith, Thou Beacon

CANON: 3 VOICES

Mozart

(1)   (2)   (3)

Faith, thou bea-con ev - er bright, Star point-ing to the

dawn a-cross the night, Cast on troub-led hearts thy heav-en-born light.

Dona Nobis Pacem

CANON: 4 VOICES

Mozart

(1) ... (2) Do - - - - - - na no - bis,

(3) ... (4) do - na da no - bis pa - cem.

How Clear Is the Trumpet

Mendelssohn

1. How clear is the trum - pet, how clear_____
2. trum - pet. How clear, how clear is the
3. trum - pet. How_____ clear,_____

_____ is the
trum - pet, how_____ clear, how clear is the
_____ how clear is the trum - - pet!

Ave Maria

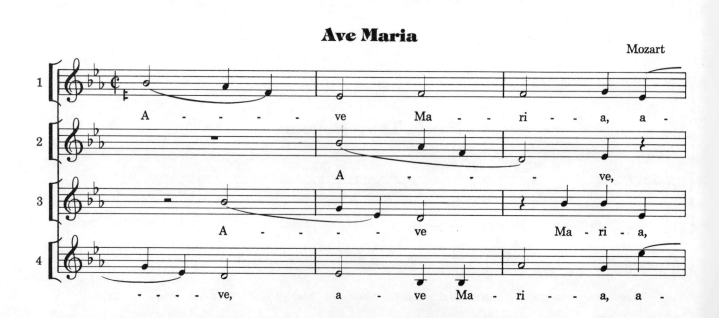

Mozart

1. A - - - ve Ma - ri - a, a -
2. A - - - ve,
3. A - - ve Ma - ri - a,
4. - - - ve, a - ve Ma - ri - - a, a -

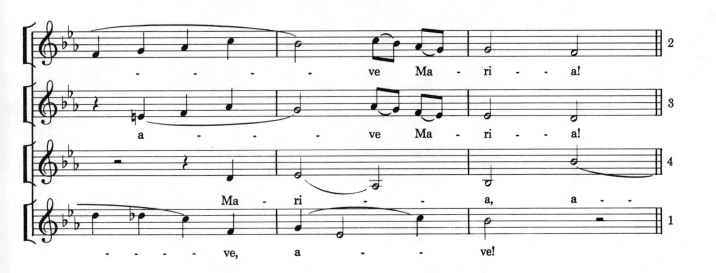

Alleluia

Mozart

(A)

(B)

NOTES (B) *is the reverse of round* (A). *Each may be sung separately as a*
3-voice round, or they may be sung consecutively as a 6-voice round.

147

Melancholy, Folly!

Mozart

Mel - - - an - - - -
fol - - - ly,
Mel - an - cho - ly is
growl - ing, moan - ing, howl - ing, dole - ful
dai - - sy, in the end will drive you
jol - ly. Woe is me and lack - a - dai - - - sy,

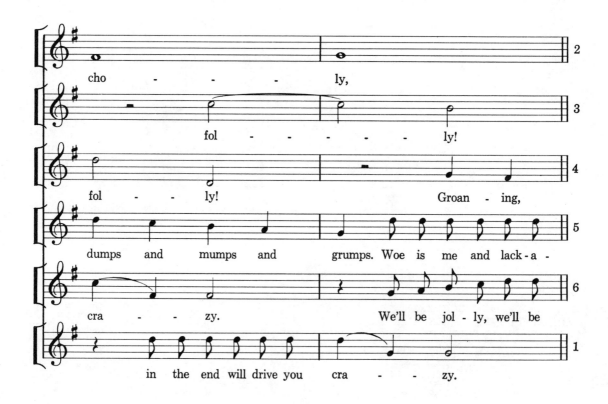

cho - - - ly,
fol - - - - - ly!
fol - - ly! Groan - ing,
dumps and mumps and grumps. Woe is me and lack - a -
cra - - zy. We'll be jol - ly, we'll be
in the end will drive you cra - - zy.

148

Bonanox

Mozart

Bo - na - nox,
not - te, lie - be Lot - te; bonne
night, heut müess ma no weit, gu - te nacht, gu - te
Schlaf sei g'sund und

bist a rech - ter Ochs; bo - na
nuit, pfui, pfui, good - night, good -
nacht'swird höchste ___ Zeit, gu - te nacht!
bleib recht ku - gel - rund.

Lacrimoso Son Io

Mozart

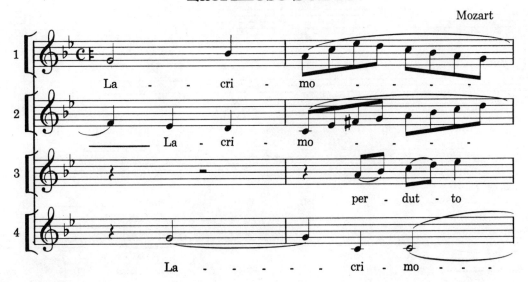

La - cri - mo - - - -
___ La - cri - mo - -
per - dut - to
La - - - - cri - mo - -

Oh Lord, Chastise Me Not

CANON: 2 VOICES   *Engilsh translation: Carol Dyk*   Telemann

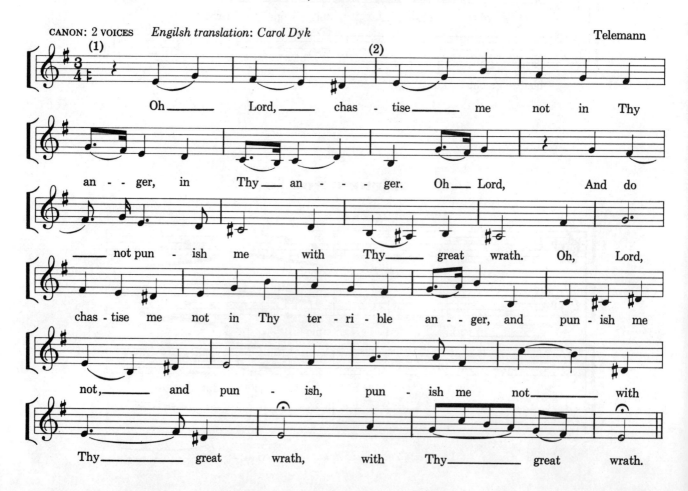

Kyrie Eleison I

Mozart

NOTE: *These are the three parts of the Kyrie of the Ordinary. They may be sung separately or one following the other, which makes a lengthy production.*

Christe Eleison II

Mozart

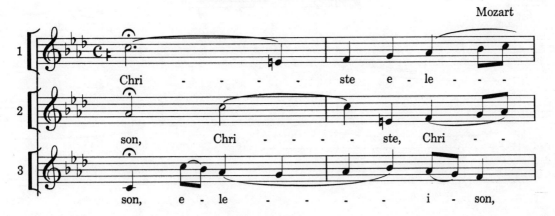

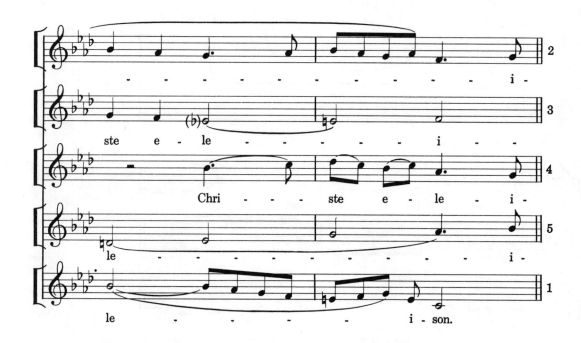

Kyrie Eleison III

Mozart

This Is One Canon (A JOKE)

English translation: Carol Dyk

Salieri

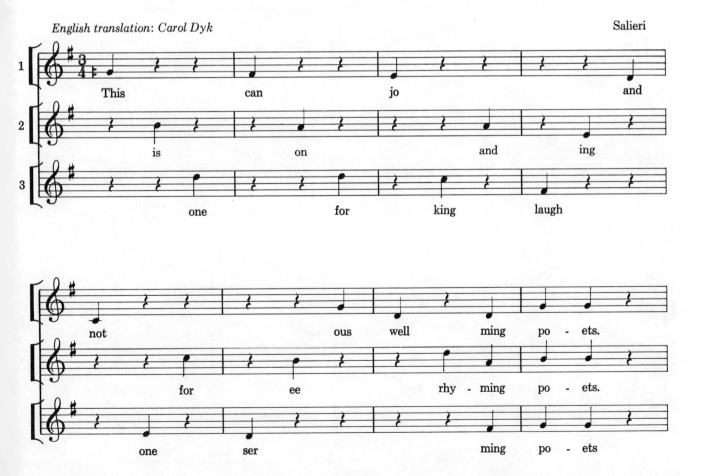

who   that   have   and

pull   leave   must   ing

pee   be   they   mean

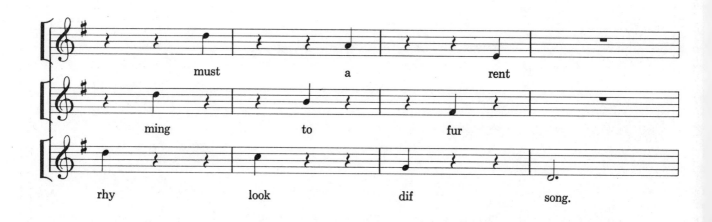

must   a   rent

ming   to   fur

rhy   look   dif   song.

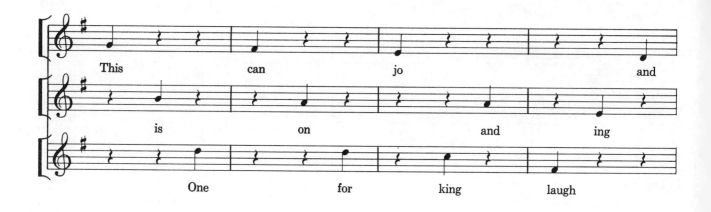

This   can   jo   and

is   on   and   ing

One   for   king   laugh

not   ous   well   ming   po - ets   **2**

for   ee   rhy - ming   po - ets.   **3**

one   ser   ming   po - ets.   **1**

PASTORAL

It Is Light

Gaily

It is light, Come, let us rise,

For the sun is In the skies.

The Morn Doth Break

Moffat

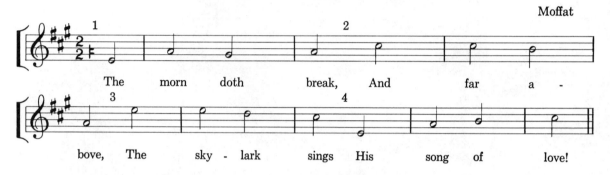

The morn doth break, And far a-

bove, The sky - lark sings His song of love!

Hark! Without

Hark! With - out the storm is loud, See, a - bove, the

black - ened cloud. Hark! Hark! Hark! Hark!

The Kine

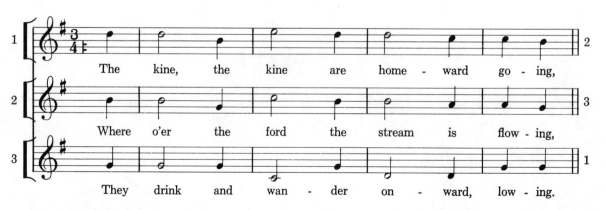

The kine, the kine are home - ward go - ing,

Where o'er the ford the stream is flow - ing,

They drink and wan - der on - ward, low - ing.

Same tune as
"A Boat, a Boat" and
"Be You to Others Kind and True"

156

Roaming O'er the Meadows

Roam-ing o'er the mea-dows far, Sing-ing gai-ly tra la la, Tra la la la la la, tra la la la la.

June, Lovely June

June, love-ly June now beau-ti-fies the ground; The notes of the cuc-koo thru the glad earth re-sound.

Purling Streams

Pur-ling streams, your sound I love,— Gently, gently glide a-long through yon-der grove.

As I Me Walked

Melvill

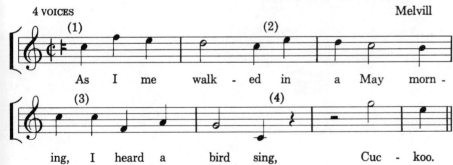

4 VOICES

As I me walk-ed in a May morn-ing, I heard a bird sing, Cuc-koo.

Farewell We Sing

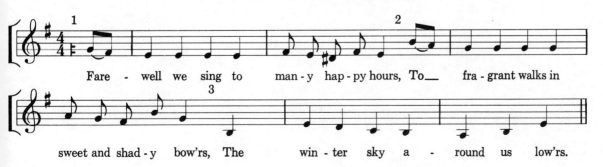

Fare-well we sing to man-y hap-py hours, To— fra-grant walks in sweet and shad-y bow'rs, The win-ter sky a-round us low'rs.

Cuckoo, Hark How He Sings

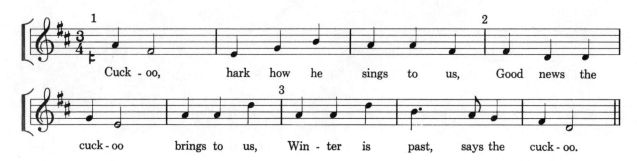

Cuck - oo, hark how he sings to us, Good news the cuck-oo brings to us, Win - ter is past, says the cuck - oo.

Mark Where the Bee

Mark where the bee, with bus - y wing,

Home to her hive the sweets does bring;

She gath - ers from the flow'rs_____ of spring.

Ye Sportive Birds

Sabbatini

Ye sport - ive birds, in cir - cles high, Your

And ye who make the woods more high, All

May joy . . . . . be yours, in__ flight and

flight for - ev - er wing - - ing.

vo - cal__ with your sing - ing.

song, To - day, and long.

When Spring Returns Again

Ferrari

When Spring re - turns a - gain, and her flow'rs once more ap - pear

Her faith - ful her - ald's strain, through the ech - oing groves we hear:

Cuck - oo Cuck - oo, Cuck - oo.

Fruitful Fields Are Waving

CANON: 2 VOICES

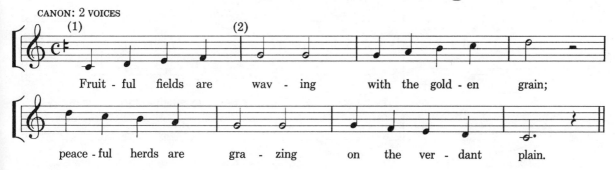

Fruit - ful fields are wav - ing with the gold - en grain;

peace - ful herds are gra - zing on the ver - dant plain.

Yes! 'Tis Raining

Yes! 'Tis rain - ing ev - 'ry oth - er morn - ing, Ev' - ry day and

ev - 'ry oth - er eve - ning. Rain, rain, go to Spain; Rain, go to Spain!

The Pigeon Is Never Woe

Deuteromelia

The pi - ge - on is ne - ver woe Till a - bent - ing* she

go, With heave and ho, So let the wind blow.

* "Benting" is the time of year when
pigeons are forced to feed on "bents",
or plantain seeds.

’Tis Blithe May Day

’Tis blithe May Day, Come, haste a - way,

Gay flags are streaming on the vill - age green, Bright fac - es beam - ing all around are seen.

Awake! Awake! Awake! Awake!

A - wake! A - wake! A - wake! A - wake! The morn with rud - dy hue!

A - rise! A - rise! Its ro - sy light to view.

O, no! No! That is no - thing new!

The Little Moon Came Out

The lit - tle moon came out too soon, and in her

The stars then shone, and ev - 'ry one

The great sun now roll'd forth in might, and

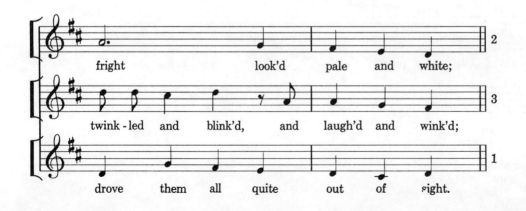

fright look'd pale and white;

twink - led and blink'd, and laugh'd and wink'd;

drove them all quite out of sight.

Mocking, Mocking

Text: Anne Greeley

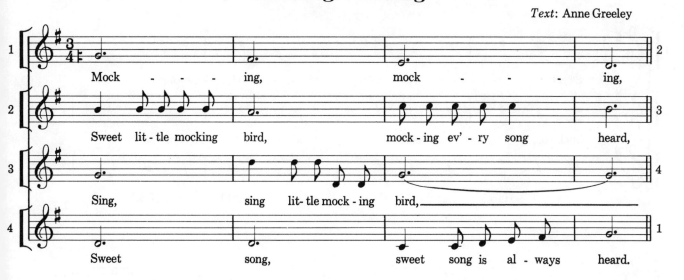

The Cheerful Day Is Dawning

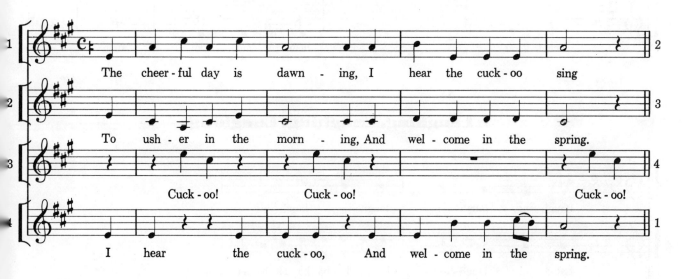

The Spring Is Come

Hayes

Sweet the Pleasures of the Spring

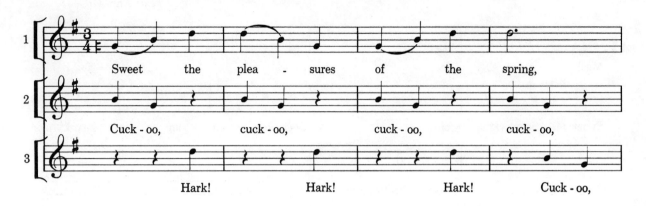

Sweet the plea - sures of the spring,

Cuck - oo, cuck - oo, cuck - oo, cuck - oo,

Hark! Hark! Hark! Cuck - oo,

When we hear the cuck - oo sing.

When we hear the cuck - oo sing.

cuck - oo, cuck - oo, hear the cuck - oo sing.

Laughing, Laughing, Laughing

Laugh - ing, laugh - ing, laugh - ing, laugh - ing

Laugh - ing, laugh - ing, ha ha ha ha ha ha ha ha

Ha ha ha ha ha ha ha ha ha ha ha ha ha ha ha ha

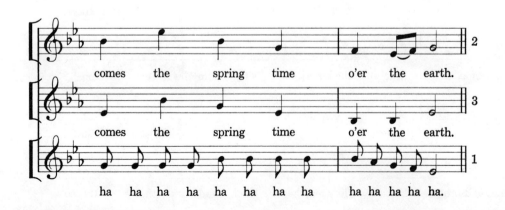

comes the spring time o'er the earth.

comes the spring time o'er the earth.

ha ha ha ha ha ha ha ha ha ha ha ha ha.

Thirty Days Hath September

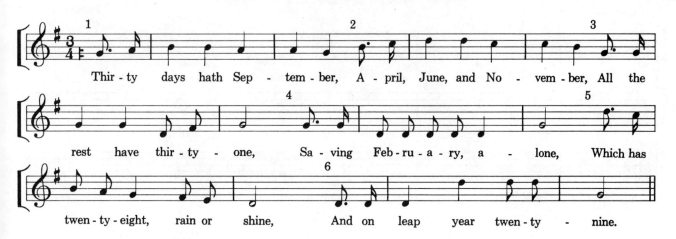

Thir-ty days hath Sep-tem-ber, A-pril, June, and No-vem-ber, All the rest have thir-ty-one, Sa-ving Feb-ru-a-ry, a-lone, Which has twen-ty-eight, rain or shine, And on leap year twen-ty-nine.

The Lark, Linnet, and Nightingale

Melvill

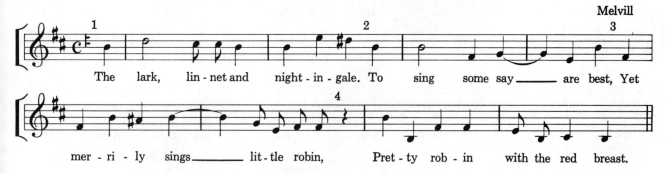

The lark, lin-net and night-in-gale. To sing some say——are best, Yet mer-ri-ly sings——lit-tle robin, Pret-ty rob-in with the red breast.

See the Raindrops

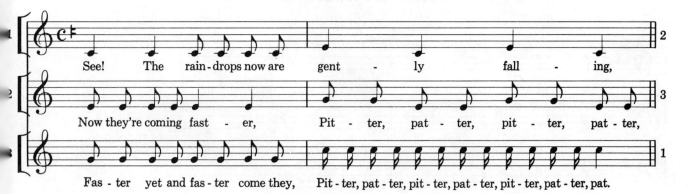

See! The rain-drops now are gent-ly fall-ing,

Now they're coming fast-er, Pit-ter, pat-ter, pit-ter, pat-ter,

Fas-ter yet and fas-ter come they, Pit-ter, pat-ter, pit-ter, pat-ter, pit-ter, pat-ter, pat.

Laughing May Is Here

Laugh-ing May is here, Blith-est of the year;

Hark! Hear the blue-bird say: Mer-ry, mer-ry, mer-ry, mer-ry May.

Note: The only thing difficult about this is keeping the 8 voices going.

The Nightingale

Quickly   Pammelia

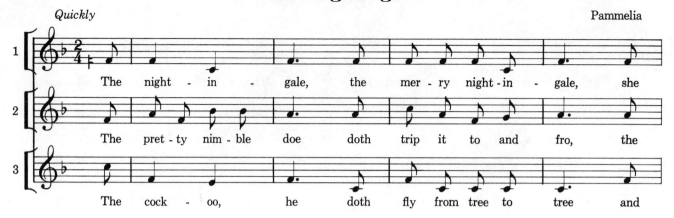

The night - in - gale, the mer - ry night - in - gale, she

The pret - ty nim - ble doe doth trip it to and fro, the

The cock - oo, he doth fly from tree to tree and

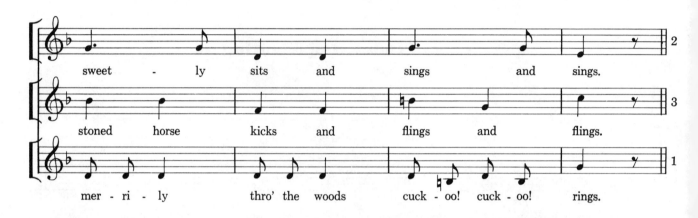

sweet - ly sits and sings and sings.

stoned horse kicks and flings and flings.

mer - ri - ly thro' the woods cuck - oo! cuck - oo! rings.

Now When the Summer's Fruits

Hilton

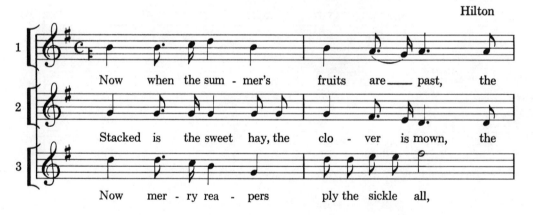

Now when the sum - mer's fruits are __ past, the

Stacked is the sweet hay, the clo - ver is mown, the

Now mer - ry rea - pers ply the sickle all,

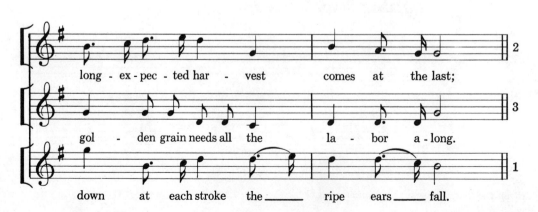

long - ex - pec - ted har - vest comes at the last;

gol - den grain needs all the la - bor a - long.

down at each stroke the __ ripe ears __ fall.

164

Haste Thee Nymph

John Milton   Samuel Arnold

Haste thee, nymph, and bring with thee Jest and youth-ful jol-li-ty;

Quips and cranks and wan-ton wiles, Nods and becks and wreathed smiles

Sport, that wrin-kled care de-rides, And laugh-ter hold-ing both his sides.

Hey, Ho! To the Greenwood

CANON: 3 VOICES

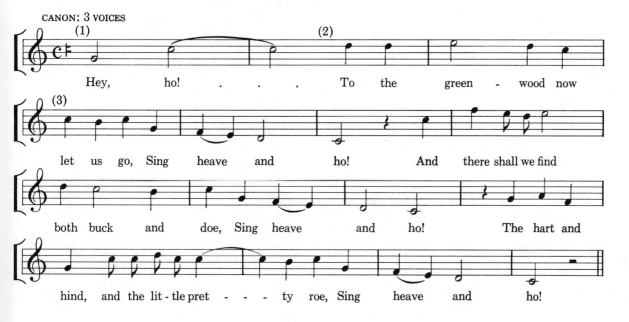

Hey, ho! . . . To the green-wood now

let us go, Sing heave and ho! And there shall we find

both buck and doe, Sing heave and ho! The hart and

hind, and the lit-tle pret - - - ty roe, Sing heave and ho!

Once in Arcadia

Alcock

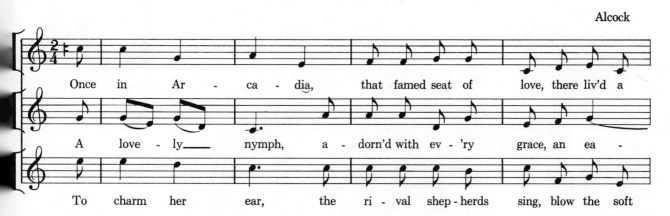

Once in Ar-ca-dia, that famed seat of love, there liv'd a

A love-ly___ nymph, a-dorn'd with ev-'ry grace, an ea-

To charm her ear, the ri-val shep-herds sing, blow the soft

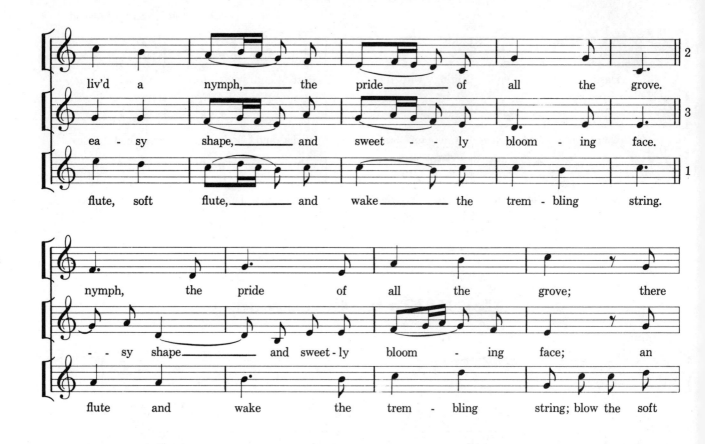

liv'd a nymph,_____ the pride_____ of all the grove.

ea - sy shape,_____ and sweet - ly bloom - ing face.

flute, soft flute,_____ and wake_____ the trem - bling string.

nymph, the pride of all the grove; there

- - sy shape_____ and sweet - ly bloom - ing face; an

flute and wake the trem - bling string; blow the soft

Jolly Shepherd

Pammelia

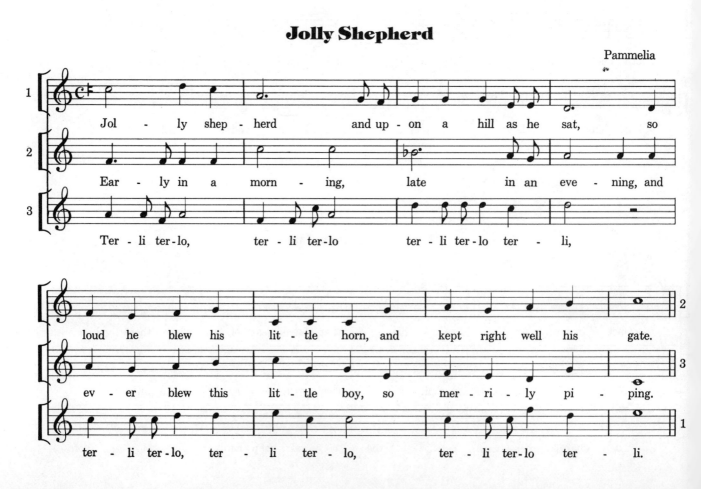

Jol - ly shep - herd and up - on a hill as he sat, so

Ear - ly in a morn - ing, late in an eve - ning, and

Ter - li ter - lo, ter - li ter - lo ter - li ter - lo ter - li,

loud he blew his lit - tle horn, and kept right well his gate.

ev - er blew this lit - tle boy, so mer - ri - ly pi - ping.

ter - li ter - lo, ter - li ter - lo, ter - li ter - lo ter - li.

166

River, That in Silence Windest

Longfellow - Martini

Riv - - er, that___ in si - - lence wind - est,

Till___ at length___ re - pose thou find - est

Riv - - er, that in si - - lence wind - est,

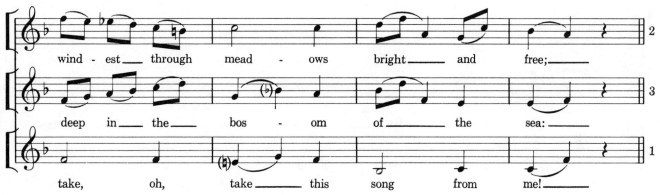

wind - est___ through mead - ows bright___ and free;___

deep in___ the___ bos - om of___ the sea:___

take, oh, take___ this song from me!___

The Winter Dark and Dreary

Mainzer

The win - ter dark and drear - y Hath fled be - fore the spring, Now

Re - sound - ing the woods with glad - ness,

Cuck - oo, cuck - oo, cuck - oo,

all is bright and cheer - y, The birds and we should sing,

Re - sound - ing the woods with glad - ness,

Cuck - oo, cuck - oo, cuck - oo.

The Winter Has Passed

The win-ter has pass'd with its frowns a-way, and the
The chil-dren are out in the field at play, and the
It seems as if Spring, with her balm-y breath, hath

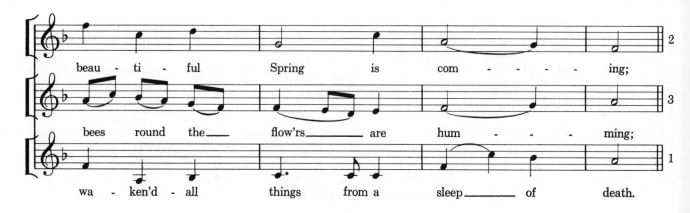

beau-ti-ful Spring is com - - - ing;
bees round the____ flow'rs_____ are hum - - ming;
wa-ken'd-all things from a sleep_____ of death.

Hallo, in Forest Track

Martini

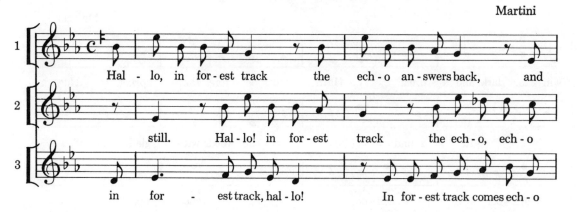

Hal - lo, in for-est track the ech-o an-swers back, and
still. Hal-lo! in for-est track the ech-o, ech-o
in for - est track, hal-lo! In for-est track comes ech-o

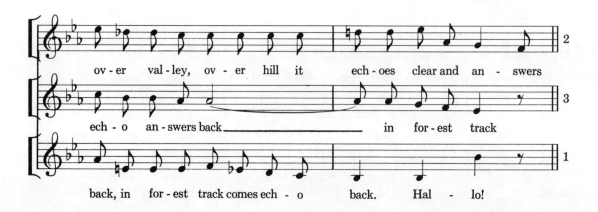

ov-er val-ley, ov-er hill it ech-oes clear and an-swers
ech-o an-swers back_____ in for-est track
back, in for-est track comes ech-o back. Hal - lo!

168

Hark! 'Tis the Cuckoo's Voice

Hark! 'Tis the cuck - oo's voice, from yon - der sha - dy grove;

Cuck - oo! Cuck - oo!

Hark! 'Tis the cuck - oo's voice, from yon - der sha - dy grove;

Hark! 'Tis the cuck - oo's voice, from yon - der sha - dy grove;

List to the mel - low notes, the song I dear - ly love.

Cuck - oo! Cuck - oo!

List to the mel - low notes, the song I dear - ly love.

List to the mel - low notes, the song I dear - ly love.

(or to Coda)

Coda to be sung together

mf *mp* *p* *pp*

Cuck - oo! Cuck - oo! Cuck - oo! Cuck - oo!

When First the Sun

Purcell

When first the sun breaks thru the shades of night, and streaks the far - off

Then co - lor comes, then co - lor comes, the plains their li - - 'vries wear; Re -

The var - ying land - scape shows its thou - sand thou - sand dyes; The

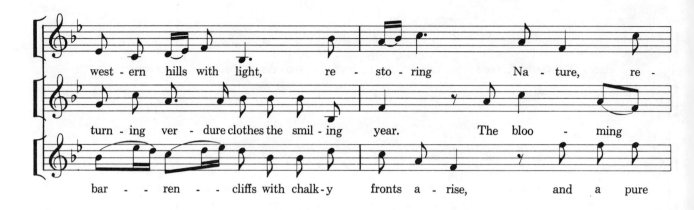

west - ern hills with light, re - sto - ring Na - ture, re -

turn - ing ver - dure clothes the smil - ing year. The bloo - ming

bar - - ren - - cliffs with chalk - y fronts a - rise, and a pure

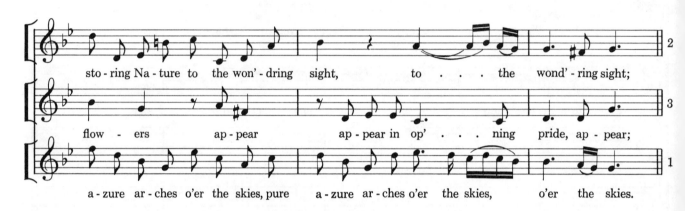

sto - ring Na - ture to the won' - dring sight, to . . . the wond' - ring sight;

flow - ers ap - pear ap - pear in op' . . . ning pride, ap - pear;

a - zure ar - ches o'er the skies, pure a - zure ar - ches o'er the skies, o'er the skies.

May Brings Round

Travers

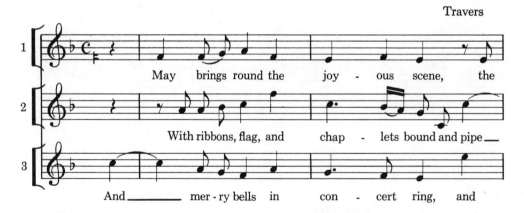

May brings round the joy - ous scene, the

With ribbons, flag, and chap - lets bound and pipe

And merry bells in con - cert ring, and

May - pole on the vil - lage green,

and ta - bor's mirth - ful sound,

mer - ry voi - ces blithe - ly sing.

170

Sumer Is Icumen In

3 or 4 voices
The 2nd, 3rd, and 4th voices enter, in turn, when the preceding part has reached
the beginning of the 3rd bar.

1 Sum - mer is a - com - ing in,_____ Loud - ly sing cuck - oo;

2 Grow - eth seed and blow - eth mead, and spring - eth wood a - new.

3 Sing, cuck - oo! E - we bleat - eth aft - er lamb, low'th

4 aft - er calf the cow; Bull - ock start - eth, buck to fern go'th,

5 Mer - ry sing cuck - oo! Cuck - oo, Cuck - oo! Well

6 sing - est thou cuck - oo,_____ Nor cease thou ev - er now.

PES

Cuc - cu, cu, cuc - cu, cu.

Cuc - cu, cuc - cu,_____ cuc - cu, cuc - cu._____

Original words, and the "Ground-Bass" or "Pes"
for two additional voices as accompaniment

Surmer is icumen in,
Lhude sing cuccur!
Groweth sed, and bloweth med,
And springeth the wde nu.

Sing cucu!

Awe bleteth after lombe,
Lhouth after calve cu;
Bulluc sterteth, bucks verteth,
Murie sing cuccu.

Cuccu, cuccu!
Wel singes thu cuccu,
Ne swik thu naver nu.

171

May Does Ev'ry Fragrance

Hayes

May_____ does___ ev' - - ry fra - grance bring,

Hap - py__ birds___ in grate - ful notes,

Blush - ing flow'rs in beau - ty rise, Dif -

All_____ the__ ver - - nal bloom_____ of__ spring;

Poor_____ their__ praise through tune - ful__ throats;

fus - ing o - dors to_____ the skies.

Hail, Hail, Green Fields

Greene

Hail, hail, green fields and sha - dy

Hail, Na - ture's un - cor - rup - ted

Free from vice,_____

woods! Hail, cry - stal streams that still run pure! Hail, crys -

goods, where vir - tue on - ly dwells se - cure, where

_____ and free_____ from care, Age has no

172

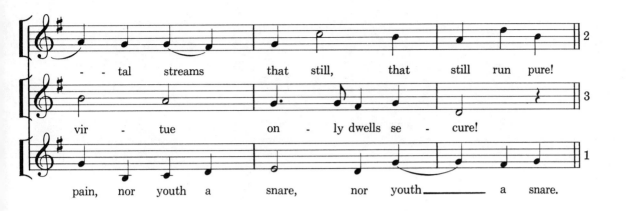

-tal streams that still, that still run pure!

vir - tue on - ly dwells se - cure!

pain, nor youth a snare, nor youth_____ a snare.

Hark, Hark, Hark to the Curfew

Arne

Hark, hark, hark, to the cur - few's

Peace and so - lemn still - ness reign, peace,

O'er the earth o'er the sky soft steals the night, soft,

And hides fair Na - ture, and hides fair Na - ture in

sound. Hark, hark to the sound;

peace and so - lemn still - ness reign_____ a - round;

o'er the earth, o'er the sky, soft steals the night,

mists from the sight, in mists from the sight.

Come, Come Away

Hayes

Come, come a - way, come, come a - way, This is a ve - ry fine

Come, come a - way, come, come a - way,

Come, come a - way,

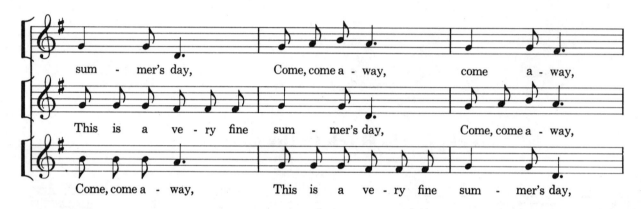

sum - mer's day, Come, come a - way, come a - way,

This is a ve - ry fine sum - mer's day, Come, come a - way,

Come, come a - way, This is a ve - ry fine sum - mer's day,

Come, come a - way, come, come a - way.

come a - way; Come, come a - way.

Come, come a - way, come a - way.

Fair Morn Ascends

Hayes

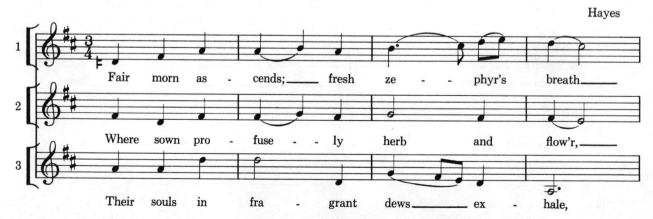

Fair morn as - cends;____ fresh ze - - phyr's breath____

Where sown pro - fuse - - ly herb and flow'r,____

Their souls in fra - grant dews____ ex - hale,

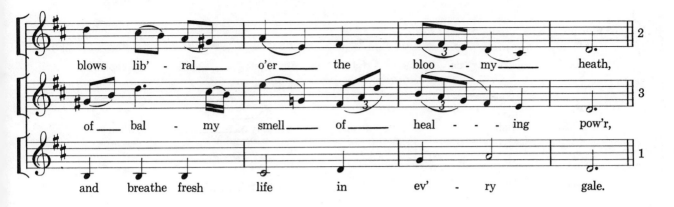

blows lib' - ral ___ o'er ___ the bloo - - my ___ heath,

of ___ bal - my smell ___ of ___ heal - - - ing pow'r,

and breathe fresh life in ev' - ry gale.

Disturb Not the Plover

Dis - turb not the plo - ver, for see she doth ho - ver so

Pee - wit,

Hear her mourn - ful cry, _____

O hear her pit - e - ous

ten - der - ly o - ver her sweet lit - tle broad;

Pee - wit,

hear her mourn - ful cry; _____

moan! _____ Pit - e - ous moan!

175

Come, Come Delightful Spring

Bononcini

Come, come delight - ful Spring,_____ choice

Birds hail the boun - teous May,_____ their

Cold Win - ter now de - parts,_____ re -

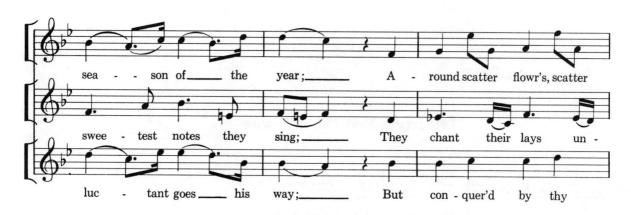

sea - son of_____ the year;_____ A - round scatter flowr's, scatter

swee - test notes they sing;_____ They chant their lays un -

luc - tant goes_____ his way;_____ But con - quer'd by thy

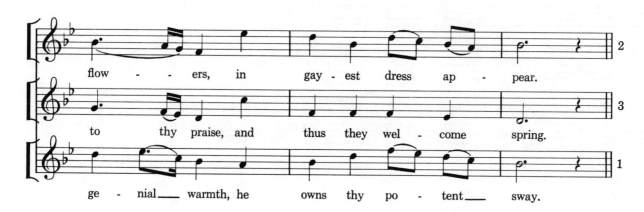

flow - ers, in gay - est dress ap - pear.

to thy praise, and thus they wel - come spring.

ge - nial_____ warmth, he owns thy po - tent_____ sway.

Come, Let Us All a-Maying Go

Hilton

Come, let us all_____ a - May - ing go, and

The bells shall ring_____ and the bells_____ shall ring and the

drums shall beat and the fife shall play and

lightly - ly and light - ly trip it to_____ and fro.

cuck - oo, the cuck - oo, the cuck - oo sing, The

so_____ we'll pass_____ our___ time a - way.

Bring Thy Treasures

Hayes

Bring thy trea - sures, smi - ling plea - sures, Love - ly

Ev - er smil - ing, care be - guil - - ing. With thy

Where can sor - row sad - ness bor - row, When a -

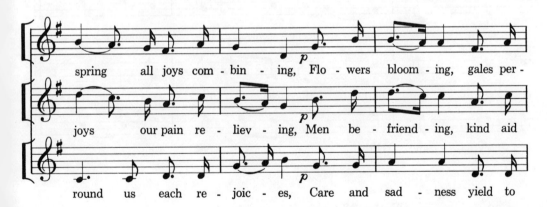

spring all joys com - bin - ing, Flo - wers bloom - ing, gales per -

joys our pain re - liev - ing, Men be - friend - ing, kind aid

round us each re - joic - es, Care and sad - ness yield to

fum - ing, All their var - - ious hues en - twin - - ing,

lend - ing To con sole____ the heart that's griev - - ing,

glad - ness, With the birds will join our voi - ces.

The Long Grass Ripples

Purcell

The long grass rip - ples in the breeze_____ which

Up, up, the birds_____ are car - ol - ing and

Mer - ry, my hearts, mer - ry, my boys, mer - ry my sprites, mer - ry, mer - ry, mer - ry,

light - ly stirs_____ a - round,_____ and a - zure sky_____ and

in - - sects on_____ the wing,_____ and blithe - ly sounds the

mer - ry, mer - ry, my hey_____ down der - ry,_____ for blithe - ly sounds the

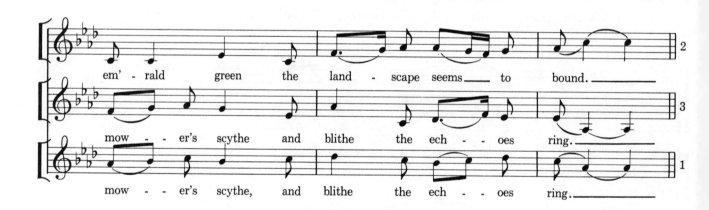

em' - rald green the land - scape seems_____ to bound._____

mow - - er's scythe and blithe the ech - - oes ring._____

mow - - er's scythe, and blithe the ech - - oes ring._____

Fair Morn

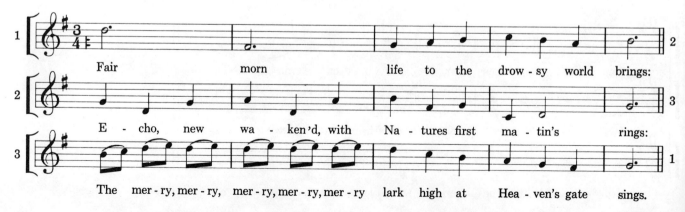

Fair morn life to the drow - sy world brings:

E - cho, new wa - ken'd, with Na - tures first ma - tin's rings:

The mer - ry, mer - ry, mer - ry, mer - ry, mer - ry lark high at Hea - ven's gate sings.

At Summer Morn

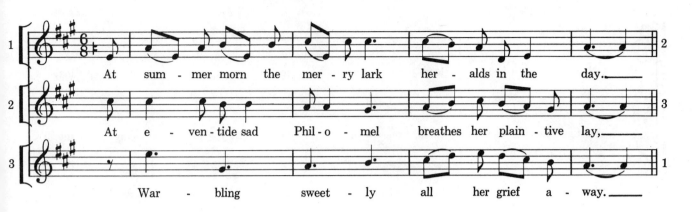

At sum - mer morn the mer - ry lark her - alds in the day.

At e - ven - tide sad Phil - o - mel breathes her plain - tive lay,

War - bling sweet - ly all her grief a - way.

Poor Robin Redbreast

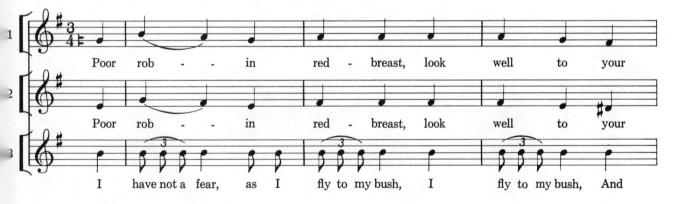

Poor rob - in red - breast, look well to your

Poor rob - in red - breast, look well to your

I have not a fear, as I fly to my bush, I fly to my bush, And

nest, The cold wea - ther, the cold wea - ther comes on;

nest, The cold wea - ther, the cold wea - ther comes on.

put my bill un - der my wing, un - der my wing, un - der my wing.

Now the Last Load

Lawes

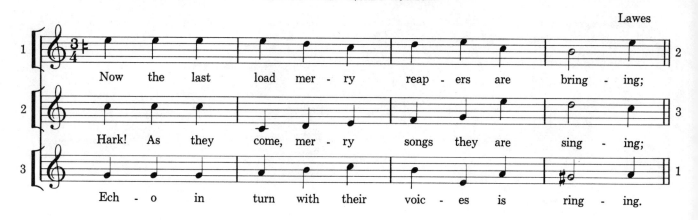

1. Now the last load merry reap - ers are bring - ing;

2. Hark! As they come, mer - ry songs they are sing - ing;

3. Ech - o in turn with their voic - es is ring - ing.

NONSENSE

Kit and Tom Chid, a!

Chidingly

Melismata

Kit and Tom chid, a! Kit and Tom chid.

Kit chid Tom, Tom chid Kit, Kit and Tom chid, a!

Uxor Mea, Uxor Polla

Ux - or me - a, ux - or pol - la, O si fram - gat

su - a col - la, Pol - la col - la, col - la pol - la.

Same time as "Hark!, Hear the Hunters"

Derry Ding Ding Dasson

Melismata

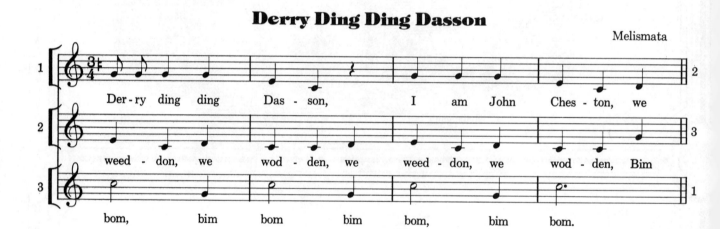

Der - ry ding ding Das - son, I am John Ches - ton, we

weed - don, we wod - den, we weed - don, we wod - den, Bim

bom, bim bom bim bom, bim bom.

The Fly She Sat

Deuteromelia

The fly she sat in Sham - ble row, the

fly she sat in Sham - ble row, and

sham - bled with, and sham - bled with her heels I trow.

NOTE *9 verses exist.*

The Wise Men Were But Sev'n

Lawes

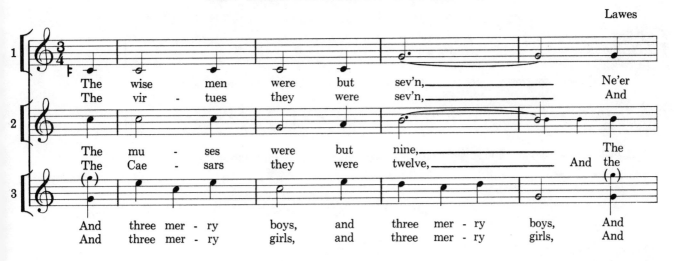

The wise men were but sev'n,_____ Ne'er
The vir - tues they but were sev'n,_____ And

The mu - ses were but nine,_____ The
The Cae - sars they were twelve,_____ And the

And three mer - ry boys, and three mer - ry boys, And
And three mer - ry girls, and three mer - ry girls, And

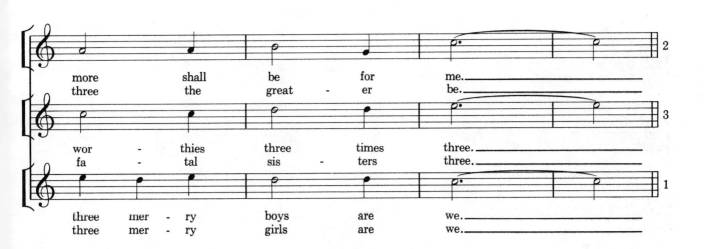

more shall be for me._____
three the great - er be._____

wor - thies three times three._____
fa - tal sis - ters three._____

three mer - ry boys are we._____
three mer - ry girls are we._____

Woe's Au Be by Wi Dinking

Lawes

Woe's au be by wi dink - - ing,

Woe's au be durke wi dink - - ing,

Gan we gang on es we be - gun

Woe's au be slay wi dink - - ing.

183

Horse to Trot, to Trot, I Say

Pierce

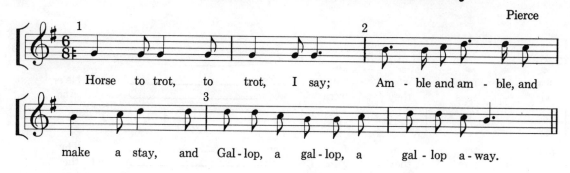

Horse to trot, to trot, I say; Am - ble and am - ble, and

make a stay, and Gal - lop, a gal - lop, a gal - lop a - way.

The White Hen

Pammelia

The white hen she cack - les and lays in the pud - dle.

Sing, Hey! Cock with - out a comb, cock ad - dle lud - dle!

As I Went by the Way

Melismata

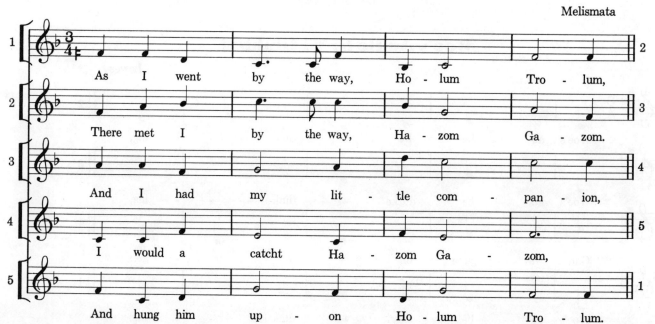

As I went by the way, Ho - lum Tro - lum,

There met I by the way, Ha - zom Ga - zom.

And I had my lit - tle com - pan - ion,

I would a catcht Ha - zom Ga - zom,

And hung him up - on Ho - lum Tro - lum.

Three Bulls and a Bear

1. Three bulls and a bear, a cob-bler and a tin-ker, 2

2. cob- tin- a cob-bler and a tin-ker 3

3. -ler, -ker, a cob-bler and a tin-ker. 1

Well Rung, Tom

Medium fast   J. Miller

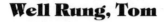

Well rung, Tom, boy, well rung, Tom, Ding-dong, cuck-oo, well rung, Tom. The

owl and the cuck-oo, the fool and the song, Well sung, cuck-oo, well rung, Tom.

Hey Ho, Behold, I Will Show

Pierce

1. Hey ho, be-hold, I will show a

2. Now he prat-tles, look ho, then

3. Thou pra-test like a cuck-oo, then

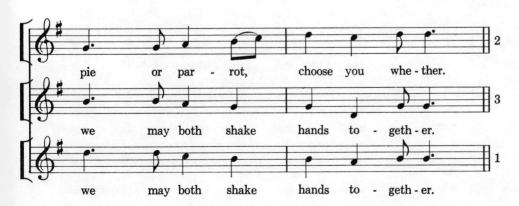

pie or par-rot, choose you whe-ther. 2

we may both shake hands to-geth-er. 3

we may both shake hands to-geth-er. 1

185

When V and I Together Meet

Purcell

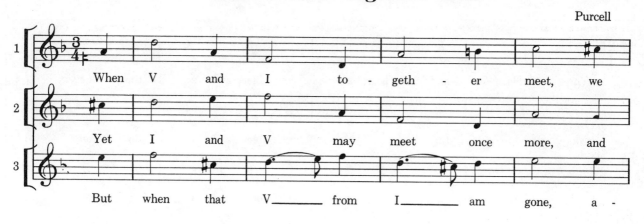

When V and I to-geth-er meet, we

Yet I and V may meet once more, and

But when that V_____ from I_____ am gone, a-

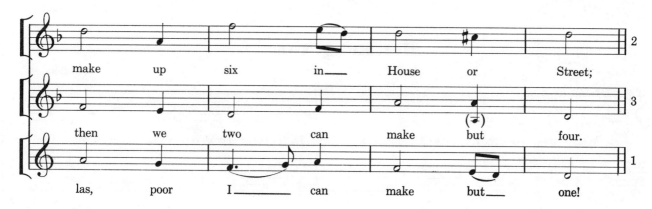

make up six in____ House or Street;

then we two can make but four.

las, poor I_____ can make but____ one!

If I Know What You Know

Fast

If I know what you know and you know what I know, then

Then I know what you know, then I know what

Then I know what you know, and you know what I know,

I know what you know and you know what I know.

you know and you know, and you know what I know.

then I know what you know and you know what I know!

MUSIC

Buzz, Buzz, Quoth the Blue Fly

Arne

Buzz, buzz, buzz, quoth the blue fly;

Buzz and hum, they cry, they cry; Buzz,

In his ear, in his nose, thus, thus do you see, thus;

He ate the dor - mouse, he ate the dor - mouse;

Hum, hum, hum, quoth the bee.

buzz and hum they cry and so,_____ so do we.

In his ear, in his nose, thus, thus do ye see.

Else it was he, else_____ it was he.

With Merry Glee

Birch

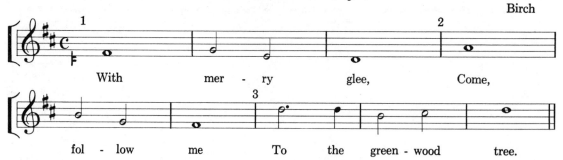

With mer - ry glee, Come,

fol - low me To the green - wood tree.

Come, Join with Me

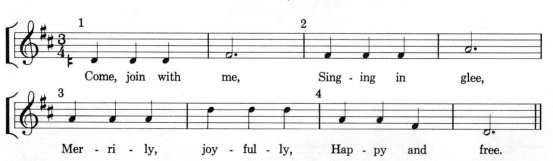

Come, join with me, Sing - ing in glee,

Mer - ri - ly, joy - ful - ly, Hap - py and free.

Warble for Us, Echo Sweet

CANON: 2 VOICES

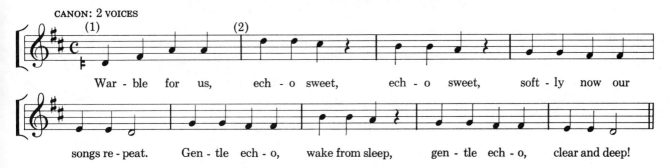

(1) Warble for us, ech - o sweet, ech - o sweet, soft - ly now our

songs re - peat. Gen - tle ech - o, wake from sleep, gen - tle ech - o, clear and deep!

We Country Clodhoppers

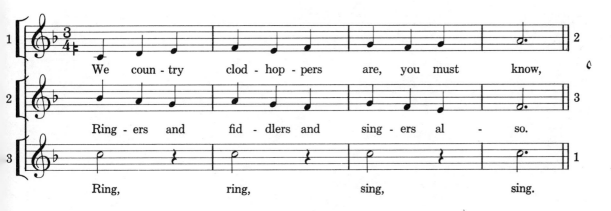

We coun - try clod - hop - pers are, you must know,

Ring - ers and fid - dlers and sing - ers al - so.

Ring, ring, sing, sing.

Merrily, Merrily, on We Ride

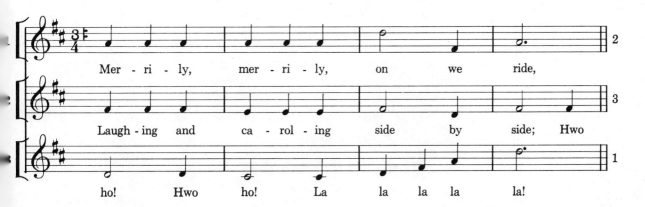

Mer - ri - ly, mer - ri - ly, on we ride,

Laugh - ing and ca - rol - ing side by side; Hwo

ho! Hwo ho! La la la la la!

Hark! The Merry Bells Are Ringing

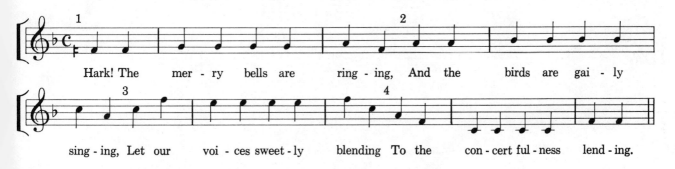

Hark! The mer - ry bells are ring - ing, And the birds are gai - ly

sing - ing, Let our voi - ces sweet - ly blending To the con - cert ful - ness lend - ing.

Let Us Endeavor

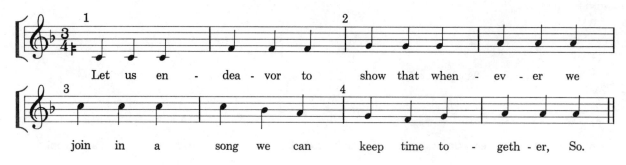

Let us en - dea - vor to show that when - ev - er we

join in a song we can keep time to - geth - er, So.

Almost the same as "Go to Joan Glover"

Johnny, Johnny

John - ny, John - ny, What? What?

So we keep sing - ing, and So we keep call - ing him.

If I Sing Ahead of You

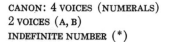

CANON: 4 VOICES (NUMERALS)
2 VOICES (A, B)
INDEFINITE NUMBER (*)

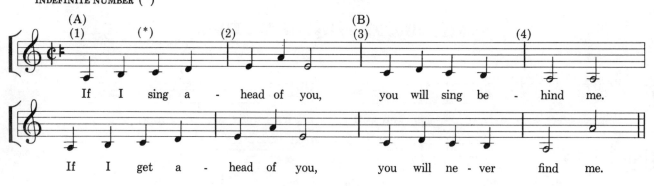

If I sing a - head of you, you will sing be - hind me.

If I get a - head of you, you will ne - ver find me.

Sing Me Another

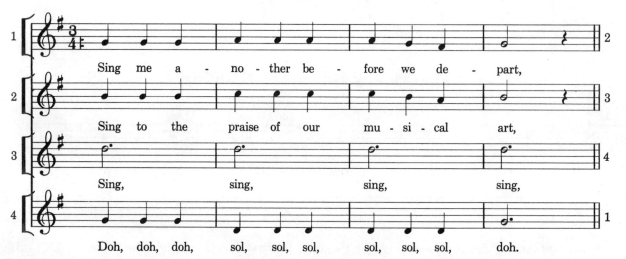

Sing me a - no - ther be - fore we de - part,

Sing to the praise of our mu - si - cal art,

Sing, sing, sing, sing,

Doh, doh, doh, sol, sol, sol, sol, sol, sol, doh.

Sing One, Two, Three

Sing one, two, three, Come fol-low me, And so shall we Good fel-lows be.

Here, Where Rippling Waters

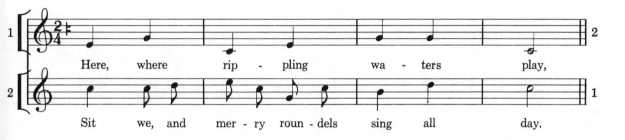

Here, where rip - pling wa - ters play,

Sit we, and mer - ry roun-dels sing all day.

Come, Count the Time For Me

Come, count the time for me,_____ come, now, be - gin,

And you shall quick - ly see_____ that thus good time we run;

Now, one, two, three, four, one, two, three, four, one, two, three, four, one, two, three.

Sing It Over

Sing it o - ver With your might;

Ne - ver leave it, ne - ver leave it Till 'tis right.

Come with Gladness

Come with glad - ness Join our song,

La la la la la la la la La la la.

Let Our Voices Now Ring Out

Let our voi - ces now ring out, Give we all a jol - ly shout,

Heart - i - ly, heart - i - ly, sit - ting here to - geth - er, Sing, sing.

Join We All to Swell the Song

Join we all to swell the song, Young and old the

strains pro - long, Mu - sic now em - ploys each tongue.

Come, Sing Along with Me

Come, sing a - long with me, And make sweet har - mo - ny.

Now loud - ly swell - ing, and now soft and low.

192

La La La Mi

Praetorius

La la la mi re do ti la ti do re mi do ti la;

La la la mi re do ti la ti do re mi la.

Sing This Grave and Simple Strain

Slowly at first—then faster and faster

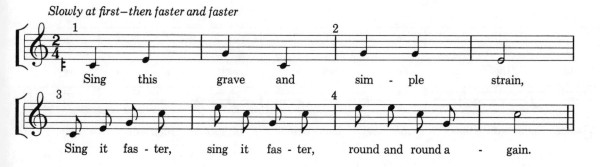

Sing this grave and sim - ple strain,

Sing it fas - ter, sing it fas - ter, round and round a - gain.

Viva, Viva la Musica

Praetorius

Vi - va, vi - va la Mu - si - ca! Vi - va, vi - va la

Mu - si - ca! Vi - va la Mu - si - ca!

Sound the Strain Again

Sound the strain a - gain, O - ver sea and main,

Tra la la la la la la la, Tra la la la la la la la.

Come Now, Let Us Jovial Be

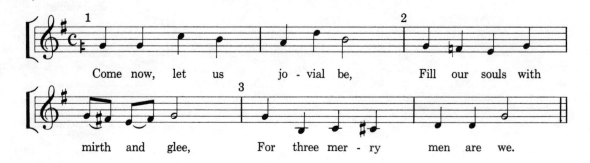

Come now, let us jo-vial be, Fill our souls with

mirth and glee, For three mer-ry men are we.

As the Moments

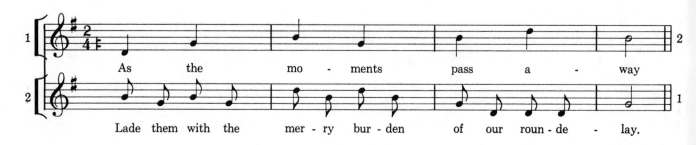

As the mo-ments pass a-way

Lade them with the mer-ry bur-den of our roun-de-lay.

Do-Re-Mi-Fa

Do, Re, Mi, Fa,

I'm quite tired of this sol-fa-ing, I've for-got all you've been say-ing.

Oh, Music, Sweet Music

Oh,— mu-sic, sweet mu-sic, thy prais-es we sing,

We'll tell of the plea-sure and glad-ness you bring,

Mu-sic, mu-sic, glad-ness you bring.

Sing We This Roundelay

Melvill

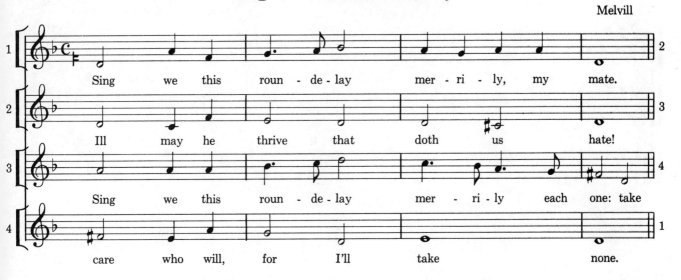

1 Sing we this roundelay merrily, my mate.

2 Ill may he thrive that doth us hate!

3 Sing we this roundelay merrily each one: take

4 care who will, for I'll take none.

How Should I Sing Well

Pammelia

How should I sing well and not be wea-ry,

and not be wea-ry? since we lack mon-ey to

make us mer-ry, to make us mer-ry;

since we lack mon-ey to make us mer-ry,

since we lack mon-ey to make us mer-ry?

All Who Sing

Goodbar of Canterbury

All who sing and wish to__ please, must

Do Re Mi Fa

Na - ture's bless - ings all should seize,__

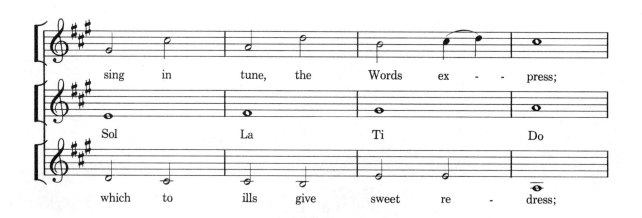

sing in tune, the Words ex - - press;

Sol La Ti Do

which to ills give sweet re - dress;

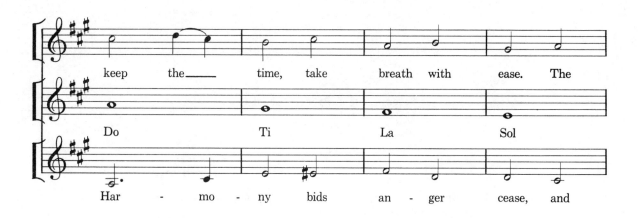

keep the__ time, take breath with ease. The

Do Ti La Sol

Har - mo - ny bids an - ger cease, and

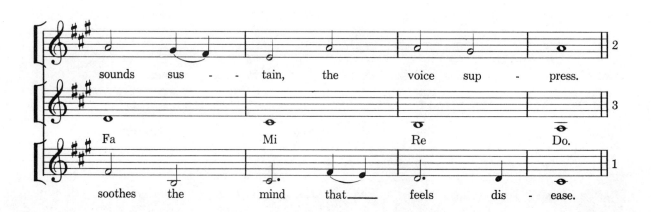

sounds sus - tain, the voice sup - press.

Fa Mi Re Do.

soothes the mind that__ feels dis - ease.

196

Oh! Ever Against Eating Cares

Hayes

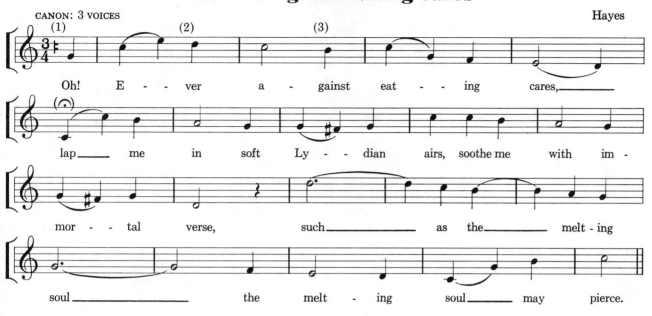

Oh! E - - ver a - gainst eat - - ing cares,

lap___ me in soft Ly - dian airs, soothe me with im -

mor - - tal verse, such___ as the___ melt - ing

soul _____ the melt - ing soul___ may pierce.

Fay Mi Fa Re

Melvill

Fay Mi Fa Re La Mi, be - gin my son and

fol - low me. Sing flat Fa Mi, so shall we well a - gree.

Hey, tro - lo - ly lo - ly - lo, hold fast good son with hey___ tro - lo - ly - lo - tro -

- - lo - ly; O sing this once a - gain lus - ti - ly.

Sing with Thy Mouth

Deuteromelia

Sing with thy mouth, sing with thy___ heart,

Like faith - ful friends sing, loath to de - part.

Though friend to - geth - er may not al - ways re - main, Yet

loath to de - part, sing once a - gain.

197

O Come, Sweet Music

CANON: 3 VOICES

Hayes

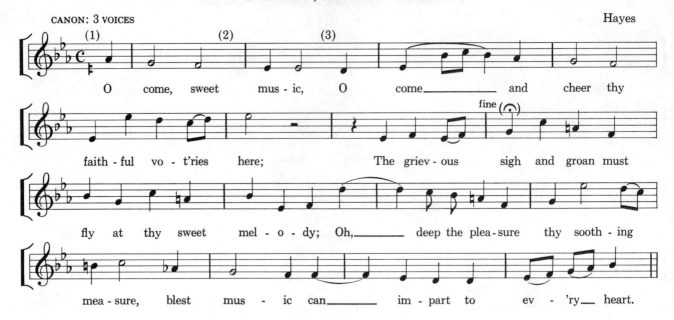

(1) (2) (3)

O come, sweet mus - ic, O come_____ and cheer thy

fine

faith - ful vo - t'ries here; The griev - ous sigh and groan must

fly at thy sweet mel - o - dy; Oh,_____ deep the plea - sure thy sooth - ing

mea - sure, blest mus - ic can_____ im - part to ev - 'ry__ heart.

Come, Let Us Laugh

Greene

1 Come, let us laugh, let us play, let us sing, The win - ter to us is as

2 care not a fea - ther for wind or for wea - ther, By night and by day we

3 fer - ing our__ notes to - ge - - - ther, con - fer - ring our_____

good as the spring, The win - ter to us is as good as the spring; We

sport and__ play, By night and by day we sport and play, Con -

notes to - geth - er, our notes, our notes__ to - ge - ther.

Jack Thou'rt a . . . Come, Come

Marella

Jack thou'rt a . . . Come, come, come, come, once

Stop, stop! Who goes, who goes the

O sir, you're quite too

more: Jack thou art . . . En - core! En - core! En -

last? That's wrong! You're much too

low. Hold, hold! You're now too

core! Once more: Jack thou art . . . I can't, I can't get

fast, too fast. I'll beat. 'Tis ver - y

slow. Oh, stay! You've got too

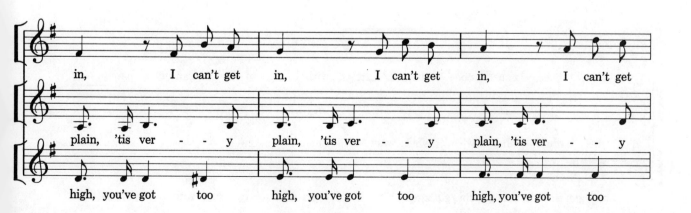

in, I can't get in, I can't get in, I can't get

plain, 'tis ver - - y plain, 'tis ver - - y plain, 'tis ver - - y

high, you've got too high, you've got too high, you've got too

in; Come, come, come, now! Do you be - - gin.

plain. Now for it once, now once____ a - - gain.

high! Good Sir,_____ pray let____ me try.

Purcell

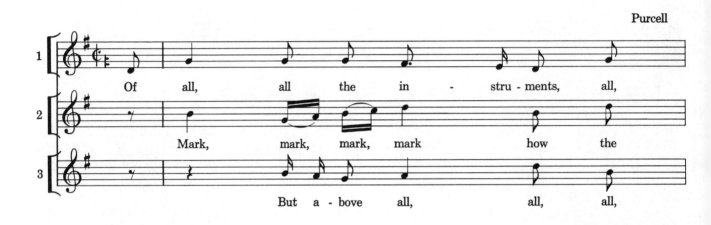

Of all, all the in - stru - ments, all,

Mark, mark, mark, mark how the

But a - bove all, all, all,

all, all, all, the in - stru - ments there are none, none, none, none, none, none,

strings, how the strings their or - der keep with a whet, whet, whet, whet, whet, whet,

all, all, all, all, this still a - - bounds with a zin - gle, zin - gle, zin - gle, zin - gle,

none, none, none, none, none_____ with the vi - - ol__ can com - pare.

whet, whet, whet, whet, whet, whet, whet, and a sweep, sweep, sweep._____

zin - gle, zin - gle, zin - gle, zin - gle, zing and a zit zan zounds.

FOREIGN

Entendezvous

En - ten - dez - vous le ca - ril -

lon, don, don, don, don, don, don, don, don, don, don, don, don?

A Ram Sam Sam

Morocco

A ram sam sam, a ram sam sam, gu - li

A ra - fi, a ra - fi, gu - li

gu - li gu - li gu - li gu - li ram sam sam.

gu - li gu - li gu - li gu - li ram sam sam.

De Bezem (The Bloom)

The Netherlands

De be - zem, de be - zem,

wat doe je er mee, wat doe je er mee,

je veegt, je veegt,

de vloer, de vloer.

La Nuit Palit

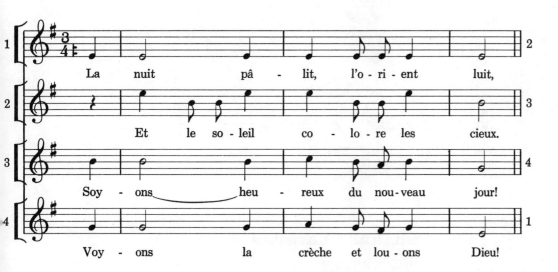

La nuit pâ - lit, l'o - ri - ent luit,

Et le so - leil co - lo - re les cieux.

Soy - ons heu - reux du nou - veau jour!

Voy - ons la crèche et lou - ons Dieu!

Toomba, Toomba

Palestinian

Toom - ba toom - ba toom - ba toom, toom - ba toom - ba toom - ba toom,

La la la la la la, la la la la la, la la la la la la, la la la la.

Toom - ba toom - ba, toom - ba.

Dans La Foret Lointaine

Dans la for - êt loin - tai - ne, on en - tend le cou - cou.

Du haut du plus haut chê - ne, il ré - pond au hi - bou:

Cou - cou, cou - cou, cou - cou, cou - cou, cou - cou!

Orleans Beaugency

Or - le - ans, Beau - gen - cy, No - tre Da - me

de Cle - ry, Ven - do - me, Ven - do - me.

Shalom Chaverim

CANON: 3 VOICES

Hebrew

Sha - lom, cha - ve - rim, sha - lom cha - ve - rim, sha - lom, sha - lom. Le -

hit - ra - ot, le - hit - ra - ot, sha - lom. Sha - lom.

Sù Cantiamo, Sù Beviamo

Lidarti

Sù can - tia - mo, sù___ be - via - mo

Ed u - ni - ti, sù___ gri - dia - mo

E la no - bil com - pa - ni - a

tut - ti quan - ti al - le - gra - men - te.

vi - va, vi - va il Pre - si - dent - e.

sti - a - mo tut - ti in al - le - gri - a.

Donna Che Un

Lidarti

Don - na che ___ un sas - - so pre -

Tor - - re in - - al - zo che re - - - -

Deh bel - la ta - i - de che mai fa - ces - ti

- - se frut - - to del suo de - lit - - to;

se at - to - ni - to l'e - git - - to;

a - des - soil pri - a - po non stà piu rit - - to.

Maudit Sois-tu

Mau - dit sois - tu ca - ril - lon - neur,

Que Dieu cré - a pour mon mal - heur!

Dès le point du jour à la cloche il s'ac - cro - che,

Et le soir en - cor ca - ril - lon ne plus fort!

Quand son - ne - ra - ton la mort du son - neur?

Cantiamo Compagni

Can - tiam - o com - pagn - i, can - tiam - o la no - ta:

Sol La Sal La Ti Do, Fa Do Ti Do.

Can - tan - do s'im - pa - re - ra, La Ti Do Re Mi Fa Re Do Do.

RIBALD

I Lay With An Old Man

Melismata

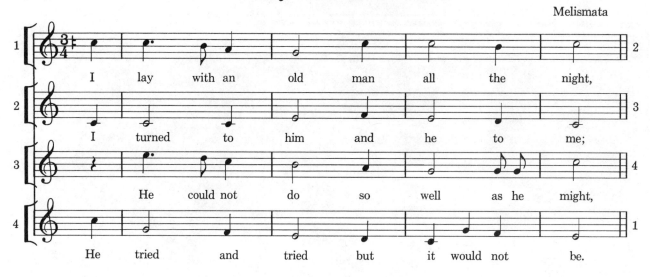

I lay with an old man all the night,
I turned to him and he to me;
He could not do so well as he might,
He tried and tried but it would not be.

Glad Am I

Melvill

Glad am I, glad am I, my mo-ther is gone to Hen-ley,
Shut the door and spare not, do thy worst I care not.
If I die up - on the same, bu - ry, bu-ry, bu-ry me a God's name.

My Wife Has a Tongue

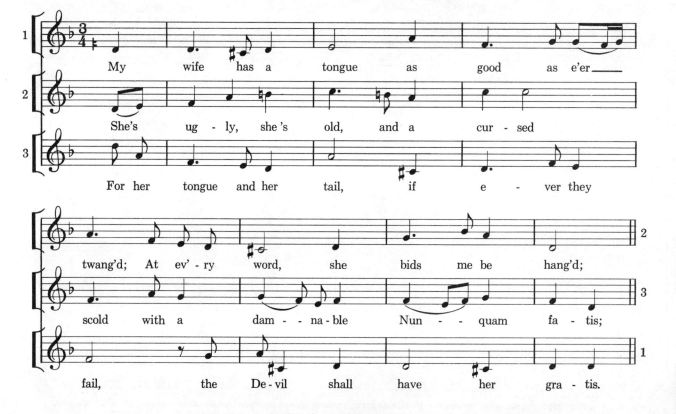

My wife has a tongue as good as e'er
She's ug - ly, she's old, and a cur - sed
For her tongue and her tail, if e - ver they

twang'd; At ev' - ry word, she bids me be hang'd;
scold with a dam - - na-ble Nun - - quam fa - tis;
fail, the De - vil shall have her gra - tis.

208

Had She Not Care Enough

Savile

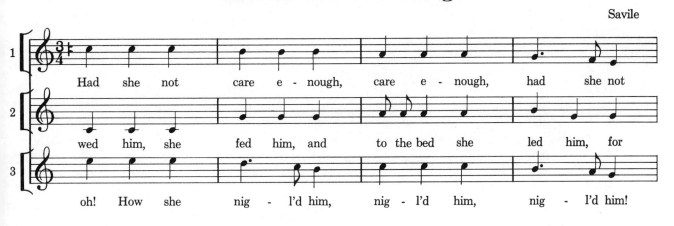

Had she not care e-nough, care e-nough, had she not
wed him, she fed him, and to the bed she led him, for
oh! How she nig-l'd him, nig-l'd him, nig-l'd him!

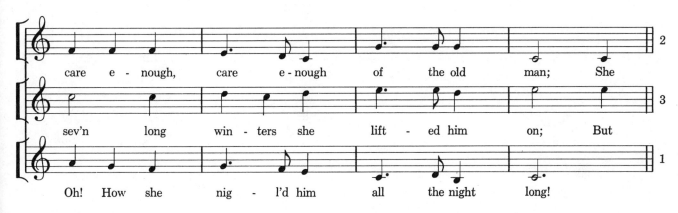

care e-nough, care e-nough of the old man; She
sev'n long win-ters she lift-ed him on; But
Oh! How she nig-l'd him all the night long!

My Mistress Will Not Be Content

Melismata

My mis-tress will not be con-tent to
But foll-'wing still the wo-man's fash-ion, al-
For with the word she'd not dis-pense and

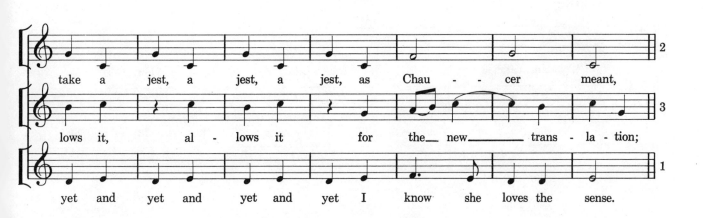

take a jest, a jest, a jest, as Chau-cer meant,
lows it, al-lows it for the new trans-la-tion;
yet and yet and yet and yet I know she loves the sense.

Ha! We to the Other World

Lawes

Ha! We to the o - - ther world, where 'tis thought they ver - y mer - ry be;

There the man in the moon drinks cla - ret, a health to thee and me.

I'll Tell My Mother

Blow

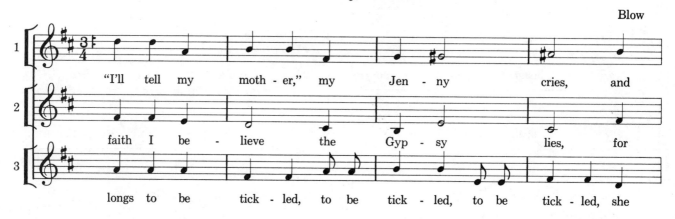

"I'll tell my moth - er," my Jen - ny cries, and

faith I be - lieve the Gyp - sy lies, for

longs to be tick - led, to be tick - led, to be tick - led, she

then a poor lan - guish - ing lo - ver dies; But by

all she is so grave and wise she

longs to be tick - led, oh, she longs to be tick - led.

Adam Catched Eve

Fairly quickly

Baildon

A - dam catched Eve by the fur - be - low,

And that's the old - est catch I know, and that's the old - est catch I

Oh, ho! did he so? Did he so? Did he so?

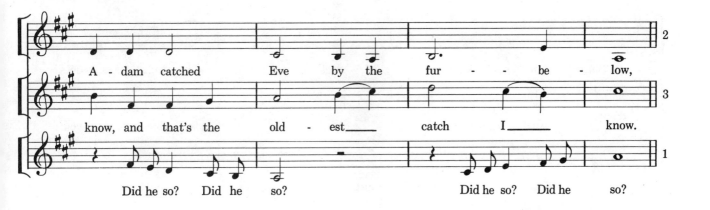

A - dam catched Eve by the fur - - be - low,
know, and that's the old - est___ catch I___ know.
Did he so? Did he so? Did he so? Did he so?

My Heart, Once as Light as a Feather

"My heart, once as light as a feather, will now, a-las, scarce hang to -
"Sweet Jen - ny, how canst thou en - dure___ it?" Quoth Thomas, "I'm
She, yield - ing with lit - tle per - sua - sion, young Thomas perform'd th'op - er -

geth - er, oh! Love, thou hast rent it in twain, thou hast
ready to cure___ it. My___ nee - dle will stitch it a - main,
a - tion, she___ cried, "It will do once a - gain, it will

rent it, thou hast rent it, oh! Love, thou hast rent it in twain."___
will stitch it, will stitch it, my nee - dle will stitch it a - main."___
do, it will do, it will do, once a - gain."___

Since Time So Kind

Purcell

1. Since time so kind to us does prove, so kind to us does prove, do not, my dear, re-fuse my love.

2. What do you mean? Oh, fie, nay, what do you do? You're the strang-est man that ev-er I knew.

3. I must, I must, I can't for-bear, I can't, I can't for-bear, lie still, lie still my dear.

When Judith Had Laid

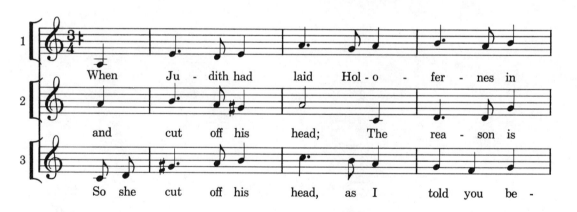

1. When Ju-dith had laid Hol-o-fer-nes in bed, she pull'd out his Fal-chion*, as I told you be-fore.

2. and cut off his head; The rea-son is plain: he'd have made her his whore;

3. So she cut off his head, as I told you be-fore.

* Falchion, a broad-bladed curved sword.

To Thee and to a Maid

Purcell

To thee, to thee, and to a maid that

And laugh___ and sing and kiss and play and

Such, such a lass, kind friends, and drink - ing,

kind - - ly will___ up - - on her back be laid; 2

wan - ton, wan - ton out a Sum - mer's day: 3

give me, Great Jove! And damn, and damn the think - ing. 1

Fair Ursley

Berg

Fair Urs - ley in a___ mer - ry mood con - sult - ed her phy - si - cian: What

Quoth Wood - ward: if my judge - ment's right and an - swer worth re - turn - ing, you'll

Quoth Urs - ley: then for plea - sure's sake each eve - ning will I take it, and

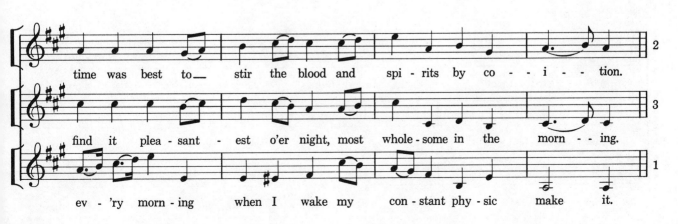

time was best to___ stir the blood and spi - rits by co - - i - - tion. 2

find it plea - sant - est o'er night, most whole - some in the morn - - ing. 3

ev - 'ry morn - ing when I wake my con - stant phy - sic make it. 1

Joan Has Been Galloping

Blow

Joan has been gal - lop-ing, gal - lop - ing gal - lop-ing,

Till her bum - fid - dle, bum - fid - dle, bum - fid - dle, un -

out e're a sad - dle up - on her old jade, to

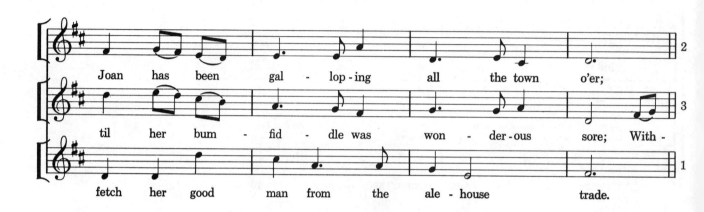

Joan has been gal - lop-ing all the town o'er;

til her bum - fid - dle was won - der - ous sore; With -

fetch her good man from the ale - house trade.

This Galloping, Galloping Joan

Lenton

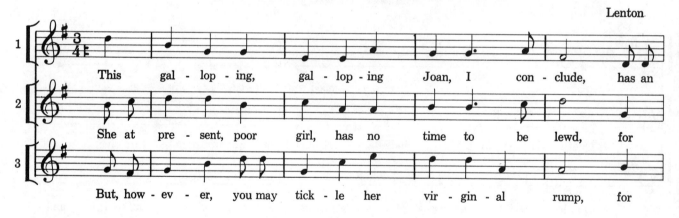

This gal - lop - ing, gal - lop - ing Joan, I con - clude, has an

She at pre - sent, poor girl, has no time to be lewd, for

But, how - ev - er, you may tick - le her vir - gin - al rump, for

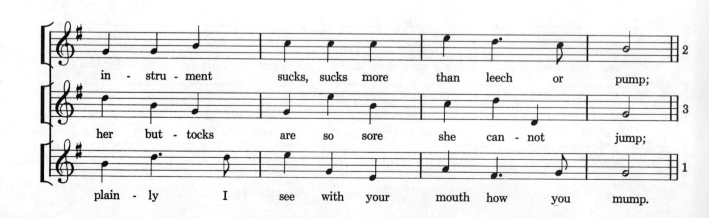

in - stru - ment sucks, sucks more than leech or pump;

her but - tocks are so sore she can - not jump;

plain - ly I see with your mouth how you mump.

214

My Lady and Her Maid

Ellis

My Lady and her maid up-on a mer-ry pin, they
made a match at fart-ing, who should the wa-ger win.

Joan lights three can-dles then, and sets them bolt up-right, with the
first fart she blew them out, with the next she gave them light.

In comes my La-dy then with all her might and main, and
blew them out, and in, and out, and in, and out a-gain.

Sir Walter, Enjoying His Damsel One Night

Purcell

Sir Wal-ter, en-joy-ing ___ his dam-sel one night, he
tick-l'd and pleased her to so great ___ a height,

That she could not con-tain t'wards the end of the mat-ter, but in
rap-ture cried out: "O, sweet Sir Wal-ter!

O, sweet Sir Wal-ter, O, sweet Sir Wal-ter, O, Sweet Sir, Sweet Sir Wal-ter; O,
swit-ter, swat-ter, swit-ter, swat-ter, swit-ter, swat-ter swit-ter, swat-ter, swit-ter, swat-ter."

When Is It Best?

Baildon.

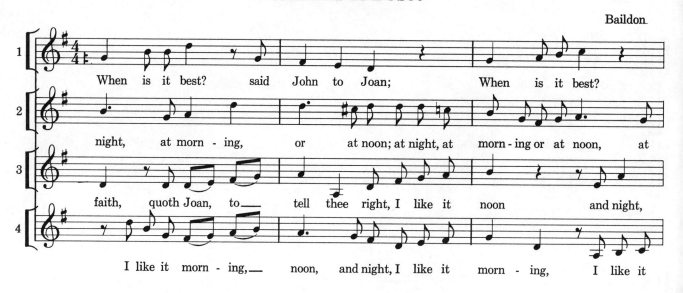

When is it best? said John to Joan; When is it best?

night, at morn - ing, or at noon; at night, at morn - ing or at noon, at

faith, quoth Joan, to__ tell thee right, I like it noon and night,

I like it morn - ing,__ noon, and night, I like it morn - ing, I like it

When is it best? When is it best? said John to Joan;

morn - ing or at noon; at night, at__ morn - ing or at noon; at night, at

and night, I like it noon, I like it night, I like it

noon, I like it morn - ing, noon, and night, and night; why faith, quoth

When is it best? When is it best?

morn - ing, at noon, at noon,

morn - ing, noon and night, I like it morn - ing noon and night; to

Joan, to tell thee right, why faith, quoth Joan, to tell you right, I

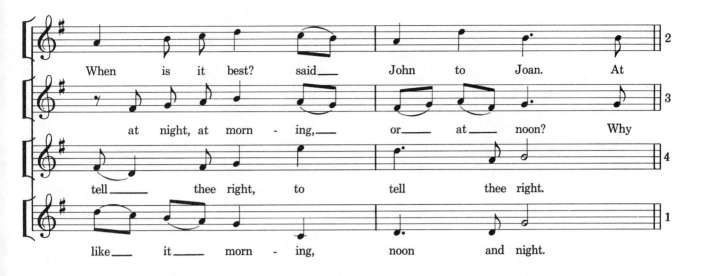

When is it best? said John to Joan. At
at night, at morn - ing, or at noon? Why
tell thee right, to tell thee right.
like it morn - ing, noon and night.

'Twixt Dick and Tom

'Twixt Dick and Tom, 'twixt Dick and Tom a
From words they quick - ly came to blows, from
"A - bout my legs the boo - bies fight the boo - bies

con - test rose of Doll's or Nan - cy's legs, Nan - cy's
words they quick - ly came to blows; Ned begg'd of Nan, Ned
fight a - bout my legs, the boo - bies fight, they say; To get be - tween,

legs, Nan - cy's legs which were the bet - ter.
begg'd of Nan to tell what was the mat - ter.
to get be - tween pray try and part the fray."

217

A Riddle: My Man John

Eccles

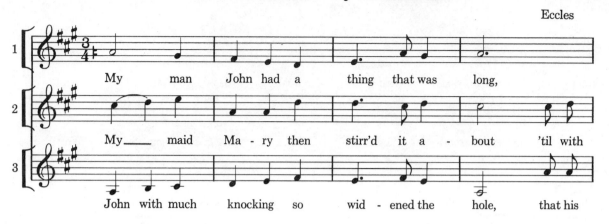

My man John had a thing that was long,

My___ maid Ma - ry then stirr'd it a - bout 'til with

John with much knocking so wid - ened the hole, that his

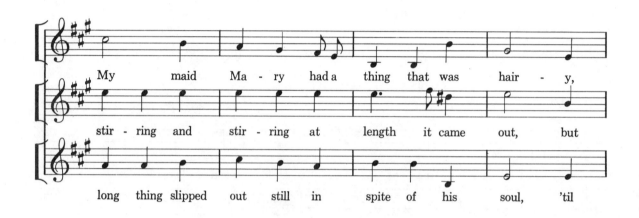

My maid Ma - ry had a thing that was hair - y,

stir - ring and stir - ring at length it came out, but

long thing slipped out still in spite of his soul, 'til

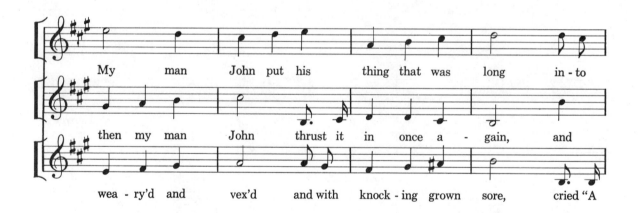

My man John put his thing that was long in - to

then my man John thrust it in once a - gain, and

wea - ry'd and vex'd and with knock - ing grown sore, cried "A

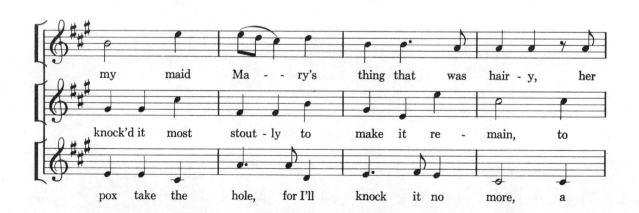

my maid Ma - ry's thing that was hair - y, her

knock'd it most stout - ly to make it re - main, to

pox take the hole, for I'll knock it no more, a

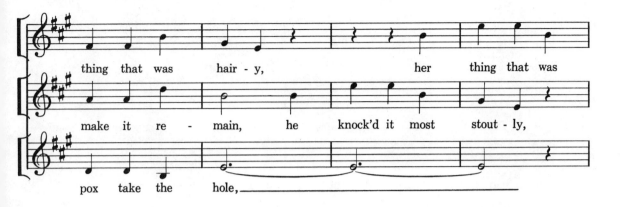

thing that was hair - y,   her   thing that was

make it re - main,   he knock'd it most stout - ly,

pox take the hole, —

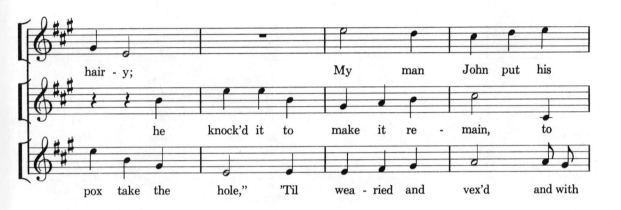

hair - y;   My   man   John put his

he   knock'd it to   make it re - main,   to

pox take the hole," 'Til wea - ried and vex'd   and with

thing that was   long   in to my   maid

make it re - main,   he knock'd it most

knock - ing grown   sore,   cried "A pox take the

Ma - - - ry's thing that was hair - y.   2

stout - ly to   make it re - main, but   3

hole for I'll   knock it no   more."   1

The riddle explained:
Maid Mary having broken the handle of her hair broom, and hearing that "My Man John" had a long stick that would fit it, desired him to put in the stick for her.

John Cooper Was Boring

Boyce

John Coop - er was bor - ing a great piece of tim - ber, he

With his break - fast his wife came jump - ing with glee and

When John had well feast - ed he bor'd with more might, his

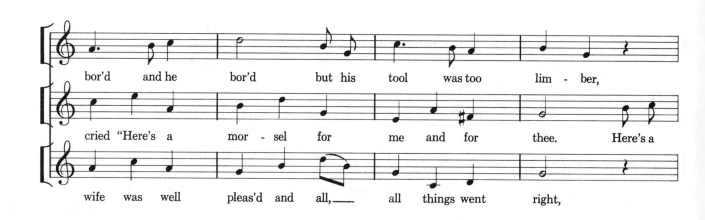

bor'd and he bor'd but his tool was too lim - ber,

cried "Here's a mor - sel for me and for thee. Here's a

wife was well pleas'd and all, ___ all things went right,

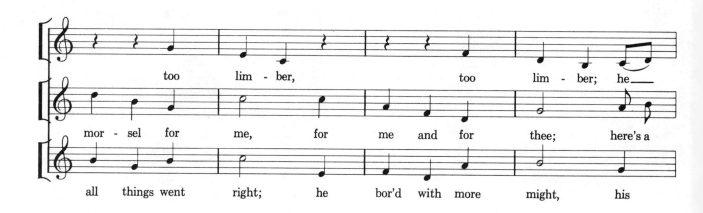

too lim - ber, too lim - ber; he ___

mor - sel for me, for me and for thee; here's a

all things went right; he bor'd with more might, his

bor'd and he bor'd but ___ his ___ tool was too lim - ber.

mor - sel for me, for me and for thee.

wife was well pleas'd, and all things went right.

The Miller's Daughter

Purcell

1. The mill-er's daugh-ter, rid-ing to the
2. "A - way, you sil - ly daugh-ter, 'tis
3. Then tak-ing her a - side, she

Fair, with-out a sad-dle up - on a scur-vy mare, cried,
ev' - ry girls' con - cern, and if you won't be - lieve me, look
made the mat-ter plain; "Oh, oh, Mo - ther, you're

"Oh mo - ther, I'm quite un - done, I'm quite un - done, I'm
here, look here, here, look here, here, look here,
ten times worse! Oh, you're ten times worse! You're ten times worse! You're

all, all o - ver - grown with hair!"
look here, here, and you may learn."
ten times worse! Why, sure, you rid up - on the mane!"

As Jenny One Morning

Berg

As Jen - ny one morn - ing was milk - ing her ass, was

And with a strong wat - tle be - la - bor'd the beast, be -

She swore she had ra - ther (in ver - y great dud - geon),

milk - ing her ass, was milk - ing her ass; as Jen - ny one morn - ing was

la - bor'd, be - la - bor'd, and with a strong wat - tle be -

she swore, she swore, she swore she had ra - ther (in

milk - ing her ass, a lust - y young fel - low close by her did pass;

la - - bor'd the beast, then laugh - ing he told her he was but in jest.

ver - y great dud - geon) than hurt the poor thing feel the force of his bludgeon.

Here Stand I

Warren

Here stand I, for whores as great to

cast a scorn - ful eye on, to cast a scorn - ful eye on; Should

each whore here be doom'd a sheet, you'd

soon want one to lie on, you'd soon want one to lie on.

ROMANTIC

Go to Joan Glover

Softly
Deuteromelia

Go to Joan Glov-er and tell her I love her and by the light of the moon I will come to her.

Oh, My Love!

Fairly slowly
Deuteromelia

Oh, my love, lov'st thou me? Then quick-ly come and save him that dies for thee.

The Moon Is Up

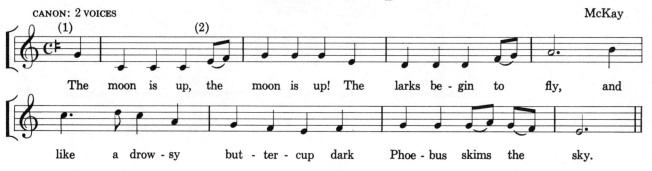

CANON: 2 VOICES
McKay

The moon is up, the moon is up! The larks be-gin to fly, and like a drow-sy but-ter-cup dark Phoe-bus skims the sky.

Joan, Come Kiss Me Now

Pammelia

Joan, come kiss me now once a-gain for my love, gen-tle Joan, come kiss me now.

"John, Come Kiss Me Now" in Melvill

224

Musing Mine Own Self

Pammelia - Melvill

Mu - sing, mu - sing, mu - sing mine own self all a -
lone, I heard a maid, I heard a maid, I heard a maid ma - king great
moan, with sobs and sighs, and ma - ny a griev - ous
groan, for that, for that, for that her mai - den - head was

In repetitions, the first measure is sung thus:

gone. Mu - sing

Adieu, Sweet Amarillis

Richard Brown

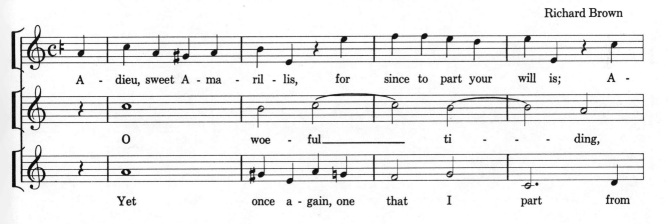

A - dieu, sweet A - ma - ril - lis, for since to part your will is; A -
O woe - ful ti - ding,
Yet once a - gain, one that I part from

dieu, sweet A - ma - ril - lis.
there is for me no bi - ding.
you, A - ma - ril - lis sweet, a dieu.

O Lady Moon

Loomis

CANON: 2 VOICES

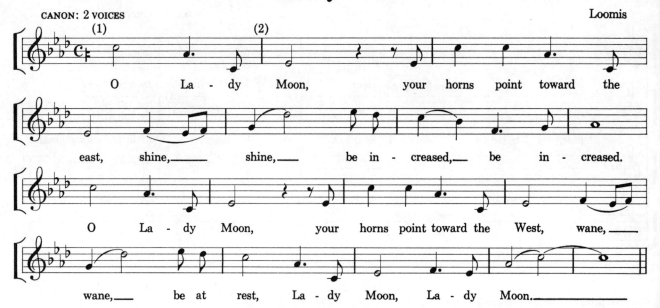

O La - dy Moon, your horns point toward the

east, shine,_____ shine,_____ be in - creased,_____ be in - creased.

O La - dy Moon, your horns point toward the West, wane,_____

wane,_____ be at rest, La - dy Moon, La - dy Moon._____

As I Went Over Tawny Marsh

John Jackson

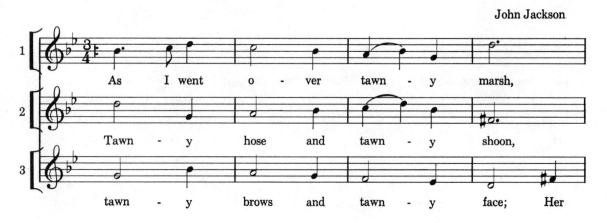

As I went o - ver tawn - y marsh,

Tawn - y hose and tawn - y shoon,

tawn - y brows and tawn - y face; Her

there I met with a tawn - y lass;

tawn - y pet - ti - coat, tawn - y gown,

tawn - y eyes put me in my place.

Love, Love, Sweet Love

Pammelia - Melvill

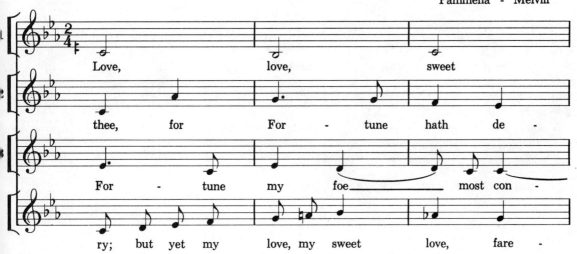

Love, love, sweet

thee, for For - tune hath de -

For - tune my foe_____ most con -

ry; but yet my love, my sweet love, fare -

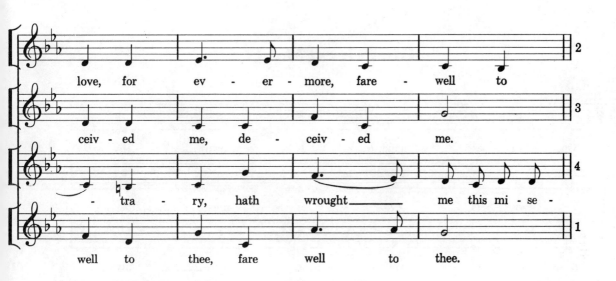

love, for ev - er - more, fare - well to

ceiv - ed me, de - ceiv - ed me.

- tra - ry, hath wrought_____ me this mi - se -

well to thee, fare well to thee.

Turn Amaryllis

Hilton

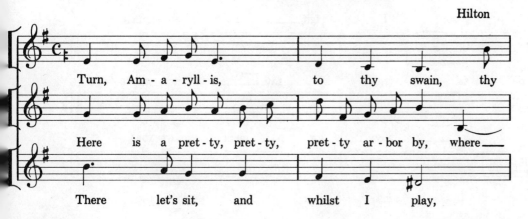

Turn, Am - a - ryll - is, to thy swain, thy

Here is a pret - ty, pret - ty, pret - ty ar - bor by, where_____

There let's sit, and whilst I play,

227

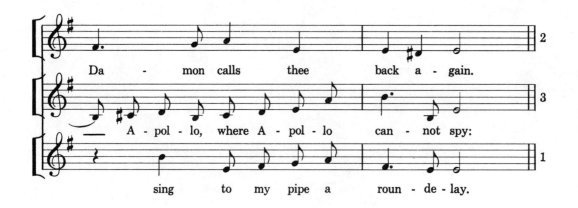

Da - mon calls thee back a - gain.

_ A - pol - lo, where A - pol - lo can - not spy:

sing to my pipe a roun - de - lay.

Oh, Fairest Maid

Nares

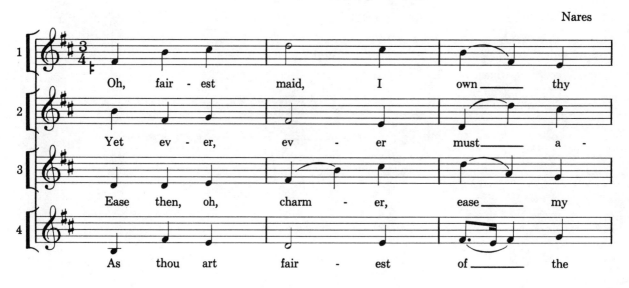

Oh, fair - est maid, I own_____ thy

Yet ev - er, ev - er must_____ a -

Ease then, oh, charm - er, ease_____ my

As thou art fair - est of _____ the

pow'r, I gaze, I sigh,_____ I lan - guish,

dore and tri - umph in my_____ an - guish.

pain and let_____ my tor - ment move thee,

fair, so I, my dear - est, love thee.

Dear Father, the Girl

Webbe

Dear fa - - ther, the girl__ you de - sign__ me in mar - riage, is she

You'd sure - ly our fam - i - ly__ keep__ from a blot? She

Ah! Now__ you de - light me, de -

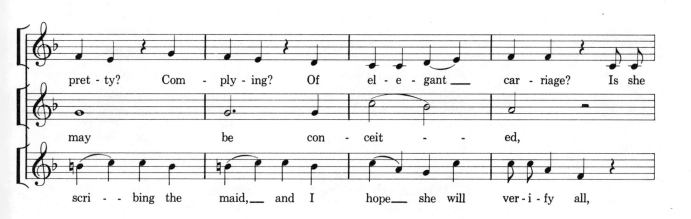

pret - ty? Com - ply - ing? Of el - e - gant__ car - riage? Is she

may be con - ceit - - ed,

scri - - bing the maid,__ and I hope__ she will ver - i - fy all,

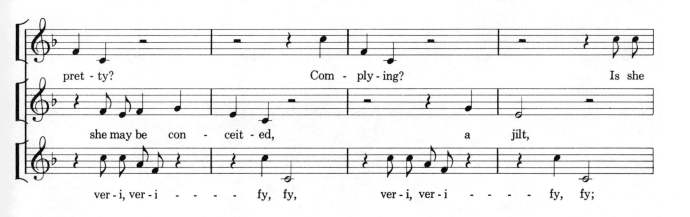

pret - ty? Com - ply - ing? Is she

she may be con - ceit - ed, a jilt,

ver - i, ver - i - - - - fy, fy, ver - i, ver - i - - - - fy, fy;

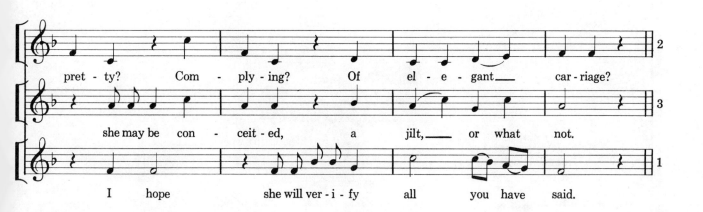

pret - ty? Com - ply - ing? Of el - e - gant__ car - riage?

she may be con - ceit - ed, a jilt,__ or what not.

I hope she will ver - i - fy all you have said.

229

O Happy, O Happy

Purcell

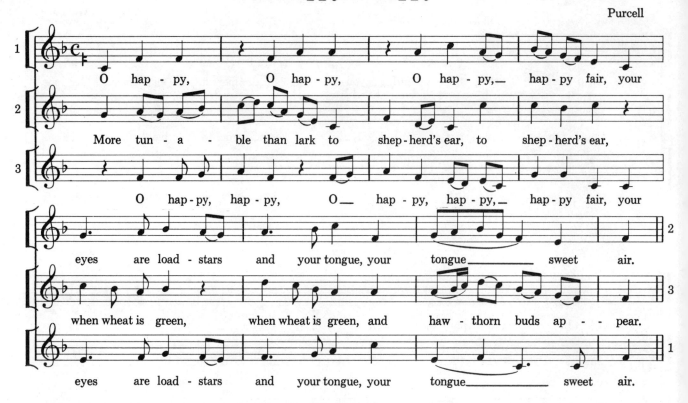

O hap-py, O hap-py, O hap-py,— hap-py fair, your

More tun-a-ble than lark to shep-herd's ear, to shep-herd's ear,

O hap-py, hap-py, O— hap-py, hap-py,— hap-py fair, your

eyes are load-stars and your tongue, your tongue_____ sweet air.

when wheat is green, when wheat is green, and haw-thorn buds ap - - pear.

eyes are load-stars and your tongue, your tongue_____ sweet air.

When o'er Earth's Face

Savage

When o'er Earth's

night, set is the sun's last ray; un -

way. Thus friendship's worth in woe's dark

in woe's dark night, un - seen in sun-ny hours un -

face de - - - scends still

seen by day, the glow worm's light shines forth to cheer our

night, thus friendship's worth_____

seen in sun-ny hours, shines bright, shines bright.

PATRIOTIC

Firmly Stand, My Native Land

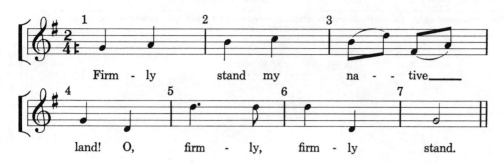

Firm - ly stand my na - tive____ land! O, firm - ly, firm - ly stand.

Hi! Cheerily Ho

with marked rhythm

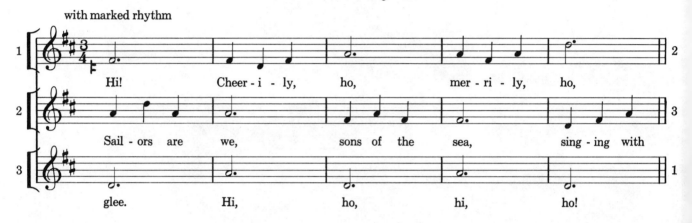

Hi! Cheer - i - ly, ho, mer - ri - ly, ho,

Sail - ors are we, sons of the sea, sing - ing with

glee. Hi, ho, hi, ho!

They March, They March

They march, they march to the roll - ing drum; The

sol - diers bold, see! They come, they come to the r - r - roll - - - ing drum!

Let the Wind Blow

Let the wind blow, High or low,

Still jol - ly tars are we, on__ the__ O - cean so free.

232

Crooked Rifles

CANON: 3 VOICES

Hayes

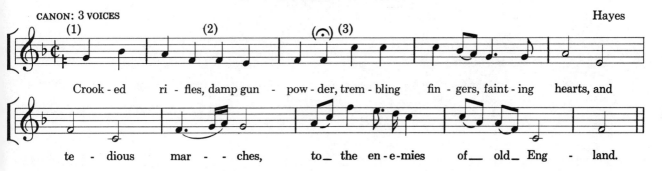

Crook - ed ri - fles, damp gun - pow - der, trem - bling fin - gers, faint - ing hearts, and

te - dious mar - - ches, to_ the en - e -mies of_ old_ Eng - land.

Long Live the King

Boyce

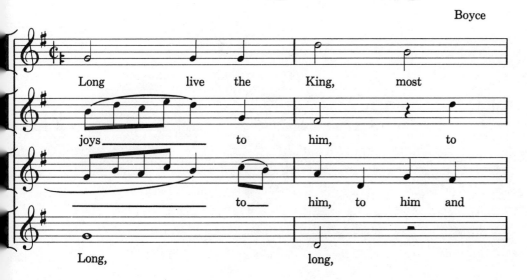

Long   live   the   King,   most

joys_____ to him, to

to_ him, to him and

Long,   long,

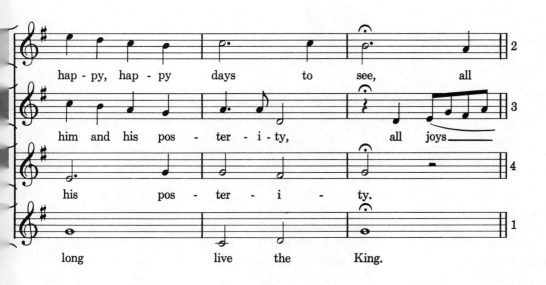

hap - py, hap - py days to see, all

him and his pos - ter - i -ty, all joys_____

his pos - ter - i - ty.

long   live   the   King.

Of Alfred the Great

Moffat

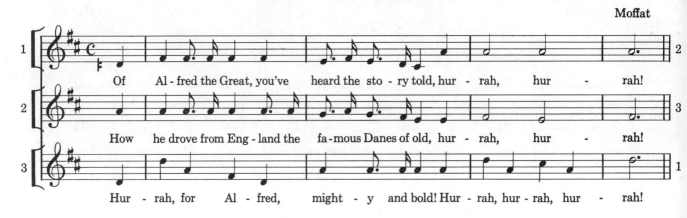

Of Al-fred the Great, you've heard the sto-ry told, hur-rah, hur-rah!

How he drove from Eng-land the fa-mous Danes of old, hur-rah, hur-rah!

Hur-rah, for Al-fred, might-y and bold! Hur-rah, hur-rah, hur-rah!

War Begets Poverty

Richard Browne

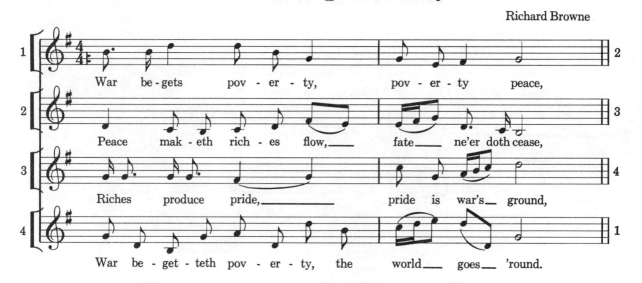

War be-gets pov-er-ty, pov-er-ty peace,

Peace mak-eth rich-es flow,___ fate___ ne'er doth cease,

Riches produce pride,___ pride is war's___ ground,

War be-get-teth pov-er-ty, the world___ goes___ 'round.

God Save the Queen

God save the Queen, Long live the Queen Let the Queen live,

Let the Queen live for-ev-er and ev-er. A - - men.

Wars Are Our Delight

Lawes

Wars are our de-light, we drink as we fight, ta-ra-ra, ra, ra,
dub-a-dub, dub-a-dub, dub, bounce, tan-tar-ra, ran, tan, tan.

As Through the Town

CANON: 2 VOICES

Boildieu

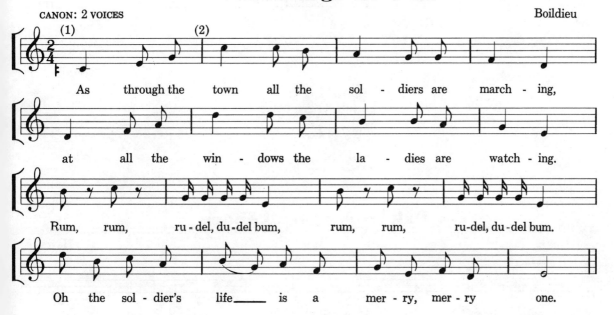

As through the town all the sol-diers are march-ing,
at all the win-dows the la-dies are watch-ing.
Rum, rum, ru-del, du-del bum, rum, rum, ru-del, du-del bum.
Oh the sol-dier's life_____ is a mer-ry, mer-ry one.

When Troy Town

Alcock

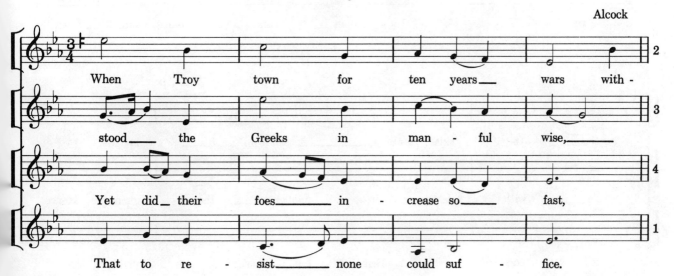

When Troy town for ten years_____ wars with-
stood_____ the Greeks in man-ful wise,_____
Yet did_ their foes_____ in-crease so_____ fast,
That to re-sist_____ none could suf-fice.

Count of Sory, Why What of He!

Aldrich

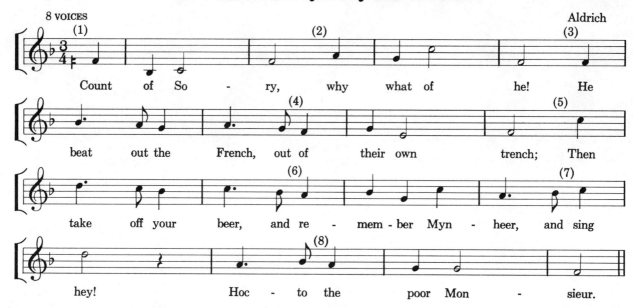

Count of So - ry, why what of he! He beat out the French, out of their own trench; Then take off your beer, and re - mem - ber Myn - heer, and sing hey! Hoc - to the poor Mon - sieur.

The Oak from a Small Acorn

Hayes

The oak from a ___ small a - - - corn grows, and

As years in - - crease, ___ it shades ___ the ___ plain, ___ then

ris - - - - es ___ safe - - ty to our shore, ___ an

to ___ the skies send up, ___ sends up ___ his ___ boughs;

big ___ with death ___ it ploughs ___ the ___ main. Hence

a - - corn gives ___ Brit - tan - nia's pow'r.

Hark! 'Tis the Indian Drum

1. Hark! 'Tis the In - dian drum!_____ The woods__ and rocks a -
2. Hark! 'Tis the In - - dian__ drum! The
3. Hark! Hark! Hark! 'Tis the In - - dian__

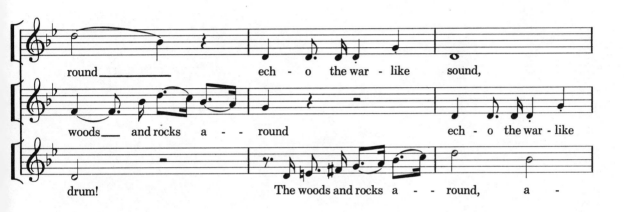

round_____ ech - o the war - like sound,
woods__ and rocks a - - round ech - o the war - like
drum! The woods and rocks a - - round, a -

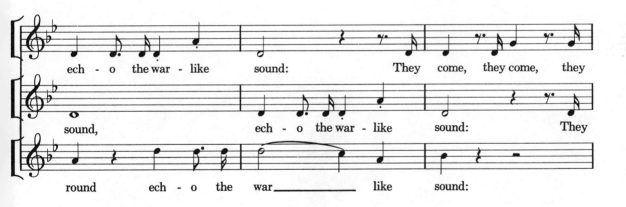

ech - o the war - like sound: They come, they come, they
sound, ech - o the war - like sound: They
round ech - o the war_____ like sound:

come,_____ they come,_____ they come!
come,_____ they come,_____ they come!
They come,_____ they come,___ they come!

237

Curs'd Be the Wretch

Carey

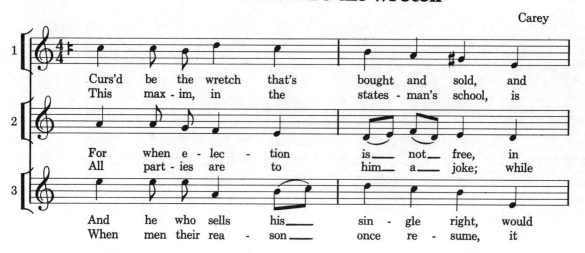

1. Curs'd be the wretch that's bought and sold, and
This max - im, in the states - man's school, is

2. For when e - lec - tion is not free, in
All part - ies are to him a joke; while

3. And he who sells his sin - gle right, would
When men their rea - son once re - sume, it

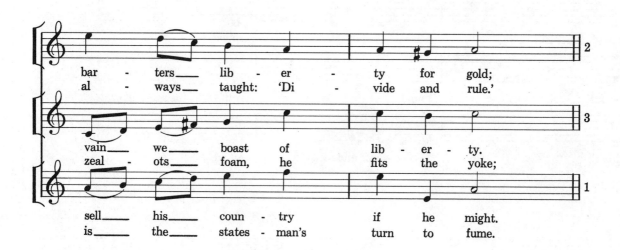

bar - ters lib - er - ty for gold;
al - ways taught: 'Di - vide and rule.'

vain we boast of lib - er - ty.
zeal - ots foam, he fits the yoke;

sell his coun - try if he might.
is the states - man's turn to fume.

238

TOASTS
AND TIPPLING

Banbury Ale

Pammelia

Ban - bur - y ale, Where, where, where? At the black - smith's house, I would I were there!

Let's Drink to All Our Wives

Richard Browne

Let's drink to all our wives, _____

Good health, and mer - ry lives! _____

But who ___ to please ___ them cares, _____

Must live old Nes - tor's years! _____

Let Us Love and Drink

Lenton

Let us love and drink our li - quor! We shall spend our

means the quick - er! Here's to thee, kind friend, a Nick - er!

Now Kiss the Cup, Cousin

Pammelia - Melvill

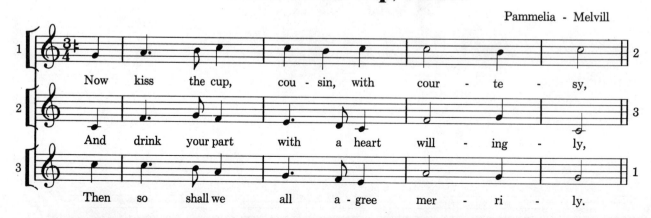

Now kiss the cup, cou - sin, with cour - te - sy,

And drink your part with a heart will - ing - ly,

Then so shall we all a - gree mer - ri - ly.

White Wine and Sugar

CANON: 5 VOICES

Pammelia - Melvill

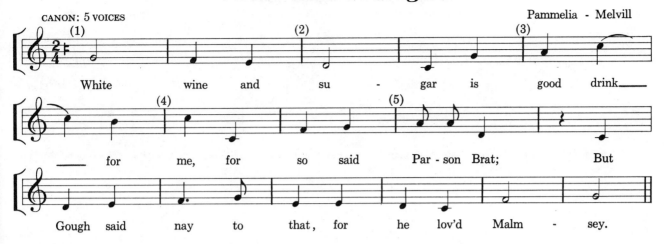

White wine and su - gar is good drink ___ for me, for so said Par - son Brat; But Gough said nay to that, for he lov'd Malm - sey.

I Am Athirst

CANON: 3 VOICES

Pammelia - Melvill

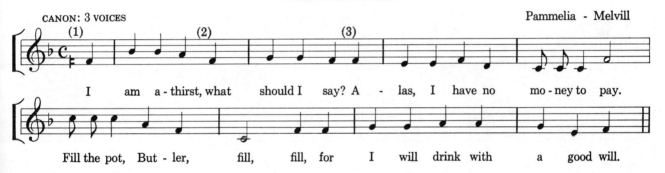

I am a-thirst, what should I say? A - las, I have no mo-ney to pay.

Fill the pot, But - ler, fill, fill, for I will drink with a good will.

A Boat, a Boat!

Jenkins

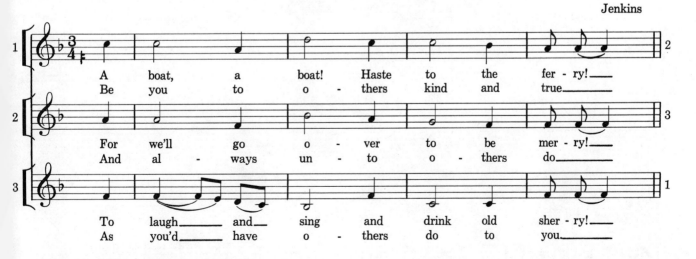

A boat, a boat! Haste to the fer - ry! ___
Be you to o - thers kind and true ___

For we'll go o - ver to be mer - ry! ___
And al - ways un - to o - thers do ___

To laugh ___ and ___ sing and drink old sher - ry! ___
As you'd ___ have o - thers do to you. ___

The second set of words comes from a later period.
Same tune as "The kine."

Go No More to Brainford

Pammelia - Melvill

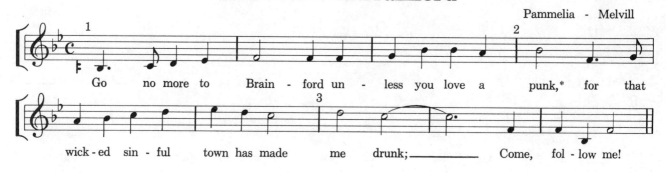

Go no more to Brain-ford un-less you love a punk,* for that
wick-ed sin-ful town has made me drunk;_____ Come, fol-low me!

*Punk = prostitute.

Hey Down a Down, Behold and See

CANON: 3 VOICES

Pammelia - Melvill

Hey, down a down, down a down, be-hold and see; Good host-ess,
fill the pot for me, and yet it is the first of
three. Take and fill this pot yet once a-gain; We will for
this time thus re-main; When this is spent, fill pot a-gain.

God Preserve His Majesty

Blow

God pre-serve His Ma-jes-ty, And for-ev-er send him vic-to-ry,
And con-found all his en-e-mies, Take off your Hock, Sir.

An ostinato which may be sung by a fifth voice throughout:

A - men!

242

O, Ale ab Alendo

Hilton

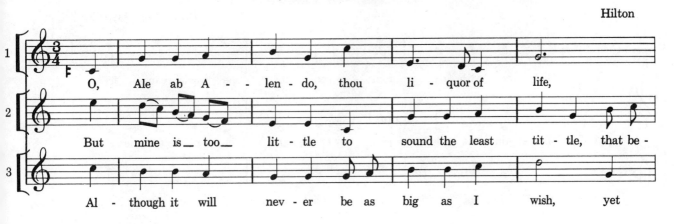

O, Ale ab A - len-do, thou li - quor of life,

But mine is_ too_ lit - tle to sound the least tit - tle, that be -

Al - though it will nev - er be as big as I wish, yet

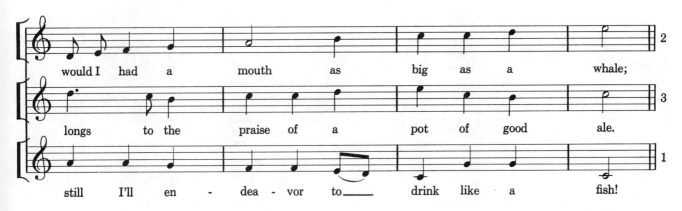

would I had a mouth as big as a whale;

longs to the praise of a pot of good ale.

still I'll en - dea - vor to___ drink like a fish!

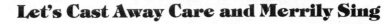

Let's Cast Away Care and Merrily Sing

Lawes

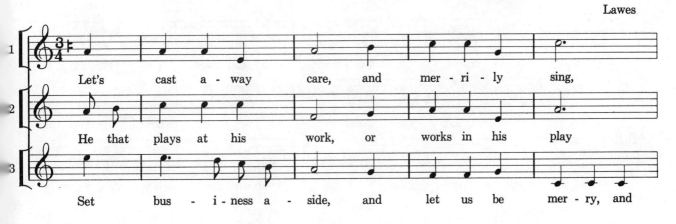

Let's cast a - way care, and mer - ri - ly sing,

He that plays at his work, or works in his play

Set bus - i - ness a - side, and let us be mer - ry, and

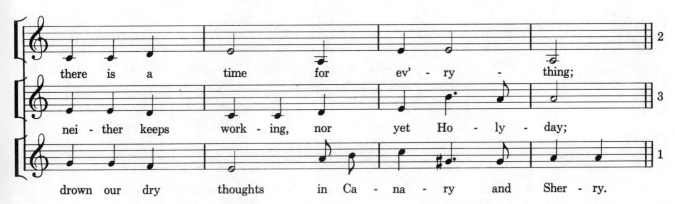

there is a time for ev' - ry - thing;

nei - ther keeps work - ing, nor yet Ho - ly - day;

drown our dry thoughts in Ca - na - ry and Sher - ry.

Now God Be with Old Simeon

Pammelia - Melvill

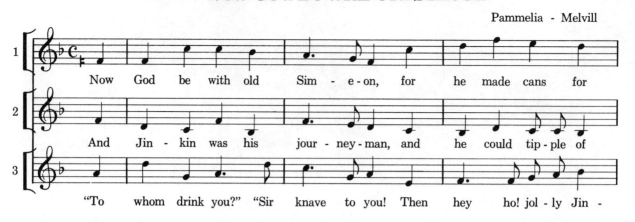

1. Now God be with old Sim-e-on, for he made cans for

2. And Jin-kin was his jour-ney-man, and he could tip-ple of

3. "To whom drink you?" "Sir knave to you! Then hey ho! jol-ly Jin-

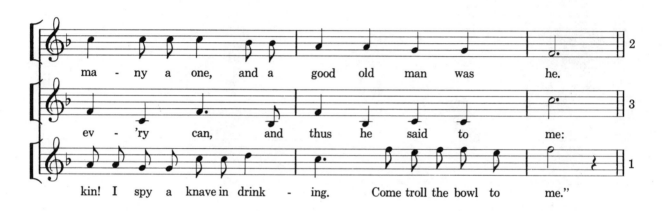

ma-ny a one, and a good old man was he.

ev-'ry can, and thus he said to me:

kin! I spy a knave in drink - ing. Come troll the bowl to me."

To Our Musical Club

Thomas Warren

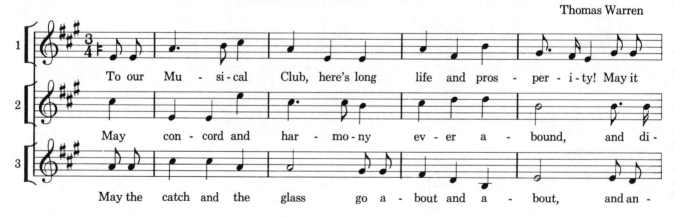

1. To our Mu-si-cal Club, here's long life and pros-per-i-ty! May it

2. May con-cord and har-mo-ny ev-er a-bound, and di-

3. May the catch and the glass go a-bout and a-bout, and an-

flour-ish with us, and so on to pos-ter-i-ty!

vi-sions here on-ly in our mu-sic be found;

oth-er suc-ceed to the bot-tle that's out!

Malt's Come Down

Deuteromelia - Melvill

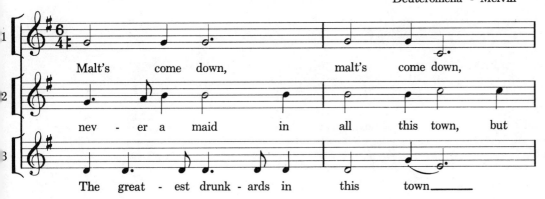

Malt's come down, malt's come down,

nev - er a maid in all this town, but

The great - est drunk - ards in this town____

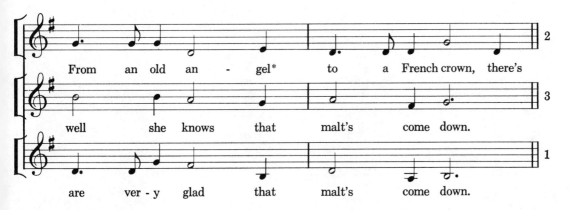

From an old an - gel* to a French crown, there's

well she knows that malt's come down.

are ver - y glad that malt's come down.

*Angel = an old English coin.

Follow Me Quickly

Pammelia - Melvill

Fol - low me quick - ly, Jack is a pret - ty boy, Round a - bout, stand - ing stout,

sing - ing ale in a bowl, Fa la fol la my de - ry com dan - dy.

Here's a Health

Here's a health to all them that we love, Here's a health to all them that love us, Here's a

health to all them that love those that love them, Love those that love them that love us.

245

If You Will Drink for Pleasure

Hilton

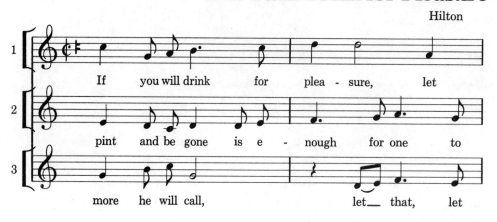

If you will drink for pleasure, let

pint and be gone is e - nough for one to

more he will call, let___ that, let

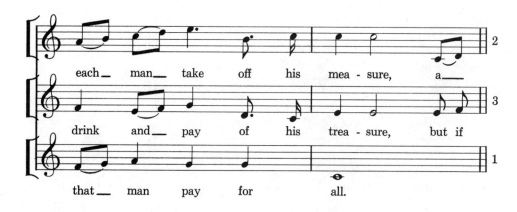

each___ man___ take off his mea - sure, a___

drink and___ pay of his trea - sure, but if

that___ man pay for all.

Once in Our Lives

Purcell

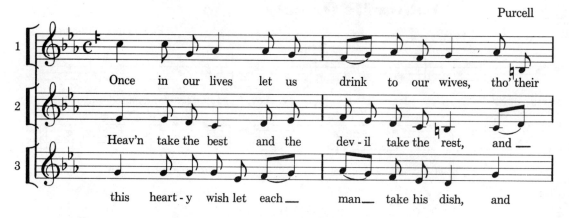

Once in our lives let us drink to our wives, tho' their

Heav'n take the best and the dev - il take the rest, and ___

this heart - y wish let each ___ man___ take his dish, and

num - ber___ be___ but___ small,

so shall we get rid___ of them all. To

drink, drink till he fall.

Now We Are Met and Humors Agree

Purcell

Now, now we are met and hu-mors a-

Fill, fill it a-bout, to me let it

A health to the King, round, round let it

gree; call, call for wine, and

come; fill the glass to the top, I'll

pass, fill it up, and then drink it

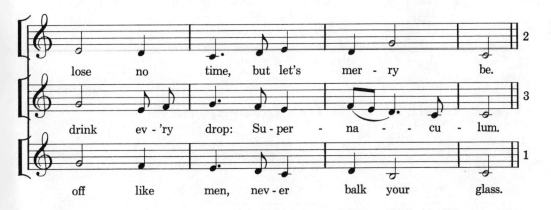

lose no time, but let's mer-ry be.

drink ev-'ry drop: Su-per - na - cu - lum.

off like men, nev-er balk your glass.

He That Drinks Is Immortal

Purcell

He that drinks is im - mor-tal, he that drinks is im -

For wine still sup - plies, for wine still sup -

How can he be dust, how

mor - - - tal and can ne'er de - - cay,

plies what age wears a - way.

can he be dust that moist - ens his clay?

Come Drink, My Friend Tom

Come drink, my friend Tom, or you'll not have your share;

Come drink, my friend Har - ry, and drive a - way care;

Come, Dick, pri - thee cir - cle the bump - er a - bout.

Come, wait - er! A - no - ther! For this bot - tle's out.

Come, Come Away to the Tavern, I Say

Come, come a - way, to the ta - vern I say, for

Leave your prit - tle prat - tle, and fill us a pot - tle, you

Draw - er come a - way, let's make it ho - ly day; A -

now at home 'tis wash - ing day;

are not so wise as Ar - i - sto - tle.

non, a - non, a - non, Sir, what is't you say?

Let's Drink and Let's Sing Together

CANON: 4 VOICES

Hayes

(1) Let's drink _____ and let's sing to - geth - er, in
(2) spite of wind or wea - ther, for here true joy is found; So
(3) let the toast go round, come here's _____ to all ho - - nest men, fill up your
(4) glass, fill up your glass, drink fair and drink a - gain.

Call for the Reck'ning

Purcell

Call for the reck - 'ning and let us, and
ring _____ the bell till the
sure, they're a - sleep, _____ a pox, _____ a

let us be gone! Such care - less at - ten - dance sure
draw - ers come up! Nay, pri - thee pull on, _____ pull
pox take 'em _____ all! Oh, now they come sneak - ing with

nev - er, sure nev - er, sure nev - er was known. Pray
on, _____ pull on tho' you break _____ the _____ rope! Why
"Gen - tle - men, d'ye call?" "Gen - tle - men, d'ye call?"

Come Let Us Cast the Dice

Lawes

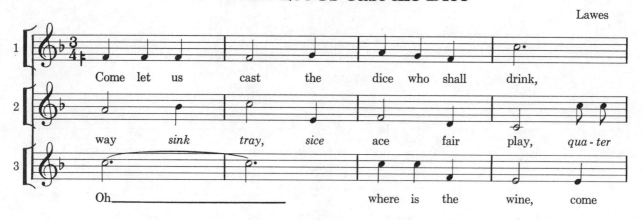

Come let us cast the dice who shall drink,

way *sink tray, sice* ace fair play, *qua-ter*

Oh_____ where is the wine, come

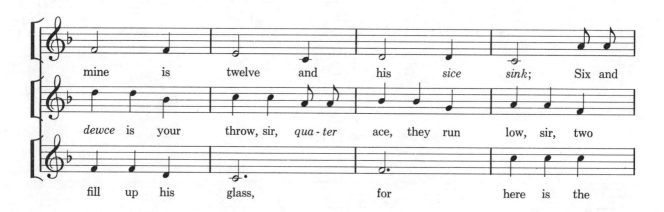

mine is twelve and his *sice sink;* Six and

dewce is your throw, sir, *qua-ter* ace, they run low, sir, two

fill up his glass, for here is the

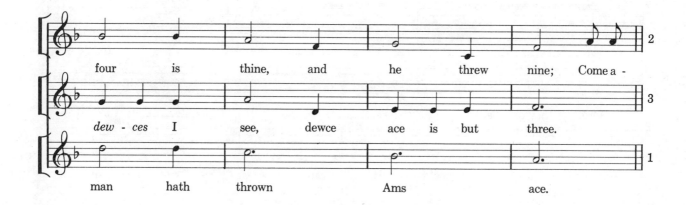

four is thine, and he threw nine; Come a-

dew-ces I see, dewce ace is but three.

man hath thrown Ams ace.

If All Be True That I Do Think

Purcell

If all be true that I do think, there

Good wine, a friend,

Or an-y oth-er rea-son, or an-y

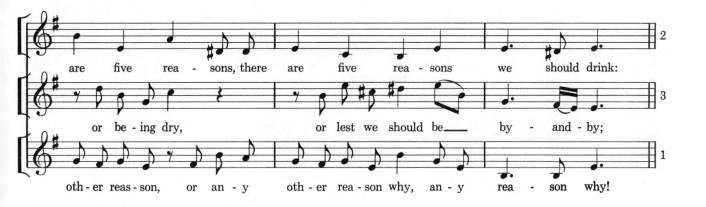

are five rea - sons, there are five rea - sons we should drink:

or be - ing dry, or lest we should be___ by - and - by;

oth - er reas - son, or an - y oth - er rea - son why, an - y rea - son why!

O! Yes, O! Yes

Hilton

O_____ yes,

If there be an - y man can tell where's the

wash - y beer lies here in my sto - mach ev - 'ry - where; come, come, let's a -

O_____ yes;

best wine: at Dog, Sun or Bell, let him come un - to the Cri - er,

way to the tav - ern, I say; a cup of rich Ca - na - ry will make my heart full

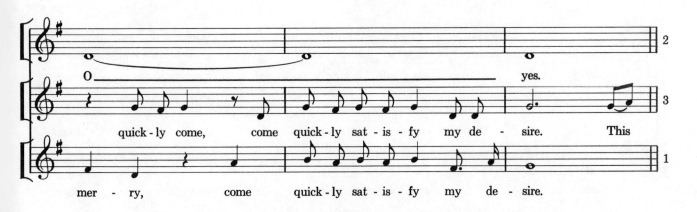

O_____ yes.

quick - ly come, come quick - ly sat - is - fy my de - sire. This

mer - ry, come quick - ly sat - is - fy my de - sire.

Come, My Hearts, Let's Now Be Merry

Hilton

Come, my hearts, let's now be mer - ry,

With a hey_____ down a der - ry,

hey, with a ho, with a hey down,

laugh__ and__ sing__ and drink old Sher - ry;

with a hey down, hey down der - ry, with a

down, down der - ry, with a hey down der - ry.

Would You Know How We Meet

Otway - Purcell

Would you know how we__ meet? O'er our__ jol - ly__ full

The__ sweet melts__ the sharp, the__ kind__ soothes the

We drink, laugh, and grat - i - fy ev - 'ry de -

bowls, as we min - gle__ our__ liq - uors, we min - gle__ our__ souls;

strong, and noth - ing but friend - ship grows all the night long:

sire; love, on - ly,__ re - mains our un - quench - a - ble fire.

At the Close of the Evening

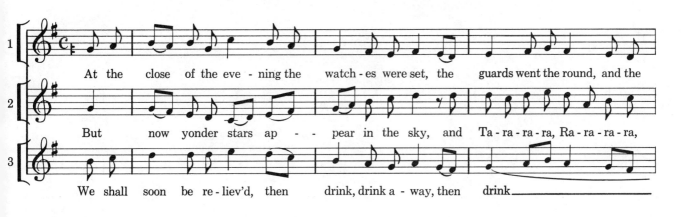

1. At the close of the eve-ning the watch-es were set, the guards went the round, and the

2. But now yonder stars ap - - pear in the sky, and Ta - ra - ra - ra, Ra - ra - ra - ra,

3. We shall soon be re - liev'd, then drink, drink a - way, then drink_____

Ta - ta - ta - too, Ta - ta - ta - too, Ta - ta - ta - too,

Ra - ra - ra - ra, Ra - ra - ra - ra, Ra - ra - ra - ra, Ra - ra - ra - ra, Ra - ra - ra - ra - ra, is

_____ a - way, then drink,_____ drink,_____ drink a -

Ta - ta - ta - too, Ta - ta - ta - too, Ta - ta - ta - ta - ta - ta -

sound - ed on high,_____ and

way; here, here's to you, and to you, and to you. Let us

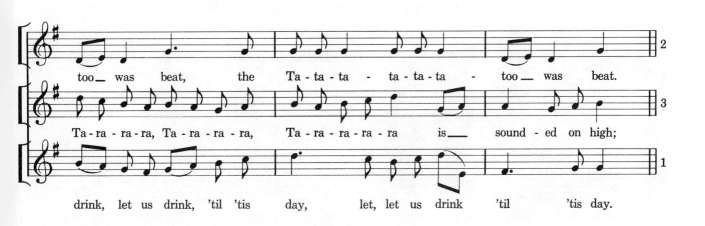

too__ was beat, the Ta - ta - ta - ta - ta - ta - too__ was beat.

Ta - ra - ra - ra, Ta - ra - ra - ra, Ta - ra - ra - ra is__ sound - ed on high;

drink, let us drink, 'til 'tis day, let, let us drink 'til 'tis day.

Drink Tonight of the Moonshine Bright

Lawes

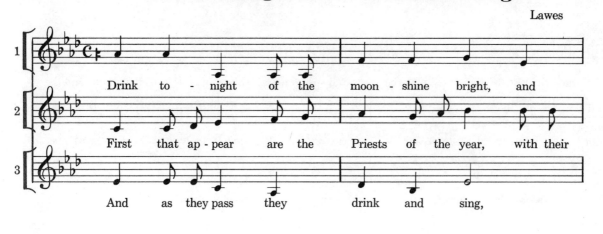

Drink to-night of the moon-shine bright, and
First that ap-pear are the Priests of the year, with their
And as they pass they drink and sing,

mark up-on her __ bor-der, some rites to be done to
cen-sers full of wine, then Cyn-tha
all health and praise to A - pol - lo their king,

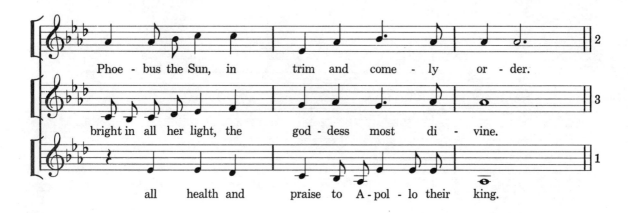

Phoe - bus the Sun, in trim and come - ly or - der.
bright in all her light, the god-dess most di - vine.
all health and praise to A-pol - lo their king.

Call for the Best

Hilton

Call for the best the __ house may ring;
And drink a-pace, and drink a - pace while breath __ you
You'll find but cold drink

Sack, wine and Cla - ret   let them bring.

have, while breath_____ you have.

in   the   grave.

Wine, Wine in a Morning

Purcell

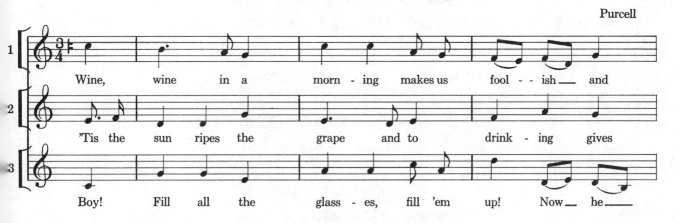

Wine,   wine   in a   morn - ing   makes us   fool - - ish_ and

'Tis the   sun   ripes   the   grape   and to   drink - ing   gives

Boy!   Fill   all   the   glass - es,   fill 'em   up!   Now_ he_

gay,   that like   ea - gles   we   soar   in the   pride of the

light;   we_   i - - - mi-tate_   him   when by_   noon   we're at

shines!   The   high - er   he   ri - ses   the   more   he re -

day.   Gout - y   sots   in the   night   on - ly   find_   a de - cay.

height.   They   steal wine,   who   take   it when   he's   out   of   sight.

fines,   but   wine   and wit_   pall   as their   ma - ker   de - clines.

Society, the Life of Man

Holmes

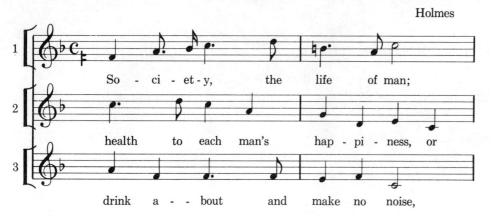

So - ci - et - y, the life of man;

health to each man's hap - pi - ness, or

drink a - - bout and make no noise,

mer - ri - ly let ev - 'ry - one take his can. 'Tis a

if you please to your mis - tress. Then

pay for what we call, and still be prec - ious, boys.

'Tis Too Late for a Coach

Purcell

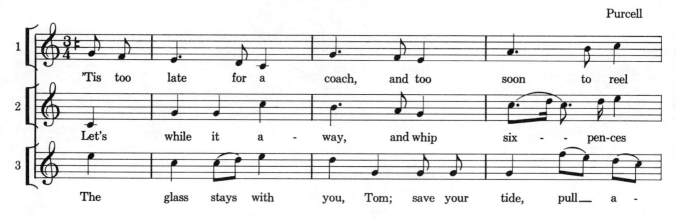

'Tis too late for a coach, and too soon to reel

Let's while it a - way, and whip six - - pen - ces

The glass stays with you, Tom; save your tide, pull - a -

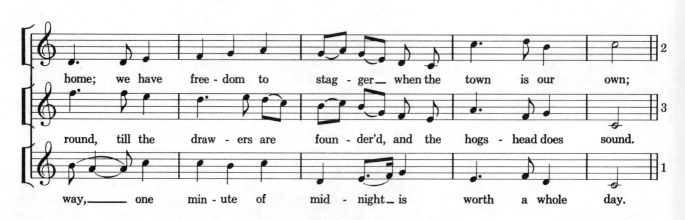

home; we have free - dom to stag - ger - when the town is our own;

round, till the draw - ers are foun - der'd, and the hogs - head does sound.

way, - one min - ute of mid - night - is worth a whole day.

Tom's Jolly Nose

Aldrich

Tom's Jol - ly nose I mean to a - buse: Thy

Thy nose,___ Tom Jol - ly, no jest it will bear, al -

Tom's nose, jol - ly Tom's nose, the

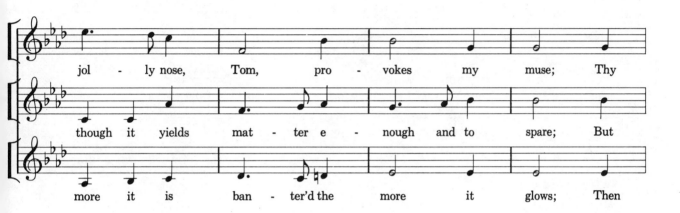

jol - ly nose, Tom, pro - vokes my muse; Thy

though it yields mat - ter e - nough and to spare; But

more it is ban - ter'd the more it glows; Then

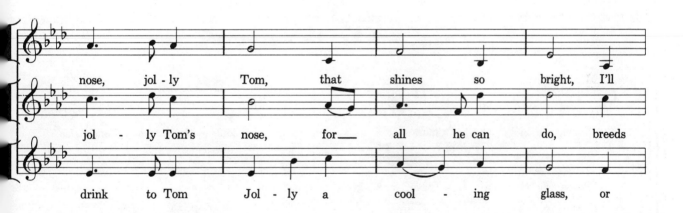

nose, jol - ly Tom, that shines so bright, I'll

jol - ly Tom's nose, for___ all he can do, breeds

drink to Tom Jol - ly a cool - ing glass, or

eas - i - ly fol - low it by its own light;

worms in it - self, and in our heads, too!

jol - ly Tom's nose will fire his face!

*To Thomas Brewer (see Introduction).

An Answer to Tom's Jolly Nose

John Jenkins

1. Al - though Jol - ly Tom, great fame thou hast won, thy
2. For the rate that we drink at each night still pro - cures such
3. And when the large bump - er floats round in the close, we'll des -

blood - y red nose shall look pa - ler e're long.
no - ses as would quite dis - count - en - ance yours.
pise thee and swear 'tis mine arse of a nose.

*To Thomas Brewer,
a fellow
composer and
drinking
companion whose
nose was very
red (see Introduction).

Come, Now Let Us Merry Be

Gregory

1. Come, now let us mer - ry be, cheer your souls with mirth and glee,
2. Those who choose to rave and drink, call it mi - se - ry to think;
3. Though we're mer - ry__ we'll be__ wise, not mirth now, to - mor - row sighs;

hearts and voi - ces shall a - gree in cheer - ful har - mo - ny.
we'll be mer - ry, yet not sink our rea - son__ in our glee.
dou - ble__ shall our__ plea - sures rise, when seen by __ me - mo - ry.

Shew a Room

Holmes

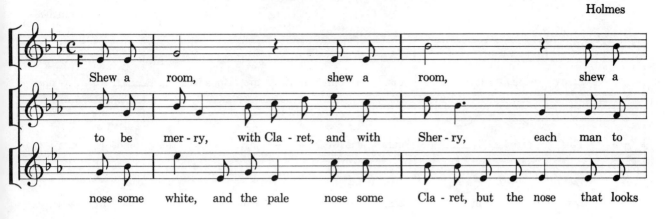

Shew a room, shew a room, shew a
to be mer-ry, with Cla-ret, and with Sher-ry,
each man to nose some white, and the pale nose some Cla-ret, but the nose that looks

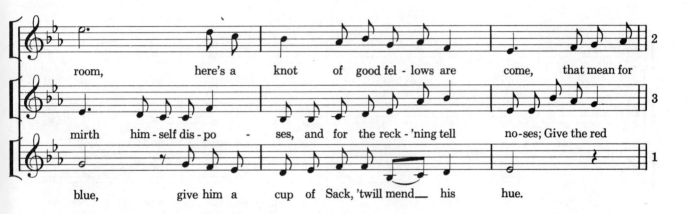

room, here's a knot of good fel-lows are come, that mean for
mirth him-self dis-po - ses, and for the reck-'ning tell no-ses; Give the red
blue, give him a cup of Sack, 'twill mend— his hue.

Drink on, Drink on, Till Night Be Spent

Purcell

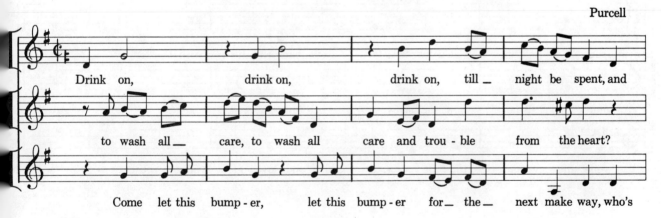

Drink on, drink on, drink on, till — night be spent, and
to wash all— care, to wash all care and trou-ble from the heart?
Come let this bump-er, let this bump-er for— the— next make way, who's

sun do shine, did— not the gods give anx-ious mor-tals wine,
Why then so soon, why then so soon should jo--vial fel-lows part?
sure to live, who's sure to live, and drink a-noth-er day.

Since Wine, Love, Music Present Are

Hughes

Since wine, love, mu - sic pre - sent are, since wine, _____ since

This night __ is ___ ours and we'll en - joy, this night is ours

Let us __ in - - dulge the joys we know, let us in - dulge

love, since mu - sic pre - sent, pre - sent are let

and we'll en - joy, this night is ours and we'll en - joy, to -

the joys we know, let us in - dulge the joys we __ know, on

each man drink his wish'd-for fair, let each man drink his wish'd - for fair.

mor - row shall not now de - stroy, to - mor - row shall not now de - stroy.

wine and love our time be - stow, on wine and love our time be - stow.

Where They Drank Their Wine in Bowls

probably Church

Where they drank their wine in bowls, to grat - i - fy, to

grat - i - fy __ their thir - sty, thir - sty, thir - sty souls.

260

Poor Owen

Church

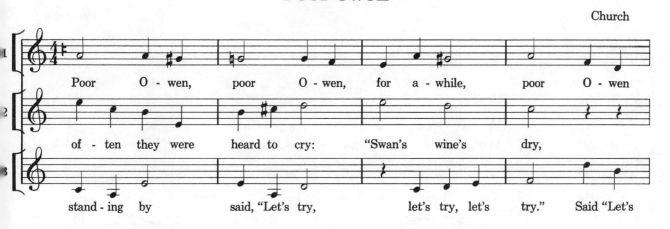

Poor O - wen, poor O - wen, for a - while, poor O - wen

of - ten they were heard to cry: "Swan's wine's dry,

stand - ing by said, "Let's try, let's try, let's try." Said "Let's

for a - while did lie, did lie de - spised by all, by

Swan's wine's dry." Of - ten they were heard to cry, were

try, let's try, let's try, let's try, let's try," One stand - ing

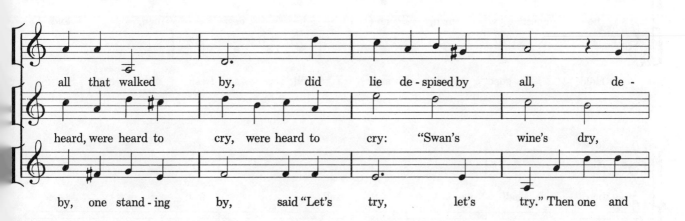

all that walked by, did lie de - spised by all, de -

heard, were heard to cry, were heard to cry: "Swan's wine's dry,

by, one stand - ing by, said "Let's try, let's try." Then one and

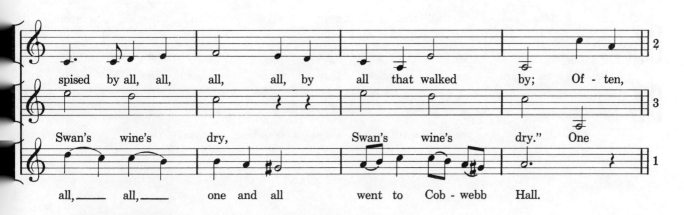

spised by all, all, all, all, by all that walked by; Of - ten,

Swan's wine's dry, Swan's wine's dry." One

all, ___ all, ___ one and all went to Cob - webb Hall.

*Mr. Owen Swan's words upon himself when he kept the Swan Tavern,
commonly called Cobwebb Hall.

261

Come, Drink to Me

Pammelia

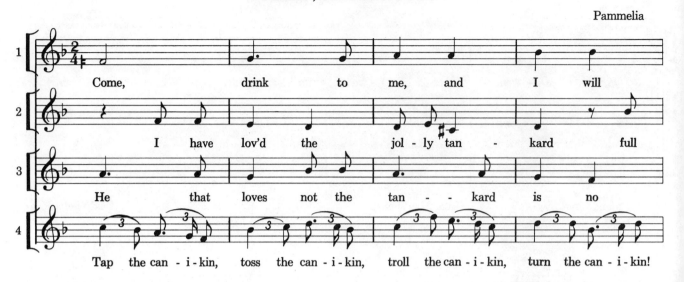

Come, drink to me, and I will

I have lov'd the jol - ly tan - kard full

He that loves not the tan - kard is no

Tap the can - i - kin, toss the can - i - kin, troll the can - i - kin, turn the can - i - kin!

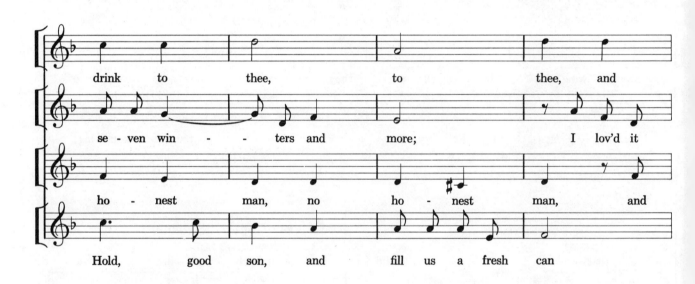

drink to thee, to thee, and

se - ven win - - ters and more; I lov'd it

ho - nest man, no ho - nest man, and

Hold, good son, and fill us a fresh can

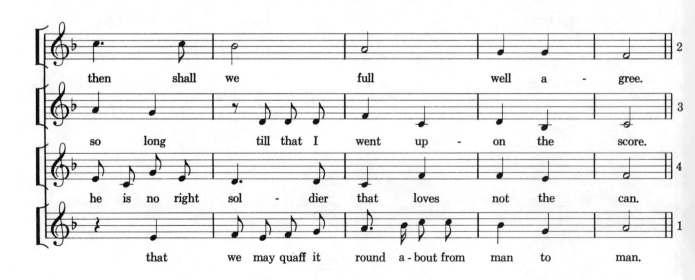

then shall we full well a - gree.

so long till that I went up - on the score.

he is no right sol - dier that loves not the can.

that we may quaff it round a - bout from man to man.

CONTEMPORARY

Crumpets

words and music
Louise Levinger

The crum-pets are sog-gy, my psy-che is grog-gy, you put me on hold, my tea's grown cold.

Trumpets (REACHING AND WINDING)

words and music
Louise Levinger

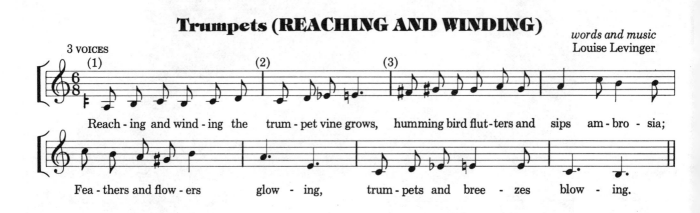

Reach-ing and wind-ing the trum-pet vine grows, humming bird flut-ters and sips am-bro-sia;

Fea-thers and flow-ers glow-ing, trum-pets and bree-zes blow-ing.

What's Icumen In?

words and music
Louise Levinger

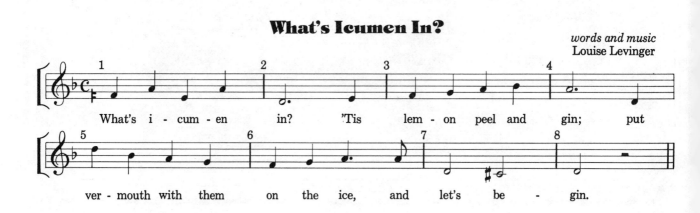

What's i-cum-en in? 'Tis lem-on peel and gin; put

ver-mouth with them on the ice, and let's be-gin.

Elephants or The force of Habit

A. E. Housman - Johan Franco

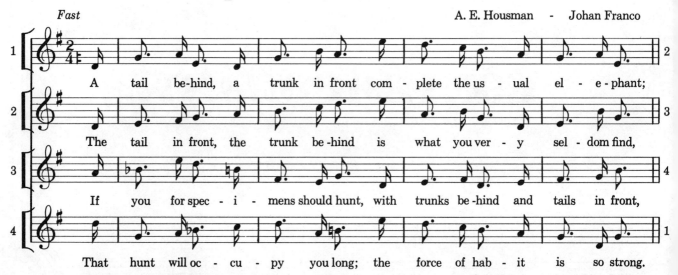

A tail be-hind, a trunk in front com-plete the us-ual el-e-phant;

The tail in front, the trunk be-hind is what you ver-y sel-dom find,

If you for spec-i-mens should hunt, with trunks be-hind and tails in front,

That hunt will oc-cu-py you long; the force of hab-it is so strong.

264

The May Queen

Emily Norcross - Mary C. Taylor

Sadly

Now the flow'rs are all a-bloom-ing, how ver-y mer-ry May can be.

Na-ture's strangely full of rich-es, best things in this life are free,

Yon a lit-tle iv-y hid-ing, un-der-neath a bud-ding tree,

Still the dear old world needs grooming, look at what it's done to me.

But dear na-ture can be vi-cious, look at what it's done to me.

Full of poi-son, there a-bid-ing, look at what it's done to me.

He Clouds Send Rain

Eluise Frano - Johan Franco

CANON: 3 VOICES   *Allegretto*

(1)   (2)   (3)

The clouds send rain down on the ground where springs come gush-ing and

brooks go rush-ing to riv-ers wind-ing 'round to meet the

sea up-on the sand where tides come flow-ing with wa-ters go-ing far a-

way from land where waves reach up-ward to the sun while clouds start drift-ing with

wa-ters lift-ing a round that won't be done un-til the world can rise a-

bove its low and dark ways in-to the bright rays of spi-rit's Light and Love!

La Musique Est un Art

John Benaglia

La_____ mu - si - que est un art,

La pa - ti - en - ce est une vir - tue,_____

La mu - si - que est un art.

I believe, O Lord

John Benaglia

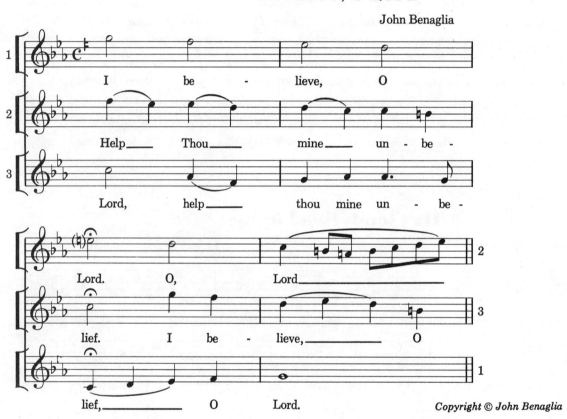

I be - lieve, O

Help____ Thou____ mine____ un - be -

Lord, help____ thou mine un - be -

Lord. O, Lord_____

lief. I be - lieve,_____ O

lief,_____ O Lord.

Gloria in Excelsis Deo I

John Benaglia

Glo - - - ri - a in ex - cel - sis De - - o,

et in ter - ra pax ho - mi - ni - bus

bo - - - - nae vo - lun - ta - - tis.

266

Gloria in Excelsis Deo II

John Benaglia

Glo - - - - - - - - - ri - a in ex - cel - sis De -
- - o in ter - ra pax ho - mi - ni - bus.

Copyright © John Benaglia

Et in Terra Pax

John Benaglia

Et in ter - ra pax
ho - mi - - - ni - - bus
Let there be peace
Lau - da - mus De - - o.

Copyright © John Benaglia

Parking a Car

In a driving tempo (of course)

Joseph Liebling

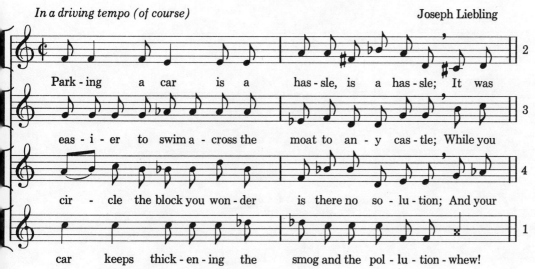

Park - ing a car is a has - sle, is a has - sle; It was
eas - i - er to swim a - cross the moat to an - y cas - tle; While you
cir - cle the block you won - der is there no so - lu - tion; And your
car keeps thick - en - ing the smog and the pol - lu - tion - whew!

Merry, Merry Christmas

John Benaglia

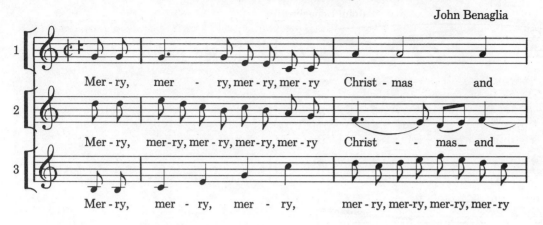

Mer - ry, mer - ry, mer - ry, mer - ry Christ - mas and

Mer - ry, mer - ry, mer - ry, mer - ry, mer - ry Christ - mas and

Mer - ry, mer - ry, mer - ry, mer - ry, mer - ry, mer - ry, mer - ry

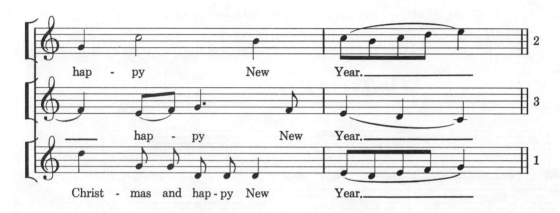

hap - py New Year.

hap - py New Year.

Christ - mas and hap - py New Year.

Sh'ma Yisroel

Joseph Liebling

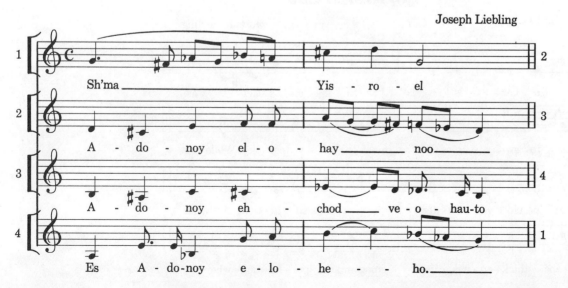

Sh'ma Yis - ro - el

A - do - noy el - o - hay noo

A - do - noy eh - chod ve - o - hau - to

Es A - do - noy e - lo - he - ho.

MISCELLANEOUS

Master, Come Help Me

Melvill

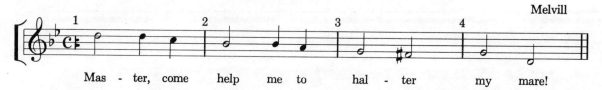

Mas - ter, come help me to hal - ter my mare!

O, Where Shall Rest Be Found?

O where shall rest be found, Rest for the wea - ry soul?

Run up the Sail

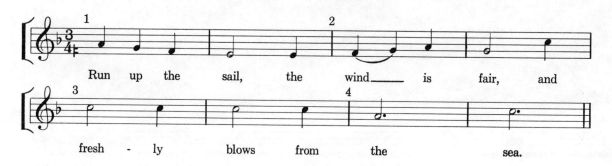

Run up the sail, the wind___ is fair, and

fresh - ly blows from the sea.

Follow Me

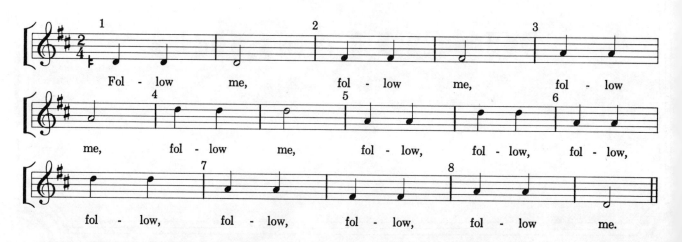

Fol - low me, fol - low me, fol - low

me, fol - low me, fol - low, fol - low, fol - low,

fol - low, fol - low, fol - low, fol - low me.

Delicta Quis

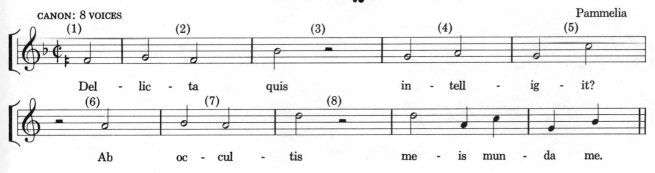

Lady, Come Down and See

The Hart, He Loves the High Wood

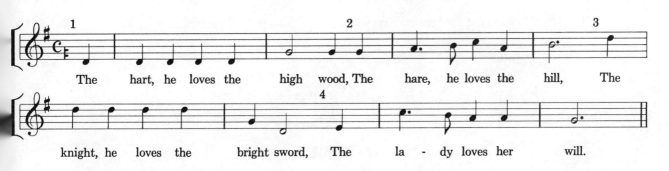

Cuckoo, Good Neighbors Help Us

Universa Transeunt

Pammelia

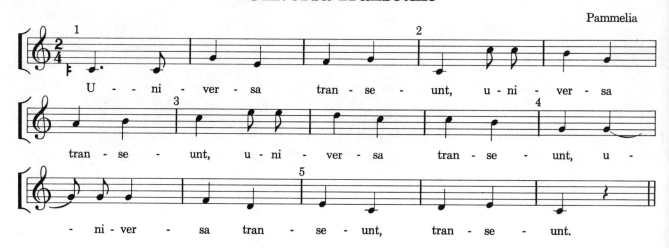

U - ni - ver - sa tran - se - unt, u - ni - ver - sa tran - se - unt, u - ni - ver - sa tran - se - unt, u - ni - ver - sa tran - se - unt, tran - se - unt.

Birch and Green Holly

Pammelia - Melvill

Birch and green hol - ly, Birch and green hol - ly, If thou be beat - en, boy, Thank thine own fol - ly.

JCUBAK

Deuteromelia

J C U B A K and ev - er - more will be, though John Cooke he saith nay, O! What a knave is he.

JCUBAK stands for "I See You Be A Knave" or "John Cooke You Be A Knave" (See introduction).

I Pray You, Good Mother

Melismata

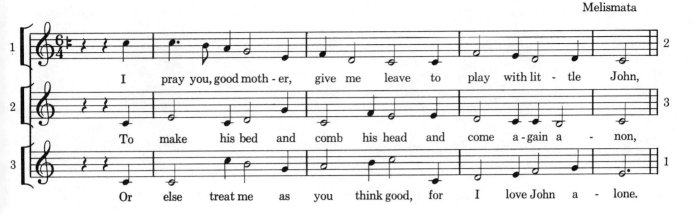

I pray you, good moth-er, give me leave to play with lit-tle John,

To make his bed and comb his head and come a-gain a-non,

Or else treat me as you think good, for I love John a-lone.

Dame, Lend Me a Loaf

Pammelia   Melvill

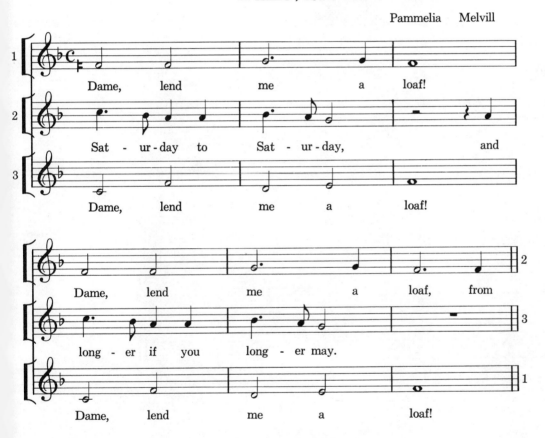

Dame, lend me a loaf!

Sat-ur-day to Sat-ur-day, and

Dame, lend me a loaf!

Dame, lend me a loaf, from

long-er if you long-er may.

Dame, lend me a loaf!

Ah Me! What Perils

Ah me!   Ah, what per-ils to en-vi-ron   He that meddles with cold i-ron,   Ah me!

Strange News from the Rose

Michael Wise

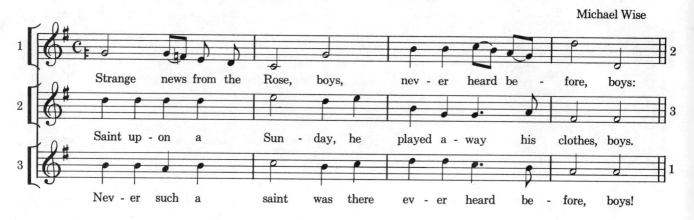

Strange news from the Rose, boys, nev - er heard be - fore, boys:

Saint up - on a Sun - day, he played a - way his clothes, boys.

Nev - er such a saint was there ev - er heard be - fore, boys!

Who Comes Laughing

Who comes laugh - ing, laugh - ing, laugh - ing,

We come laugh - ing, Ha ha ha ha ha ha ha ha,

Ha ha ha ha ha ha ha ha, ha ha ha ha ha ha ha ha,

who comes laugh - ing here a - - gain?

we come laugh - ing here a - gain.

ha ha ha ha ha ha ha ha, ha ha ha ha ha.

Si Non Paruisti

CANON: 5 VOICES

Pammelia

Si _____ non _____ pa - - -

- - ruis - ti, oc - ci - - dis - ti.

Oaken Leaves

Pammelia

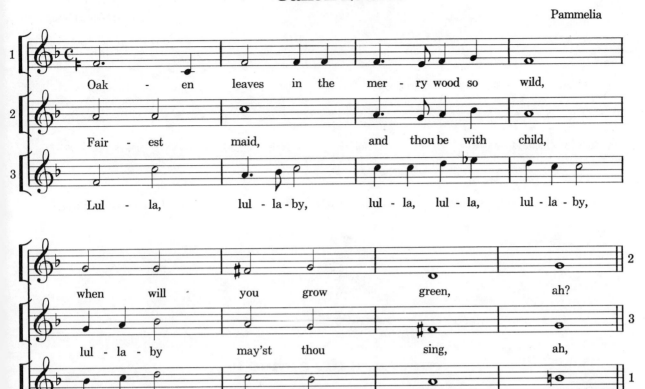

Oak - en leaves in the mer - ry wood so wild,

Fair - est maid, and thou be with child,

Lul - la, lul - la - by, lul - la, lul - la, lul - la - by,

when will you grow green, ah?

lul - la - by may'st thou sing, ah,

lul - la - by may'st thou sing, ah.

Ars Longa, Vita Brevis

Hayes

Ars lon - ga, vi - ta___ bre - vis, vi - ta bre -

- vis, Ars lon - ga, vi - ta bre - vis, vi - ta___ bre - vis.

C-o-f-f-e-e

Translation: Carol Dyk

Hering

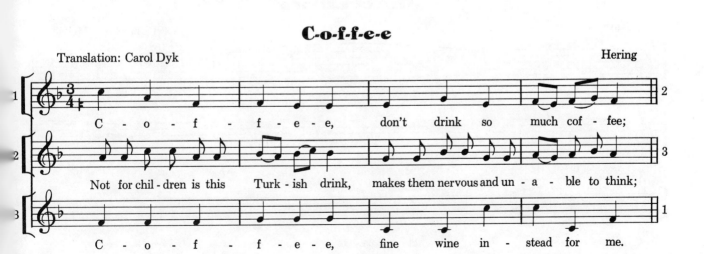

C - o - f - f - e - e, don't drink so much cof - fee;

Not for chil - dren is this Turk - ish drink, makes them nervous and un - a - ble to think;

C - o - f - f - e - e, fine wine in - stead for me.

Come, Follow to the Greenwood Tree

Quickly

Hilton

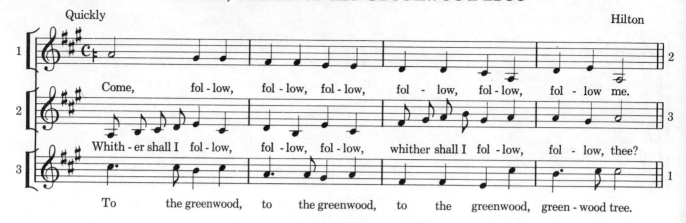

Come, fol - low, fol - low, fol - low, fol - low, fol - low, fol - low me.

Whith - er shall I fol - low, fol - low, fol - low, whither shall I fol - low, fol - low, thee?

To the greenwood, to the greenwood, to the greenwood, green - wood tree.

Sweet Are the Sounds

Wilson

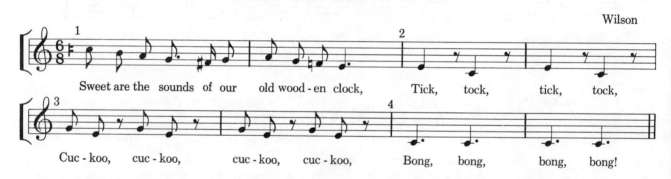

Sweet are the sounds of our old wood - en clock, Tick, tock, tick, tock,

Cuc - koo, cuc - koo, cuc - koo, cuc - koo, Bong, bong, bong, bong!

Ora et Labora

CANON: 4 VOICES

Pammelia   Melvill

O - ra - - - - - - - - et la - bo -

ra, et la - bo - - - ra. O - ra - -

- - - - - - et la - bo - ra, et la - bo - - ra.

This Is the Way the Ploughboy Goes

Pearson

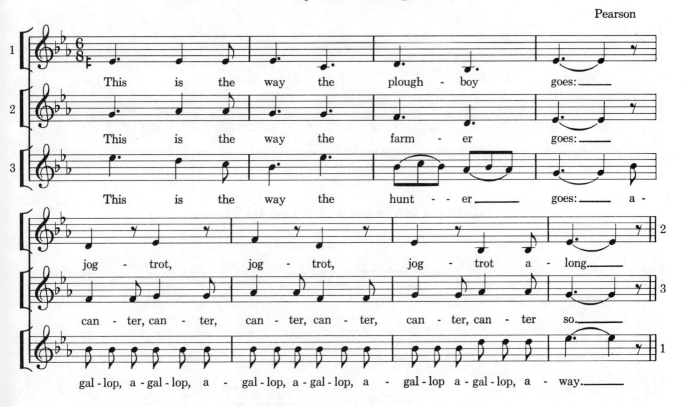

Let Us Be Merry in Our Old Clothes

Gregory

Come to the Old Oak Tree

Come to the old oak tree, Fol - low, fol - low, fol - low, fol - low, fol - low, fol - low me,

Quick - ly, quick - ly, quick - ly, quick - ly, quick - ly fol - low me, And we there will jol - ly be.

Mister Chairman, I Rise to Move

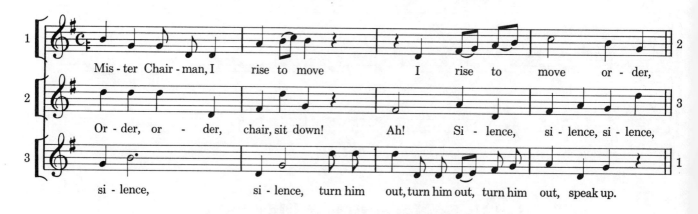

Mis - ter Chair - man, I rise to move I rise to move or - der,

Or - der, or - der, chair, sit down! Ah! Si - lence, si - lence, si - lence,

si - lence, si - lence, turn him out, turn him out, turn him out, speak up.

All We Here, or, The Agreement

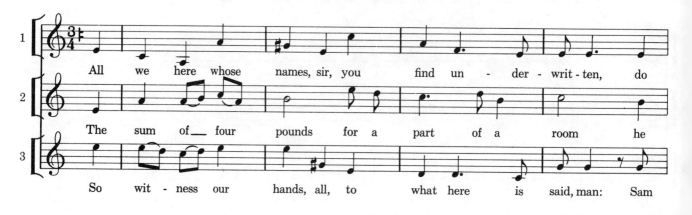

All we here whose names, sir, you find un - der - writ - ten, do

The sum of__ four pounds for a part of a room he

So wit - ness our hands, all, to what here is said, man: Sam

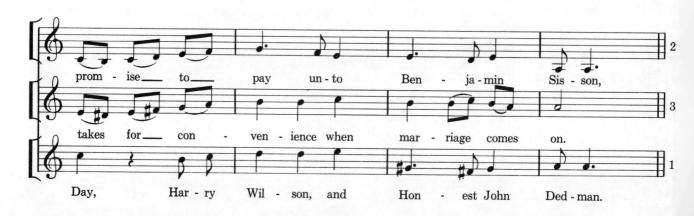

prom - ise__ to__ pay un - to Ben - ja - min Sis - son,

takes for__ con - ven - ience when mar - riage comes on.

Day, Har - ry Wil - son, and Hon - est John Ded - man.

Wind Gentle Evergreen

Hayes

1. Wind gen-tle ev - er-green, to form a shade a-round the tomb where So - pho-cles is laid;

2. Sweet i - vy bend thy boughs and in - ter-twine with blush - ing ro - ses and the clus - t'ring vine.

3. Thus will thy last - ing leaves with beau - ty hung, prove grate - ful em - blems of the lays he sung.

The Prophet's Old Dog

Browne

The pro - phet's old dog was a man - ner - ly cur, his mast - ter went first and he fol - low'd his sir.

But Jer - ry's old Turn - spit, such man - ners not know - ing, to the boat, or the coach, first of all will be go - ing,

At which Jer - ry smiles, 'cause his hu - mor he pricks, and swears 'tis too late to teach old dogs new tricks.

Hark, the Nightingale

J. S. Smith

Hark, hark, hark, the night-in-gale in her mourn-ful lay;

She tells her sto-ry's woe - - - ful tale to

Warn ye if she may, to warn ye if she may.

We Cats When Assembled

Browne

We cats when as-sem-bl'd at mid-night to-geth-er, for

If dogs be in ken-nel, all fast in the straw, we

But if they sur-prise us, and put us to flight, we

in - - no-cent purr - ing, purr - ing, for in - no-cent

march and we meow, me - - ow,

fret, fret and we spit, fret, spit, spit, give a squall,

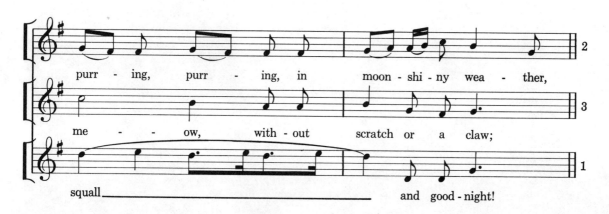

purr - ing, purr - ing, in moon-shi-ny wea - ther,

me - - ow, with-out scratch or a claw;

squall and good-night!

Down in a Dungeon Deep

Hilton

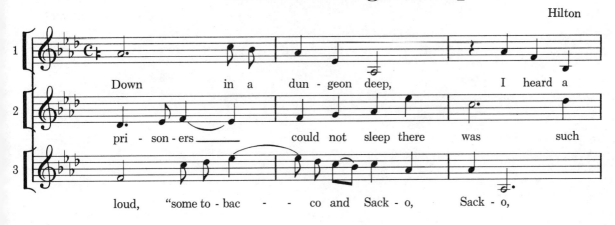

Down in a dun-geon deep, I heard a
pri-son-ers could not sleep there was such
loud, "some to-bac - - co and Sack-o, Sack-o,

fear - ful, fear-ful noise; the
roar - - - - - ing; "Boys," they cried a-
quick-ly quick-ly quick-ly, quick-ly,— quick - ly, boys."

Money, Money, 'Tis That Only

Holmes

Mo - ney, mo-ney, mo - ney, 'tis that on - ly
though some men of vain be -
mo - ney, mo - ney, mo - ney, mo-ney is the chief;

can give life to the__ soul of a man; What
lief do o-ther aid wish and im - plore; Money, mo - ney,
Give me but that, I ask no more.

The Mate to a Cock

"Mr. Tomlinson"

John Lenton

1. The mate to a cock, and corn tall as wheat, is his Chris - tian name, who in mu - sic's com - plete, po - et de - serves a good kick on the shins!

2. His sur - name be - gins with the grace of a cat, and con - cludes with the house of a her - mit, note that!

3. His skill and per - form - ance each au - di - tor wins, but the

Galli marita par tritice seges,
  Proenomen est ejus, dat chromati leges.
Intrat cognomen blanditiis cati,

Exit eremi in oedibus stali,
Expertum effectum ommes admirentur.
Quid merent poetoe? Ut bene calcentur.

One Industrious Insect

"Mr. Tomlinson"

Purcell

One in - dus - tri - ous in - sect, and the sign he hangs out is half flesh and half fish, and he

His sur - name the room where the sweet - ness of the oth - er, is the Chris - tian

The sign he hangs out is half fire's in the mid - dle, and some say he sells as true

name of our well____ be-lov'd broth-er.

plays____ ver-y well on the____ fid-dle.____

wine as good fel-low can wish.

*"Who keeps the Mermaid Tavern in Oxford, and plays his part very well on the violin."

Miss Sue

Howard

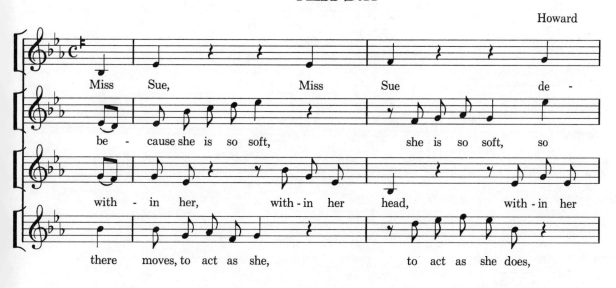

Miss Sue, Miss Sue de -

be - cause she is so soft, she is so soft, so

with - in her, with - in her head, with - in her

there moves, to act as she, to act as she does,

clares, Miss Sue de - - clares her dar - - ling cat she loves

soft, and purrs so____ sweet-ly; She says, with - in her head,

head a mind there moves, with - in her____ head a mind

to act as she does so dis-creet-ly, dis - creetly

Ye Heavens, If Innocence Deserves Your Care

Baildon

1. Ye heav'ns, _____ if in - no - cence de - serves your care, if in - no - cence de - serves your care, why have you made it fa - tal, fa - tal to _____ be fair?

2. Base man, base man, the ru - in of our sex was born, the ru - in of our sex was born, the beau - teous are his prey, the rest, the _ rest _____ his scorn;

3. A - like un - for - tu - nate, our fate, our fate is such: we please too lit - tle or too much, we please, we please too lit - tle, or we please too much.

Dainty, Fine Aniseed Water

Lawes

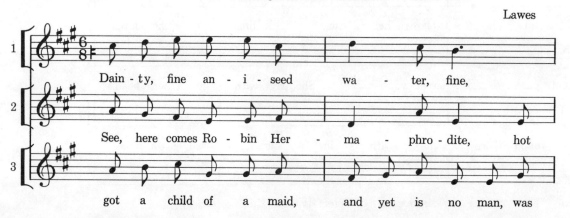

1. Dain - ty, fine an - i - seed wa - ter, fine,

2. See, here comes Ro - bin Her - ma - phro - dite, hot

3. got a child of a maid, and yet is no man, was

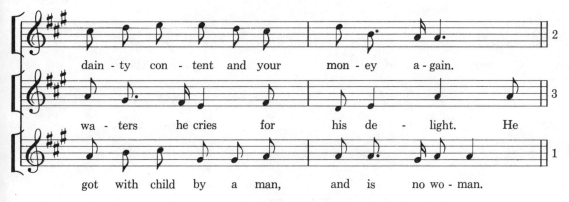

dain - ty con - tent and your mon - ey a - gain.

wa - ters he cries for his de - light. He

got with child by a man, and is no wo - man.

Let Me Sleep This Night Away

Webbe

Let me sleep

till the dawn - ing of the day,

o - - - pening of mine eyes, at the

and all the world shall

this night a - way,

till the dawn - - ing of the day; Then at the

o - - - pening of mine eyes, I

rise, I and all the world shall rise.

With a Down, Down, Hey, Derry Down

Birch

With a down, down, hey, der-ry down, with a

With a down, der-ry down,

With a down, der-ry down, with a

With a down, der-ry down,

down, hey, der-ry down, der-ry, with a down, down,

with a der-ry down, der-ry down, der-ry, with a down,

down, a der-ry down, der-ry down, der-ry, down,

with a der-ry down, der-ry, down, down, with a

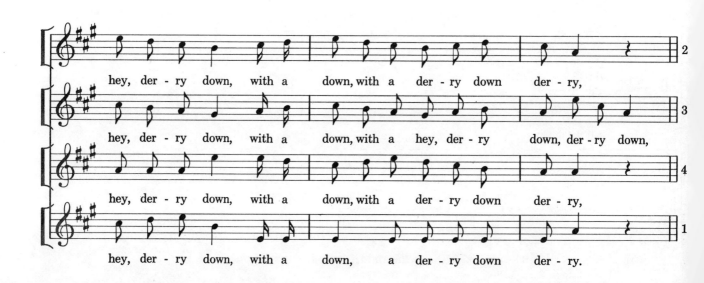

hey, der-ry down, with a down, with a der-ry down der-ry,

hey, der-ry down, with a down, with a hey, der-ry down, der-ry down,

hey, der-ry down, with a down, with a der-ry down der-ry,

hey, der-ry down, with a down, a der-ry down der-ry.

Dost Thou Not Remember, Ned?

Aldrich

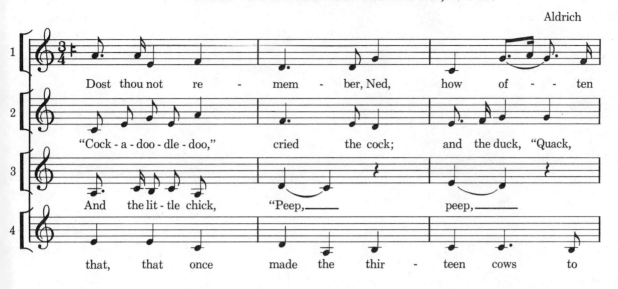

Dost thou not re - mem - ber, Ned, how of - ten

"Cock - a - doo - dle - doo," cried the cock; and the duck, "Quack,

And the lit - tle chick, "Peep,_____ peep,_____

that, that once made the thir - teen cows to

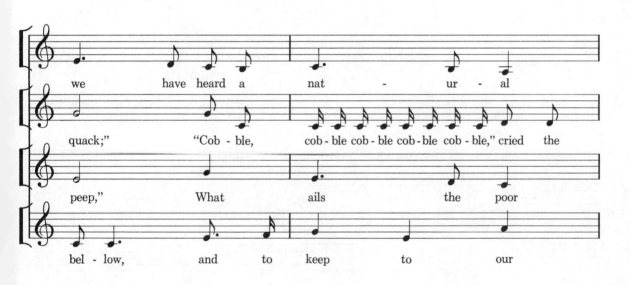

we have heard a nat - ur - al

quack;" "Cob - ble, cob - ble cob - ble cob - ble cob - ble," cried the

peep," What ails the poor

bel - low, and to keep to our

chor - us of brutes in Fa - ther Dod - well's yard?

tur - key cock; "We-hee, we - hee, we - hee," the hack.

crea - tures, such a coil_____ to keep? E'en

au - thor, here's to thee, my good fel - low.

If Hungry My Nose

Paxton

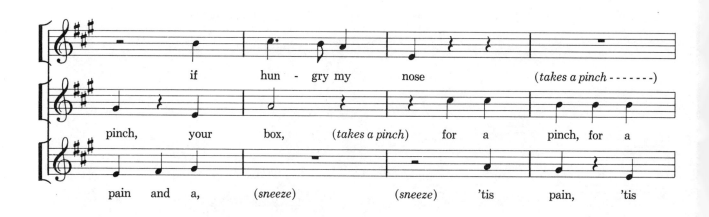

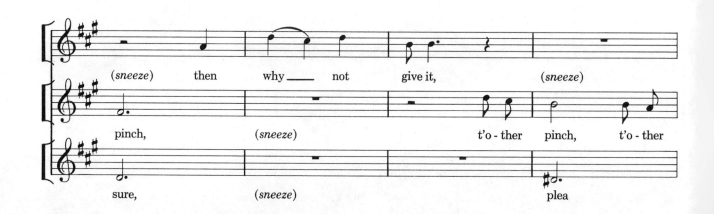

then why_____ not give it, *(take a pinch)*

pinch, t'o - ther pinch, t'o - ther

sure, a plea - -

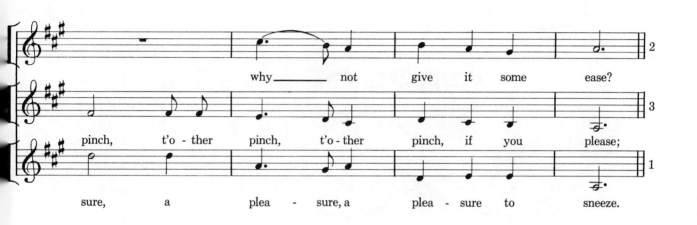

why_____ not give it some ease?

pinch, t'o - ther pinch, t'o - ther pinch, if you please;

sure, a plea - sure, a plea - sure to sneeze.

INDEX OF TITLES